Beth Ann Nunn

SEPARATE COUNTRY

For Carleton Adair

SEPARATE COUNTRY

a literary journey through the American South

Paul Binding

PADDINGTON PRESS LTD

NEW YORK & LONDON

Library of Congress Cataloging in Publication Data
Binding, Paul
  Separate country.

  Bibliography: p.
  Includes index.
    1.   American literature—Southern States—
History and criticism.   2.   Authors, American—
20th century—Interviews.   3.   Southern States—
Description and travel—1951–   I.   Title.
PS261.B54   818'.5'403   79–1412

ISBN 0 448 22072 5 (U.S. and Canada only)
ISBN 0 7092 0050 1

Filmset in England by SX Composing Ltd., Rayleigh, Essex.
Printed and bound in the United States.

Designed by Patricia Pillay
Map illustration by Eileen Batterberry

In the United States
PADDINGTON PRESS
Distributed by
GROSSET & DUNLAP

In the United Kingdom
PADDINGTON PRESS

In Canada
Distributed by
RANDOM HOUSE OF CANADA LTD.

In Southern Africa
Distributed by
ERNEST STANTON (PUBLISHERS) (PTY.) LTD.

In Australia and New Zealand
Distributed by
A. H. & A. W. REED

CONTENTS

ACKNOWLEDGMENTS

FIRST I THANK, for their hospitality, cooperation and generosity with time the writers who feature in this book and their families: Wendell Berry, James Dickey, Madison Jones, Andrew Lytle, David Madden, Marion Montgomery, Walker Percy, Reynolds Price, Allen Tate, Peter Taylor, Anne Tyler and Eudora Welty.

I would also like to thank the following for contributing to the pleasantness and interest of my stay in America and helping me in my task there: Carleton Adair, Dr. and Mrs. Charles Adair, Ruth and Paul Barolski, Lucy and Gerald Cadogan, Walker Cowan, David Dionne, Mr. and Mrs. Hervé Dionne, David Dobson, Col. and Mrs. Melvin Dobson, Harry Ford, Margaret Game, Elaine Gordon, Reina and Wayne Gunn, Cathy and Skip Hardin, Dale Hardman, Lowell Kelly, Nancy and Charles Marion Crawford, Jim Marks, Cabell Marshall, Margaret McElderry, George Mitchell, David Roscoe, John Saumarez Smith, Martha and Jerome Stephens, Mary Wimbush, David Winter, and Carol and Peter Zerner.

And I thank, too, Mark Todd for reading this book in its various stages before completion, and my editor Catherine Carpenter for her considerable help.

AUTHOR'S NOTE

FOR MANY YEARS now I have admired a considerable number of novelists from the American South. This admiration led me to ask myself what qualities they had in common and why the South had produced so many fine writers. This book is the result of these inner questions. For six months I journeyed around the Southern states, visiting the living writers I most admired and discussing their work with them in their own homes. In my book I give accounts both of my own literary-oriented travels and of my meetings with the writers.

Inevitably limits had to be set. My definition of which states constitute the South will be found in the first chapter. As for the writers, I decided to include only those who still lived and worked in the South.

Allen Tate died recently. I have chosen, however, not to alter my chapter on him. I count myself exceedingly fortunate to have met, so near the close of his life, a man who, when the century's achievements are reviewed, will surely stand as one of the few giants of its literature in the English language.

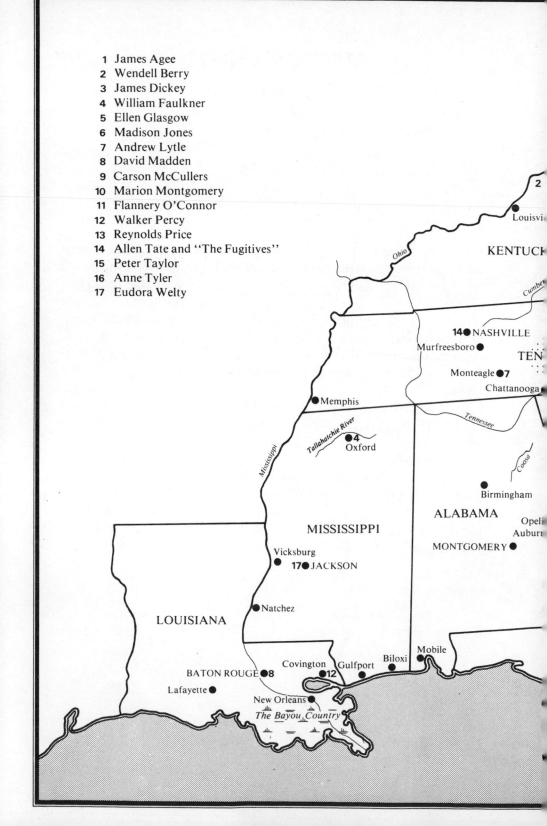

1 James Agee
2 Wendell Berry
3 James Dickey
4 William Faulkner
5 Ellen Glasgow
6 Madison Jones
7 Andrew Lytle
8 David Madden
9 Carson McCullers
10 Marion Montgomery
11 Flannery O'Connor
12 Walker Percy
13 Reynolds Price
14 Allen Tate and "The Fugitives"
15 Peter Taylor
16 Anne Tyler
17 Eudora Welty

2

Louisvi•

Ohio

KENTUCK

Cumbe

14● NASHVILLE

Murfreesboro ●

TEN

Monteagle ●7

Chattanooga

Tennessee

● Memphis

Tallahatchie River

Coosa

●4
Oxford

Mississippi

● Birmingham

ALABAMA

Opeli
Auburr

MISSISSIPPI

Vicksburg
●   MONTGOMERY ●
17● JACKSON

● Natchez

LOUISIANA

Mobile ●

Covington Gulfport   Biloxi ●
BATON ROUGE ●8   ●   ●

Lafayette ●   ●12

New Orleans ●
The Bayou Country

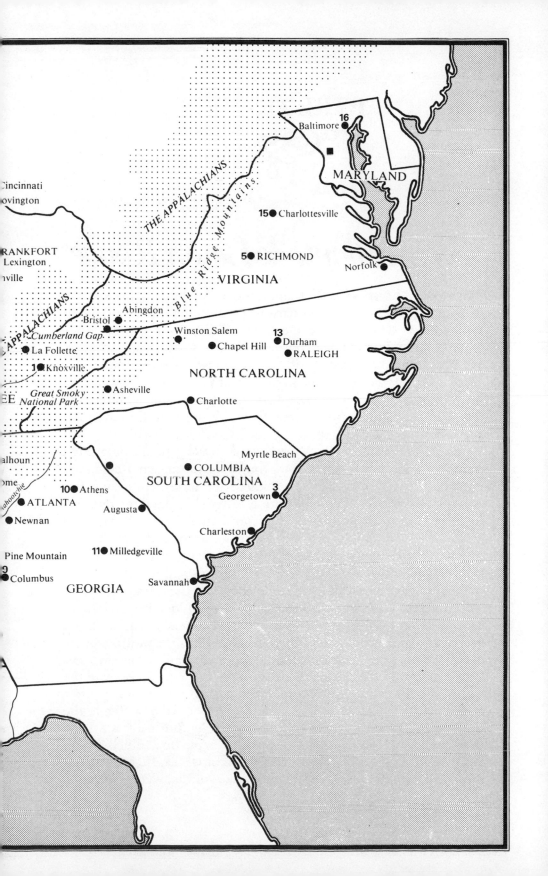

1: THE TRAVELS

From Atlanta to Baton Rouge

THE SOUTHBOUND EXPRESS train came to a sudden, unexpected stop. A few minutes later a guard told passengers why: a flock of wild turkeys had settled on the track. Although it was not quite 6 A.M. I knew I would sleep no more. I looked out of the window at a lightening sky streaked with green and pearly pink, and, below that, at still shadowy woodland moist with dew. The train moved on. The offending turkeys became briefly visible, angrily retreating into waste ground. I tilted my seat forward into its upright position and settled to watching morning come to South Carolina.

I had left Charlottesville, Virginia, still in the grip of a protracted winter—many trees leafless, the ground hard, the wind cold, and patches of snow up on the Blue Ridge Mountains. But now, after a night's travel, I had entered spring. Growing daylight revealed in the woods a prolificacy of blossom—dogwood, wisteria and lilac, gleaming whites, pinks and purples among the fresh light green of the newly leaved trees. The attendant came by to tell us that breakfast was being served, and though still a little sleepy I made my way to the dining car. I decided that the train, the Southern Crescent, was the most elegant I had ever ridden in: its sleeping cars, its washrooms, its restaurant were all touched with a certain grandeur like that of luxury hotels in 1930s films. Its motion, however, left much to be desired, not through any fault of its own but because the tracks beneath it were in such poor condition. And the fate of the Southern Crescent itself was, I had read in notice after notice, uncertain. I myself was getting off at Atlanta, while the train was to continue to New Orleans today. But no train made this journey every day, and it was questionable how much longer one would do so at all. Trains and railroad tracks, such recurring subjects in Southern folk, country and blues music, were threatened

10

in the very country that had most apostrophized them. Later in New Orleans I was to hear a group of young people in the street singing a tuneful elegy to the American railroad.

Breakfast, like most Southern breakfasts, was delicious—a huge plateful of pancakes, fried eggs and grits, hot biscuits with apple jelly, and many cups of strong coffee with cream—a sensually satisfying accompaniment to the view flying past the windows. It was all I could do not to exclaim with joy at this landscape, for it was the very South that I had long dreamed of seeing, the South that its writers, no matter where they came from, celebrated. Beyond the unkempt railroad track were dense deciduous woods, plantations of pine, cabins with porches, bigger houses with verandas, abrupt creeks of limpid water, straight roads with untidy shoulders and, to the right and continuously in the background, mountains. These mountains, lying to the west as they did and so remaining in shadow for quite some time, seemed unbearably enticing. The ridges that give the Blue Ridge Mountains their name are more broken in South Carolina and Georgia than to the north in Virginia. Thickly wooded valleys smash their way into them, making mountains of some 5,000 feet stand out as intriguing individual peaks, and I was to find that their romance did not diminish at closer quarters. As the train exchanged South Carolina for Georgia the countryside became a little more populous.

I found myself remembering that poem of Walt Whitman's which begins "O Magnet South! O glistening perfumed South! My South!" (*His* South? Whitman was born on Long Island and spent his childhood in Brooklyn.) The poem continues with a list of the region's fascinations:

> *I see where the live-oak is growing, I see where the yellow-*
> *pine, the scented bay-tree, the lemon and orange, the*
> *cypress, the graceful palmetto . . .*
> *The range afar, the richness and barrenness, the old woods*
> *charged with mistletoe and trailing moss,*
> *The piney odor and the gloom, the awful natural stillness,*
> *(here in these dense swamps the freebooter carries his gun,*
> *and the fugitive has his conceal'd hut;)*
> *O the strange fascination of those half-known half-*
> *impassable swamps, infested by reptiles, resounding with*
> *the bellow of the alligator, the sad noises of the night-owl*

11

and the wild-cat, and the whirr of the rattle-snake,
The mocking-bird, the wild turkey, the raccoon, the
opossum;
A Kentucky corn-field, the tall, graceful, long-leav'd corn,
slender, flapping, bright green, with tassels, with beautiful
ears each well-sheath'd in its husk;
O my heart! O tender and fierce pangs, I can stand them
not, I will depart;
O to be a Virginian where I grew up! O to be a Carolinian!
O longings irrepressible! I will go back to old Tennessee
and never wander more.

Whitman, I recollected, had spent a mere few months in the South in 1848, mostly in a New Orleans newspaper office. Then in 1862 he had seen the South again, during the Civil War in the most unhappy circumstances: he went to Fredericksburg, Virginia, to visit his wounded brother. For the next two years he lived in and around Washington, D.C., tending casualties of one of the bloodiest civil wars to date—one which, it could be said, had been started by Southerners. So one would have thought Whitman had little cause to feel affection for the South. Yet he did; every line of the poem proclaims it. "My South!" he says. And now, gazing at the Southern landscape through the train windows, I felt the same rush of personal emotion toward it that Whitman must have felt— "Mine," I wanted to exclaim. Even now, back in England, I can still feel this as I remember Southern scenes, and the last lines of Whitman's poem arouse an almost painful nostalgia in me.

If these are the feelings of visitors, how much more intense must be those of the natives of the country. There is no major Southern novel—no matter how ugly its central incidents, no matter how tragic its vision of life—that does not pulsate with a love for the land in which it is set. And that love extends to those parts that are bypassed, neglected or shunned:

A place that ever was lived in [says Eudora Welty] is like a fire that never goes out. It flares up, it smolders for a time, it is fanned or smothered by circumstances, but its being is intact, forever fluttering within it, the result of some original ignition. Sometimes it gives out glory, sometimes its little light must be sought out to be seen, small and tender as a candle flame, but as certain.[1]

It was, I think, the ubiquitous love for their country among the Southern writers that first made me want to see the South for myself, to see a place that could generate such intensity of feeling. I was impressed too by the assumption throughout Southern literature that there was a landscape, an amalgam of buildings, plants and natural features that was thought to belong to the South as an entity (however it was defined), though I knew, of course, that the word South had emotional as well as geographical connotations. I remembered Quentin Compson's Harvard roommate in William Faulkner's *Absalom, Absalom* asking him, "Tell me about the South. What it's like there? What do they do there? Why do they live there? Why do they live at all?" I remembered also that rhetorical passage in the same author's *Intruder in the Dust* (the first Southern novel I ever read):

> For every Southern boy fourteen years old, not once but whenever he wants it, there is the instant when it's still not two o'clock on that July afternoon in 1863, the brigades are in position behind the rail fence, the guns are laid and ready in the woods and the furled flags are already loosened to break out . . . and it's all in the balance, it hasn't happened yet, it hasn't even begun yet, it not only hasn't begun yet but there is still time for it not to begin. . . .

There was a song, "Flyin' South" by Hank Locklin, that was popular in my adolescence, which had the refrain, "In the South is where I want to be." And now I was seeing it for myself.

When I left the train at Atlanta I would spend only a morning there, and perhaps an afternoon, for I was to return for an extended stay later in the summer. It was April 7, a Saturday; on Wednesday the eleventh I was to see the novelist Madison Jones in Auburn, Alabama, where he teaches and lives. I could therefore make my way there slowly and be reasonably free with my time. After Auburn I would go to Montgomery, Mobile, New Orleans, Lake Pontchartrain, Covington, and Baton Rouge, and then back via Gulfport and Biloxi to my base in Charlottesville, Virginia.

I was still at the stage of traveling when a recitation of the names of places shortly to be seen produces a frisson of excitement as at the prospect of romance about to be realized. I found at that time (though familiarity with the place has since diminished it) a romance about the name *Atlanta*, perhaps because it sounds like

13

Atlantis and Atalanta; certainly there seemed to me something mythological about its syllables. An image would come to me of a city rising above devastation like a phoenix from the ashes, for the best known fact about Atlanta's history is that in the last weeks of 1864 General Sherman left 90 percent of the city in smoldering ruins. Atlanta is thus a forebear of those European cities which were destroyed not by marauding barbarians but by civilized neighbors using all the achievements of their civilization to insure the maximum destruction. This thought was a further reminder to me of what I feel is too often forgotten—that the American Civil War, so smothered in the popular mind by subsequent picturesque and romantic treatment, was in many important respects the first *modern* war, its tragedies belonging to our century as much as to its own. After all, one of the reasons why we all know so much about it was that it was the first war to be photographed—Atlanta, Richmond and Jackson are thus kin to Warsaw and Hamburg, Saigon and Phnomh Penh, in that their death agonies were recorded by the media.

Nevertheless, Atlanta had risen anew and now was said to be the capital of the New South. I felt there should be something triumphant about it, and indeed there was. But its railroad station—delightfully called Peachtree—was a disappointment; the Southern Crescent slid into it before I was really aware of our having entered a city at all, and indeed it turned out to be a small and rather forlorn affair, its hall deserted except for one student who lay sprawled across a bench, unshaven and fast asleep. There is something alarming about arriving at a place which looks nothing like one's expectations of it (I had imagined a bustling station fit for a metropolis of almost two million people), and my consequent feeling of slight panic was intensified when I stepped out into a wide and empty tree-lined road which again in no way seemed part of a huge, thriving city. I consulted a map, worked out where I must be in relation to what I took to be the heart of Atlanta, and set out toward it. It was 8:30 A.M. I could tell from the sky and the air quivering above the surface of the road that the day would be hot, my first hot day since I'd arrived in the United States at the beginning of March.

There was, of course, a very good reason for the curious sleepiness of the station: hardly anyone ever arrives in Atlanta by train.

I had walked for some time down a pleasant but uninteresting suburban road before, standing at the crest of a downward-sloping avenue, I saw—as if placed there for my benefit only instants before—downtown Atlanta. I think there can be no urban landscape in the world more dramatic than Atlanta seen from a short distance. It is a dense, sudden, strange cluster of skyscrapers, diverse in shape and height but all at a casual glance seemingly made of polished glass. Since that first moment I have seen the prospect of Atlanta many times and from almost all points of the compass, and I suppose it looked most beautiful seen at dawn from the southwest. Then the rising sun shone through that abrupt and soaring forest of buildings and made the most extraordinary of them all— the round, gigantic, dominating Peachtree Hotel—a burning column of green and orange.

The other day I had cause to look at Bunyan's *The Pilgrim's Progress*, in particular at the account of the Vale of Beulah, so rich in flowers, from which pilgrims could see the Celestial City. I found that, immediately and unbidden, the image of Atlanta came to me as seen from the top of an avenue lined with springtime gardens.

A bus stop nearby made me realize that it was not necessary to walk all the way into downtown Atlanta. While on the bus I searched my mind for references to Atlanta in Southern fiction. In *Gone with the Wind*, in which the city burns so memorably, Scarlet O'Hara describes it as "full of pushy people." The four men in James Dickey's *Deliverance* want to escape from Atlanta to find adventure and reality in the wild country beyond it, but such is the power that life in the city has exercised over them that they are woefully ignorant of what could happen to them away from it. And I remembered an interview with the experimental novelist from Georgia, Marion Montgomery, in which he voiced fears of an "Atlanta-ization" of the rest of the state. All these references were uncomplimentary. Yet from the moment the bus entered the downtown area I felt I was in a great city. It was only afterward that I realized that these literary instances actually paid tribute to a sort of greatness about the place.

I call a city great if it possesses not only a uniqueness but a palpable awareness of its uniqueness, and conveys equally palpably a sense of the interestingness of its present life. It must be of a certain size (say, five hundred thousand inhabitants or more) and contain a number of beautiful or impressive buildings and streets. Atlanta has all these attributes. It is a city of Promethean architectural

15

ambition. A restaurant revolves on the top of the bizarrely shaped tallest hotel in the world. A narrow-looking covered passageway—like some futuristic Bridge of Sighs—spans Peachtree Street, linking one skyscraper to another at a giddying altitude above street level. Nor have the depths been ignored: there are sunken shopping arcades and sunken gardens, fountains and restaurants. There is also the famous Underground Atlanta, to which I made my way during the course of that first morning. (Hardly anyone was there; its subterranean length, lit by gas lamps and lined by fake old shop and cafe façades, looked melancholy as only places meant for pleasure but lacking in revelers can look.)

I shall write more fully of Atlanta later in the book, for I lived there for some time and came to know it rather well. This particular day I spent my time desultorily, in the uncertain and fitful way one too often does in a strange city to which one is ignorantly anxious to do swift justice. Underground Atlanta, as I have said, turned out to be unsatisfactory; I lost the way to the Joel Hurt Memorial Park; I searched—for a long time in vain—for film for my camera; I had several coffees to enable me to fight a rising tiredness. I noticed many gaps and clearings in the central forest of high buildings due to excavations, demolitions and construction. The city, I realized, is set in a permanent quest for change. I tried later to get Atlantans to describe to me how such a street, so patently new, had looked five years or perhaps ten years ago, but they were unable to remember. They could only recall a difference in overall effect. I left the heart of the city and found myself in a complex of streets on its southern side, separated from the center by a chasm of excavations later to become the Atlanta Metro. Gone were the rich and well-dressed people; in this quarter the streets were dirty and the shops scruffy. The people were almost without exception black.

Toward midday, hot and somewhat weary, I walked back into the main part of downtown Atlanta toward the square at the lower end of Peachtree Street, and here a great surprise awaited me. In my absence crowds of considerable size had gathered on the sidewalks, crowds that renewed themselves and indeed swelled as midday gave way to afternoon. There came a noise of brass instruments and beating drums. Then, down the street and around the square came group after group of marchers and float after float. Two hours later the parade still continued. It was as if, I thought,

16

the whole of humanity had decided to go "razzmatazz." My arrival had coincided with the first day of Atlanta's annual Dogwood Festival.

Perhaps to an American it would not have seemed as remarkable as it did to me. There was a near-tangible delight among the spectators—men and women, young and old, black and white; office workers and salesgirls kept coming out to watch happily. There were drum majorettes; black boys in guardsmen's uniforms with bearskins, who, at the beat of a drum, did a curious twisting dance on the burning street; city dignitaries who waved at the crowds like royalty; men riding on an old fire engine, dressed in the bright clothes of the 1920s; and children from North Georgia who carried sprays of blossoms, branches of trees and huge brooms. I must confess I was delighted. To celebrate the coming of the dogwood, the most splendid of all those woodland blossoms I had admired earlier from the train, seemed such a nice thing to be doing. It appears to me now to confirm the closeness almost all Southerners, however urban their lives, feel to nature.

Had, I wondered, a similar scene been described by a Southern writer? Yes—Anne Tyler, whom I had already visited in Baltimore, had written about such a parade in her fine latest novel, *Earthly Possessions* (1977). It provides a sort of epiphany for her three delightful but hopeless and ill-assorted runaways:

> . . . here came another high school band. Everybody clapped and waved. But then there must have been a hitch of some kind, somewhere up front. They came to a halt, still playing, then finished their tune and fell silent and stood staring straight ahead. You could see the little pulses in their temples. You could see the silver chain linking a musician to his piccolo, giving me a sudden comical picture of the accident that must once have happened to make them think of this precaution. I laughed—the loudest sound on the street. For the clapping had stopped by now. There was some understanding between players and audience: each pretending the other wasn't there. Till finally the parade resumed and so did the clapping, and the audience was filled with admiration all over again as if by appointment. The players marched on. Their legs flashed as steadily and evenly as scissors. I was sorry not to have them to watch any more.

17

"I would think a drum would be a right good instrument,"
Jake told me, gazing after them.[2]

I was conscious of a good nature in those Atlanta spectators
comparable to that of the audience Anne Tyler described.

It was a young desk clerk at the Greyhound bus station who suggested I go to Newnan, just over an hour's journey southwest of
Atlanta. He said it was a pretty place, particularly at this time of
year, so I followed his advice. The bus took me through flat farm
country of peach orchards, small woods, hog pastures and corn-
fields. The young man turned out to be right; in any season
Newnan would be delightful, but on this late spring afternoon it
seemed an astoundingly perfect fusion of the beauties of nature and
civilization. People had built the houses, some antebellum, some
in antebellum style, some graced with turrets and other Gothic
appendages, the majority, however, of a classical plainness, and all
proudly verandaed. But nature had profusely and sumptuously
filled the gardens of the houses. Wisteria and lilac grew so tall they
towered over the roofs, scattering petals down on them. Because
the town was long and narrow, one often found oneself walking
down a charming residential street only to encounter rich woodland or meadow a moment later.

At the bus station—if the small, untidy building could be so
called at which I was the only passenger to alight—I was accosted
by two pleasant-looking, plump young girls who said that I looked
lost; could they help? I said I wanted a comfortable, cheap hotel for
the night. They kindly said they would drive me around the town
to find one. Was I English? They both came from originally
British families, though of course their ancestors had been living
in Georgia for the last 120 years, and the uncle of one of the girls
was working on an amateur genealogical study of the main families
of the neighborhood.

This brings me to a great difference I had already noticed between
Southerners and other Americans (Yankees, Californians, etc.),
who seem to me to commit a sort of cultural parricide. These often
betray very little interest in the Britain, Germany or Italy that their
ancestors left behind; indeed, they are frequently extremely vague
and ill-informed about their origins. Most Southerners, on the
other hand, a good proportion of whom have been in their particular area, and often in their own particular corner of it, for a very

18

long time, know much more about where their antecedents came from and are anxious too to increase that knowledge. The explanation may lie in the far greater ethnic homogeneousness of the South; except in Louisiana, most white Southerners come ultimately from Britain, and Scotland and the Ulster Plantations account for a good proportion of these. Looking through a Tennessee or North Georgia telephone book, one encounters the same names as in Glasgow or Edinburgh. At one time I made quite an extensive study of certain aspects of Scottish culture during the course of biographical work on Robert Louis Stevenson, and during my Southern journey I noted many distinctive features of life which seemed to me to have Scottish parallels and therefore roots. These I shall record later.

Early evening and country surroundings meant a pleasant reduction in the heat of the day; those bearskin-wearing young black men in Atlanta had been capering in the street at noon in a temperature somewhere in the 80s. The evening air was fragrant with blossom, the warmth was caressing, and the light was soft and golden. I felt disinclined to read in my motel room but uncertain, with the gathering dusk, how to spend the evening. Then I saw that a movie theater in the main street was showing a film I had missed that winter in London and had wanted to see, a film moreover with a Southern setting—*Ode to Billy Joe*, based on a novel by Herman Raucher. It was filmed in and around Tallahatchie, Mississippi, which I was later to see. I could not have been more pleased at the entertainment offered.

The story of both the novel and film was inspired by a curious ballad sung by Bobby Gentry which, with its baffling words and insistent tune, swept America in the mid 1960s. The plot, as elaborated in longer form, tells of a boy who is something of a misfit in his Mississippi community and who falls in love with a girl. Despite the intensity of his longing, he cannot consummate a relationship with her. He realizes (though for some time the audience does not) that the reason for this is his own latent homosexuality. After a sexual experience with an older man he becomes so disgusted with himself, and so upset at the loss of the girl, that he commits suicide by jumping off the Tallahatchie Bridge into the river.

In view of the grim subject matter, I was surprised to see a great number of children in the small but full theater; indeed, the audience seemed to consist *principally* of children. Directly in front of me was a party of little girls aged six or seven, dressed as for an old-fashioned Sunday School outing in flouncy dresses and ribbons. They seemed to enjoy the film very much and giggled happily at fights, arguments and car crashes. The older members of the audience also found amusement: in the movie the "rednecks" who cause such mayhem drive a truck with an Alabama license plate; this provoked raucous cheers, for Alabama lies close by to the west of Newnan. What these spectators thought of the more serious aspects of the film I do not know. I must confess to being disappointed myself. One receives a sense of the roughness and narrow-mindedness of a Mississippi community, and one sees how an eccentric and sensitive boy such as Billy Joe could not cope with that community's harsh, limited definition of masculinity. In response he turns to homosexual activity. But I found myself regretting the histrionics that seemed to lurk near the surface at the movie's unhappy end.

On Sunday morning the whole of Newnan seemed to be going to church. How different the atmosphere was here from that of an English country town on Sunday, where bells ring out from lofty old churches over deserted, sad-looking streets to summon nobody. The churches in Newnan—Baptist or Presbyterian—were plain, white, and humble in size, although their severe façades were attractively framed by trees in blossom. At church porches many people, soberly dressed and of all ages, greeted one another with a solemn joviality. Then I thought of Sunday mornings in country towns in Ireland or Scotland, but the people here appeared more formal than in the former and more cheerful than in the latter. I crept up with my camera on several groups of worshipers, gathered outside churches and commenting to one another on the loveliness of the day, until several women asked me, in the nicest manner, whether I would like to attend their service. I declined. Why? Because I was shy; because I looked scruffy in T-shirt and jeans. But most of all because I felt, as Thomas Hardy said:

> *That with this bright believing band*
> *I have no claim to be.*

This was only the first of many times when, confronted by the intensity of Southern religious belief, I was to feel this way. I think it is no rash generalization to say that England is, and has been for at least the past forty years, an agnostic country. I grew up and live today in a society in which few people go to any church, where formal religion plays little part and is seldom discussed, and in which most people not only have no coherently formulated faith, but have never made a conscious decision on the matter. Things are very different in the South, particularly in the rural South, as I was to discover. It is strange and not a little alarming for someone from a secular country to find himself in a community where believers are in the majority. But I was to find that witnessing Southern religion and the prominent part it plays in so many lives stirred within me atavistic religious emotions, which I shall refer to again.

Between Newnan and Auburn, Alabama, I broke my journey twice, staying one night in Pine Mountain and the other in Columbus, Georgia, birthplace of the novelist Carson McCullers. Toward Pine Mountain, as its name suggests, the countryside changed to one of wooded hills, though the woods were more deciduous than pine in composition. And not only did the countryside change, but the weather did, too; sun and showers now followed each other in confusing succession. Hills would be all but obscured by curtains of rain, only to stand shimmeringly green and almost tangibly near minutes later.

Pine Mountain is the village from which to see the famous Calloway Gardens, an extensive sanctuary for southern Appalachian flowers, shrubs and trees. One could rent bicycles; I did so and rode for two hours through the gardens. The effect of rain, fitful sunshine and rainbow on the lake, hills and woodland inevitably brought to my mind once again Ireland and Scotland. The first settlers from these countries must have felt quickly at home here; at certain moments, by a bend of the lake or before a prospect of hills, one could have fancied oneself near Innisfree or in Galloway. Then I remembered that ahead lay months of concentrated heat quite unlike anything known in Britain. Yet even in these hottest months—and I was to find them astoundingly, painfully hot—I discovered that the air in the Appalachians is moist and humidity of 98–9 percent can be recorded. For me the azaleas for which Calloway Gardens are famous were the most impressive of all the spring blooms—bank upon bank of exuberant colors that I had never encountered in these flowers before.

Pine Mountain itself is a pleasant enough, rather impermanent-seeming village, nicely permeated by the smells and sounds of woodland but a little too obviously consecrated to tourism to be altogether likeable. I had met the place before in a novel, I knew, but it was some time before I could recollect the exact reference— the judge in Carson McCullers' *Clock without Hands* attended Ku Klux Klan meetings here. It seemed incongruous to relate the infamous Klan to the azaleas, tourists on bicycles, and cabin-style restaurants serving Southern dinners, and yet it was not inconceivable that it met here.

The next morning a couple staying at my motel offered to give me a lift into Columbus. The husband was Canadian and the wife English, though she had lived in North America for over thirty years. They both preferred the United States—and in particular the South—to either Canada or Britain, mainly because they felt it was more capable of resisting "creeping socialism" than other places. They were afraid however that President Carter was flirting with socialism; they hoped his native Georgia upbringing and commonsense would come to his rescue. They intended to retire to Georgia, for they felt that the South was almost the only bastion of Christianity and wholesome values, of antisocialism and political conservatism, left in the world. While they talked we drove through woods of a tender beauty and caught glimpses of a gentle but wild hillscape to the north and south. There *was* one thing about Georgia, though, that the man didn't like: he had once seen, along this very road, a chain gang. The sight of men chained together had been unpleasant enough, but what had really upset him was the way the man in charge of the prisoners, all black, had bullied and abused them.

Columbus seemed to me a dreary, formless town although I cannot pretend to know it well. It vies with Savannah for a place as the second city of Georgia. Its older part is the west end, down by the Chattahoochee River; its newer east end, which contains the smarter residential area, is situated on a small hill. To walk from one end to the other, one has to cross the railroad track, and when I reached this point I had to wait for some time while a freight train passed by. I remembered the lines of a Southern song:

> *The train I ride on*
> *Is a hundred coaches long,*
> *You can hear the whistle blow a hundred miles.*
> *If that train was right,*

I'll be home tomorrow night,
'Cause I'm nine hundred miles from my home.
An' I hate to hear that lonesome whistle blow.

The train that passed me in Columbus, Georgia, did not have a hundred coaches—only forty-seven—but they seemed more like a thousand as one followed the other in heavy, slow rhythm. The South and the freight train have an intimate relationship, as I mentioned before. In their book *Folk Song USA* two eminent experts on American folk music, John and Alan Lomax, have this to say about it:

All through the strip of country that runs from Maryland, south and west to Oklahoma, which is the land of fiddlers, guitar players, banjo pickers, and harp blowers, you can hear them making lonesome whistle tunes on their instruments. A fiddler will pull his bow in a low, minor moan across his top string and then start jerking it in quick, raspy strokes until you close your eyes and hear a heavy freight train running away down a steep grade. A harmonica player will blow out the high, hollering notes of a fast passenger engine, while the guitar player will make a rhythm on his bass strings like a train crossing a trestle. Together they'll play in the rhythm of car wheels clicking over sleepers as counterrhythm, they'll whip out the rattling bounce of a caboose as it shakes and jounces along a rough roadbed. Then they'll throw back their heads and holler.

"Lord, Lord, I hate to hear that lonesome whistle blow."

These folk musicians and the people they're playing for listen to railroad whistles the way fisherfolk listen to bell-buoys and foghorns. Out in the country they tell time by the whistles of the trains that fly past their fields. The railroad whistles bring them good news and bad news. The whistles talk to them about the places they have never been, the women they've never seen, the fine clothes they've never worn. . . . The whistles talk to them about the folk who have gone down that long, lonesome road and won't be back again. . . . The whistles talk to them about the great big raw country they live in. The whistles remind them that every man is a traveler on a lonesome road. . . .[3]

23

The very names of many Southern folk tunes proclaim the inspiration of the railroad: "Cotton Blossom Special," "Orange Blossom Special" and "Wabash Cannonball."

Wandering around the older parts of Columbus I did not find the yearning to be free and away hard to understand. Too many American commercial towns produce this through their cheerlessness, ugliness and sense of impermanency. Downtown Louisville, Kentucky; downtown Durham, North Carolina; Charlotte, Raleigh, Columbia—all seemed so forlorn, unhomely and unloved that a loneliness and a pining to be elsewhere would sweep through me. Perhaps the builders of these towns were in their hearts so deeply antiurban that they did not wish them to seem like home; for them happiness and reality may have been the country, while a town was something necessary, alas, but by its very nature temporary and unimportant. Their creations, however, have taken revenge on them for this attitude, not least in the violence their drabness engenders in the inhabitants. (I was warned, with tales of shootings and muggings, by two couples in Columbus to stay inside my motel after dark.)

Standing in Main Street at the decline of afternoon I experienced again this sense of forlornness, which receives such powerful expression in the works of Columbus' most famous offspring, Carson McCullers (1917–1967).

Her sister Margarita Smith, in her moving introduction to *The Mortgaged Heart* (a collection of Carson McCullers' miscellaneous writings), says that of all her characters the one who resembled the writer most was the girl Frankie in *The Member of the Wedding,* with her search, born of isolation, for the "we of me"; her sense of kinship to the freaks she has seen at the fair, her painful crossing of the threshold of puberty, marked by a heightened intimation of mortality. But imaginative and finely wrought though *The Member of the Wedding* is, I find myself thinking more often of Carson McCullers' first and last novels, *The Heart Is a Lonely Hunter* (1940) and *Clock without Hands* (1961). Both are redolent of a deep conviction of loneliness as an essential, perhaps *the* essential, fact of human existence; both attest to dreams and emotions that neither life in a dreary Southern town, nor perhaps life anywhere, can ever gratify.

The Heart Is a Lonely Hunter must be one of the most remarkable first novels ever written. (Incidentally, it is fascinating to compare the novel as published with Carson McCullers' original notes for it, preserved in *The Mortgaged Heart*.) In a "fairly large," hot, dull town of cotton mills and mean streets, where you can see in the faces a "desperate look of hunger and of loneliness," a town of heavy afternoons and pointless eruptions of strong pent-up feeling, we meet four people, all of whom are ravaged by a seemingly unappeasable hunger of the spirit. Mick is a "gamine" girl of fourteen from a ramshackle, financially unstable family; random encounters with classical music, heard drifting from radios as she roams the streets on warm evenings, awaken yearnings in her of near-unbearable force. Jake at twenty-nine is a confirmed alcoholic who was once convinced he had a mission to convert his fellow workers to socialist brotherhood. Benedict Copeland is a black doctor, and in some ways his is the most disturbing of the four portraits. Ascetic, proudly dedicated to the lonely perusal of Marx and Spinoza, and obsessed by the injustices perpetrated on his race (and more particularly on himself as an intelligent person), he is in fact arrogantly disdainful of most of his fellows, shut off from the common joys and feelings of normal life. Fourth is Biff Brannon, a lovelessly married cafe proprietor, whose sex drive has virtually ceased and who looks instead for affection and a breaking away from the narrow definitions of masculine and feminine.

These four people, so different in personality and situation, all find themselves deeply affected by a deaf-mute, John Singer, who seems to them at once noble, wise and compassionate—aloof from humdrum human entanglement yet kindly perceptive of it. Each of the four uses Singer as the receptacle of his or her frustrations, pouring out to this strange-faced man, who can neither speak nor hear, ceaseless sagas of their unhappy predicaments. They are not wholly wrong about Singer, for he does possess a certain nobility and he is altruistic. But his reactions to the stories he receives are very different from what their tellers imagine. For Singer's heart is elsewhere, committed irretrievably to a fellow deaf-mute, an obese and mentally retarded Greek who at the beginning of the novel is taken off to an institution. When the Greek dies, John Singer kills himself for he has no further reason to live. He leaves the four confessing souls bewildered and more lonely than ever.

The Heart Is a Lonely Hunter is not a flawless book. To me Carson McCullers brings alive two of her four main characters—the hoydenish Mick and tortured Dr. Copeland—more successfully than the others. The social criticism is at times too overt, too little assimilated into the texture of the novel. And the explosions of violence, though intended to surprise and shock, are sometimes inadequately anticipated. This said, it is a haunting, poetic and intricately worked novel and a complex, organic metaphor of human existence; one takes away from it a chastening sense of lives trapped together with a not altogether dispiriting awareness of the blazing intensity of frustrated aspirations.

The Heart Is a Lonely Hunter brought Carson McCullers almost instant fame; with this one book she became one of America's most acclaimed novelists. However her last novel, *Clock without Hands,* has not had quite the salute it deserves. Carson McCullers was a sick woman when she wrote it; had she been stronger she may have amplified certain parts of the novel, for here and there I feel we ought to know and hear more than we are given. Nevertheless, it remains for me one of the best Southern novels, and (Madison Jones' *Cry of Absence* excepted) the very best of those which have the period of desegregation or imminent desegregation as their subject. This tense, unhappy and completely necessary stage is not its only subject though, nor even its principal subject, which, it seems to me, is death. The novel begins authoritatively and frighteningly: "Death is always the same, but each man dies in his own way. For J.T. Malone it began in such a simple ordinary way that for a time he confused the end of life with the beginning of a new season."

J.T. Malone owns a drugstore but once cherished intellectual ambitions. Now he has incurable leukemia, and on the last page of the book he dies. But as in *The Heart Is a Lonely Hunter*, we are concerned not with one man but with four whose lives interconnect, even interact, without their being fully aware of the fact. The others are J.T. Malone's old friend, an octogenarian judge who is obsessed by the majesty of the Southern past; Jester, his imaginative adolescent grandson, uncertain and sexually ambivalent; and a strange, psychopathic Negro with blue eyes, Sherman Pew. The crises in these individual lives are heightened by the tensions of the Civil Rights movement. Beyond these four people are the dead—the loved, once-known dead and the "great" dead of the South's glorious years.

There are times in this novel when Carson McCullers seems to sound the very note of heartache, of apprehension of life's terrors, that eludes all but the greatest novelists. Here is Judge Clane, who spends a great deal of his mental energy brooding on a crazy scheme to restore the South through the recovery and realization of confiscated Confederate bonds, remembering his cherished dead:

> Several months ago he had read . . . the words: "How can the dead be truly dead when they are still walking in my heart?" It was from an old Indian legend and the Judge could not forget it. He had seen in his mind's eye a barefooted, bronzed Indian walking silently in the forest and heard the silent sound of a canoe. He never cried about his wife's death. . . . When his nervous system and tear ducts made him cry, he thought of his brother Beau, and Beau was like a lightning rod that could ground and safely conduct his tears. Beau was two years older than he was, and had died when he was eighteen years old. As a young boy Fox Clane had worshiped his brother, yea, worshiped the ground he walked on. Beau acted, could recite, was the president of the Milan Players Club. Beau could have been anything. Then one night he had come in with a sore throat. The next morning he was delirious. It was an infected throat, and Beau was muttering "I am dying, Egypt, dying, ebbs the crimson life tide fast." Then he began to sing, "I feel, I feel, I feel like the morning star; I feel, I feel, I feel like the morning star. Shoo, fly, don't bother me!" At the end Beau had begun to laugh although it wasn't laughter. The young Fox had shuddered so violently that his mother had sent him to the back room. It was a bare bleak room that was a sickroom, playroom where the children had their measles, mumps and childhood diseases, and where they were free to roughhouse when they were well. The Judge remembered an old forgotten rocking horse, and a sixteen-year-old boy had put his arms around the wooden horse—and cried—and even as an eighty-five-year-old man he could cry whenever he wanted to, just thinking about that early sorrow. The Indian walking silently in the forest and the silent sound of the canoe. "How can the dead be truly dead when they are still walking in my heart?"[4]

The novel culminates in an appalling act of violence—the mad, depraved Negro boy, whose blue eyes proclaim that he is part white, is murdered by a handful of white citizens of the town because he

has taken rooms in a white quarter. The dying J. T. Malone, however, will have nothing to do with the killing; the shadow of
death, Carson McCullers suggests, should surely make us fearful of
doing harm to another human being. We are all fellow-victims of
life; why must we compound its cruelty?

If she had sustained these finest moments, Carson McCullers
would be among the best American novelists. She does not, however; a preoccupation with the bizarre, the freakish and the
hysterical undercuts for me even her most successful work. The
edge between exploration of life's darkest sides and morbid indulgence is a fine one, and Carson McCullers strays too often over
it. This is a pity, though she cannot be wholly blamed for it. For
the obsessive harping on the freak, the maimed and the eccentric
is something encountered so often in Southern literature that
it must be the result of something within Southern experience.
But what? I did not feel ready even to attempt guesses. Loneliness—
yes, in these Columbus streets, as in Louisville and Durham earlier,
I could sense why this should stalk the pages of the Southern novel.
But the freakish? All the other guests at the motel were Southern.
The early evening was hot, and the morning's rain seemed a
distant event. Families were dipping in and out of the pool, and a
more healthy-looking group of people it would be hard to envisage.

Carson McCullers' position in Southern literature is an uncertain
one. In the world outside the South she was for many years thought
of as the very pattern and exemplar of the Southern writer;
throughout the 1940s and early 1950s she was second only to
Faulkner in fame. However, this is not the case today. Carson
McCullers' tragically short life—marred by much physical and
emotional suffering—was led for the most part away from the
South, in New York City, and it is principally as a New York
bohemian that she emerges in the stories told about her. Southerners
say she lived too long away from the places of her fiction, and
that her particular brand of grotesquerie has given Southern fiction
a bad name. Nevertheless, the people and places of her formative
years and the people and places of her novels were all unquestion-
ably Southern, and among the ranks of Southern writers she must
be accorded a place.

Carson McCullers wrote some poetry (mostly later in her life);
it is not of particularly high quality and lacks the originality of her
prose. But there are three lines of hers which occur to me often

when I think of the South and its relation to its past:

> *The dead demand a double vision. A furthered zone,*
> *Ghostly decision of apportionment. For the dead can claim*
> *The lover's sense, the mortgaged heart.*[5]

At the Alabama border one goes back in time, so that I arrived in Auburn, Alabama, at the very hour that the bus had left Columbus, Georgia. One should not make an easy symbol out of this, but it is tempting to do so. For while Georgia, epitomized by big, booming Atlanta, is the vaunted cradle and apotheosis of the New South, Alabama, whose present capital Montgomery was the capital of the Confederacy itself, has come to represent in the popular mind the Old South and its reactionary perpetuation. Its very name, picturesque in sound, has an effect on people who know little about the state and its history. Its images are potent. A primary one is the plantation myth, encapsulated in popular songs such as "Alabama Moon," "Alabama Jubilee," "The Midnight Train to Alabam'," and "O Susannah." But its recent fame and resulting images have been exceedingly grim. The ugly incidents of the Selma-to-Montgomery march; white Alabamians preventing blacks from voting; Governor George Wallace personally blocking the doors of a university to black students—such hideous visions do not easily fade. They come swiftly to my own mind when Alabama is mentioned. The state must accept the consequences of its past deeds, however unfair this may seem to its people later when times have changed. I fear it will be a long time before these memories altogether recede in outsiders' minds. (The word *Alabama*, incidentally, has a charming derivation. According to my guidebook, the migratory Indians who first reached it exclaimed "Alba Amo," which means "This is a goodly land. Clear the thickets. Plant the seed. Here we rest!" How two words as short as these can mean something so long was not explained.)

Founded by the Spanish, colonized by the French, conquered by the British, sold to the new United States government after the Revolution and admitted as a state in 1819, Alabama's history has been a varied one. It was one of the first states to follow the secession of South Carolina from the Union, after which it existed for a month as an independent republic and then joined the Confederacy, whose center it became for a time. Its people were savagely punished during the Reconstruction, and in more recent times it

29

has been the scene of some of the most bitter and violent racial clashes.

The weather was proving changeable. The evening before had been warm, but I made the journey to Auburn (through thickly wooded, rolling countryside and via the pretty town of Opelika) in driving rain. By the time I was dropped off beside a gas station in Auburn the sky was really black and the rain was dense, fast and noisy. The garage owner suggested that I take shelter inside his establishment and I gladly accepted his invitation.

I made for a room adjacent to the mechanic's workshop where a television set stood. From its screen a serious, well-dressed man looked out; he was seated at a desk and his expression was both businesslike and intent. He was about to speak, I heard him say, on a matter of the greatest importance to the world at the present time. I settled down to listen to what I thought would be a program of a political nature, but the man soon disabused me of this idea. People would think, he said, that by this he meant a Middle Eastern crisis or a failure in the dollar. That wasn't what he'd come to talk about at all. It was the dreadful truth, and one that contemporary society failed to face up to, that every man would suffer eternal damnation unless he came to believe in the Lord Jesus Christ. His tone was at once matter-of-fact and missionary. The rain continued to pour down, the men at the garage went about their tasks unheeding, and I went on listening to this man, who looked like (and indeed may have been) a sensible company president, speaking measuredly of hell and how it surely awaited the majority of mankind.

The rain abated a little, so I made my way to the Heart of Auburn Hotel. Auburn, where I was to stay for the best part of three days, is a small town devoted almost entirely to the university's spacious, attractive campus with lawns, gardens, bowers and one tall building in its midst, in which Madison Jones has his office. The rest of the town consists principally of two straggling commercial streets which give way without much effort to woodland, along with residential roads of pleasant houses and gardens full of azaleas.

I made contact with Madison Jones, who not only lent me various periodicals and reviews relating to his work but also an advance copy of his latest book *Passage through Gehenna*, a powerful novel which I spent some of that wet afternoon reading. I was to spend most of the next day with Madison Jones and his family and then saw him again the following morning. But I will give an account of my conversations with him in the next chapter, which deals not with my travels but with the writers.

I had an invitation for my first evening in Auburn—from Anne, a girl I'd met by chance near my motel who had shown me around the campus that morning, sheltering me from the rain with her umbrella. I was to go to her house for supper and beer. Anne lived in an old clapboard, verandaed house which turned out to be pleasantly full of cats. Here I met a young writer whom I shall call R.

I greatly enjoyed the vigor of R's conversation, which was at the same time both personal and revelatory of a stimulating, objective interest in literature and social culture. Later he gave me a volume of his poems, a number of which I found impressive and as thoughtful and energetic as his talk. I look forward to later books from him—he is still in his twenties. I do not name him only because I want to record here remarks made in the informality of a social evening; to ascribe them to him as a named individual might give them a significance he did not intend. Nevertheless they made a strong impression on me.

R had grown up in the rural South though not, in fact, in Alabama. His career had been interrupted, like that of too many Americans of his generation, by the war in Vietnam, an experience which haunted him even now. I asked him if he had ever contemplated dodging the draft. He said never; the atmosphere of his home would have made it impossible for him not to have gone— it was expected of him. After all, he had been taught to handle and revere guns since his earliest years, and even now he accepted them as a part of his heritage. I suppose, he added, the South is the nearest approximation ever to the culture of Sparta.

Indeed, in spite of his abundant literary preoccupations, he had by no means turned his back on the way of life of the rural South. He was fond of escaping from the atmosphere of the university by going to Veteran Farm Workers (VFW) socials. It was through meeting people here that he had become interested in what he thought was one of the liveliest subcultures of the region, cock-fighting. (He added that he was unsure of the morality of this cruel sport.) What fascinated him about cock-fighting were its rituals and mythology; the cult of the individual birds, the knowledge of pedigree and the excitement generated by their performance. The other evening he'd been to a VFW dance and had begun talking to a man about this. "Do you want to see a fight tonight?" the man had asked him. "Come with us afterward!"

A convoy of cars had drawn up by the roadside, parked in such a way that passersby could not see what was happening beyond, birds were produced, and fights began. I asked if any women were present at these deplorable affairs. He said yes, but they were not what you would call "ladies." Later I was to hear that in the country-side of Virginia cock-fights were also held, promoted by certain uppercrust families.

R. also told me about snake-handling churches, institutions hitherto unknown to me. R. had relations who belonged to them. They are mostly to be found in the mountains of Tennessee and North Carolina. Their curious practices derive from equally curious words in the now disputed last chapter of the Gospel of St. Mark:

> He that believeth and is baptized shall be saved, and he that believeth not shall be damned. And these signs shall follow them that believe; in my name shall they cast out devils; they shall speak with new tongues; They shall take up serpents; and if they drink any deadly thing it shall not hurt them.

The New English Bible, in addition to stating the probable apocryphal nature of this coda to the Gospel, not only softens these dreadful words but suggests that they only apply to those who came in contact with the eleven Apostles whom Christ was addressing.

R. told me that in the churches snakes of the deadliest kinds—rattlesnakes and copperheads—are thrown around, caught and stroked as proof of the worshipers' salvation. R. said that all states have made snake-handling illegal with the exception of Tennessee in whose eastern part it is strongest; he knew in fact of one village there in which all the churches practiced snake-handling.

Back in my motel I began to make a list of questions to ask Madison Jones during our meeting in the morning. And at this stage I feel I should state my purpose in interviewing the Southern writers I had asked to see, which will be to state my ultimate purpose in writing this book. "The South," wrote Reynolds Price in "Dodo, Phoenix or Tough Old Cock," an essay on the Southern novel, "can come honorably out of a cool exam-ination of its fiction in the past forty years. In fact its record as a

country can stand with the simultaneous record of any country—
with France, Britain, Germany, the rest of America. . . . And whatever new subjects, new forms of life the New South is offering . . .
the Old South will go on offering its life as subject for another fifty
years at least—the working life of those who are children in it now.
Not offering but *imposing*."[6]

"As a country"—I remember the intellectual excitement I felt
when I first read these significant words. They seemed to help
answer a question that had been perplexing me for some time. The
rollcall of Southern writers since 1920 (I slightly extend Reynolds
Price's period) is a most impressive one: Ellen Glasgow, John Crowe
Ransom, Donald Davidson, William Faulkner, Allen Tate,
Andrew Lytle, Robert Penn Warren, Caroline Gordon, Katharine
Anne Porter, Thomas Wolfe, Carson McCullers, James Agee,
Flannery O'Connor, William Styron, Eudora Welty, James
Dickey, Peter Taylor, Walker Percy, Madison Jones, Reynolds
Price, Anne Tyler and others. . . . It hardly needs to be said that
these are writers admirable for their artistry, insight, sensibility,
intellectual vigor and individuality. And these qualities are what is
most important about each of them; William Faulkner's *The
Sound and the Fury*, Allen Tate's *The Fathers*, Carson McCullers'
The Heart Is a Lonely Hunter, Eudora Welty's *The Optimist's
Daughter*—these masterworks could be (and indeed are) enjoyed
and respected by readers with no knowledge of or concern for the
South. This fact, true of the books by each of the people listed, at
once removes the possibility of their being considered merely
regional. For a regional writer is interesting *primarily* because of
his relation to his particular area. Nevertheless, all these writers
have set their work in the South, dealt with specific Southern
issues or situations, and show themselves to be obsessed with
Southern history and culture. But out of Southern themes they
have made complex statements of universal reference and truth.

To say this is to leave a lot unsaid. Could one subtract the South
from their work? Certainly not. Universal they may be, but these
writers think of themselves as Southerners; they frequently acknowledge kinships with one another which they do not feel with
writers from elsewhere; and clearly their visions of life have been
shaped by their Southern experience and awareness of the uniqueness of the South.

But if one regards the writers as coming from a separate

country—and after all, the South was once the independent Confederate States of America—then much in their curious position is explained. A serious novelist is usually concerned with the problems and culture of his own country, at the same time that he or she takes it for granted that the subject matter will be interesting and important to the readers. Thus the Southern writer can tackle plights peculiar to the South in terms that make them seem part of the world's experience, and at the same time feel free to be him or herself.

Common nationality among writers means the sharing of important qualities. Ever since the late 1950s when, still in my teens, I became a confirmed reader of fiction, I have admired various Southern novelists, finding in them a respect for the individual human being, a nondetached relationship to society, a poetic apprehension of time and place, and an emotional intensity that I encountered in few other contemporary writers. And yet these books, which I found so refreshing in their humanity, were coming from a society which as the 1960s progressed was increasingly open to censure for its stubborn inhumanity. Here seemed another paradox.

In talking to the writers I wanted to ask them about their work, about the relationship of their life to their fiction, and about the obsessions and preoccupations that drove them to this art form. I was interested in them as novelists first and Southerners second. But I felt there might emerge from the conversations I had with them, and from ensuing serious consideration of their books, some glimmer as to what unique features the South's culture possessed.

As I climbed the flight of steps up to the capitol building in Montgomery I inevitably thought again about the South as a "separate country." For it was on the topmost step, on February 18, 1861, that Jefferson Davis proclaimed the Confederate States of America and took his oath of office as their first president; a star-shaped brass plaque marks the spot today. The morning of the proclamation was fair and balmy, and this was interpreted as a good omen for the new nation's future.

Montgomery's capitol, which dates from 1851, dominates the city in much the same way as the United States Capitol dominates Washington, D.C. Not only its elevated situation but its dome, its whiteness, and its classical façade bring the more famous building to mind. I was not surprised, therefore, to find out that its architect, George Nichols, based his designs on the Washington capitol, a curious presage of the fate that was to overtake Montgomery ten years later when, like Washington, D.C., it too became the capital of a nation.

The morning of my own walk to the capitol was fair, too, with bright but kindly sunshine and a cloudless sky; the many blossoms of magnolia and camellia which flourished in the parks and gardens of Montgomery showed their colors against a vivid blue backcloth. I turned around and looked at the city below me. The broad, dignified length of Decatur Street sweeps up to the capitol and it was along this, as part of the pageantry that heralded Jefferson Davis' inauguration, that Confederate troops marched to a new tune, "Dixie," the future anthem of the South. As I stood surveying the town the street was quiet, and I saw that the last twenty years had added a dreary crop of new buildings to Montgomery's otherwise pleasant townscape. But all the same I found it easy to imagine that band playing its way up the avenue, easy to imagine the emotions that swelled within the people of Montgomery as they listened to its tune.

Surely no more stirring march than "Dixie" has ever been written. Its romantic swagger must appeal to even the least martial of hearts:

> *I wish I was in Dixie, hooray, hooray!*
> *In Dixieland I'll take my stand*
> *To live and die in Dixie*
> *Away, away, away down South in Dixie!*

Madison Jones had told me that, sadly, you could no longer hear "Dixie" played in the South, whereas until the late 1960s it still had currency as a Southern anthem and was to be heard at most public functions. Certainly this is not the case today; the march of a pro-slavery army is considered offensive by black Southerners. But you *can* hear it, and witness the tremendous response the tune elicits, which I was to do later.

A few yards from the capitol steps stands a statue of Jefferson Davis, put up like the star-shaped plaque by the Daughters of the Confederacy, so that his craggy, intellectual, half-blind face still stares down at the street up which his army once marched so joyously. Around the pedestal beneath his feet are carved the names of those states which made up the Confederacy. By the day of his inauguration there were seven—South Carolina, the first to secede as it is still proud to announce; Georgia; Florida; Alabama; Mississippi; Louisiana; and lastly, the biggest, Texas, which seceded on February 1, 1861. In April and May of that year the states of the upper South joined them: Virginia, Arkansas, Tennessee and North Carolina. Later still the Confederacy admitted the divided Kentucky and Missouri, though neither of these actually seceded and were represented only by "governments in exile."

Is the term *South* as used today synonymous with the old Confederacy? This issue had much exercised me, as it must anyone who is concerned with Southern culture. The answer is no. That the South means Virginia, North Carolina, South Carolina, Tennessee, Georgia, Alabama, Mississippi and Louisiana no one would dispute, least of all the citizens of these states (though northern Virginia does contain dormitory towns for Washington, D.C., and the inhabitants of these may or may not think of themselves as Southerners). Of the other Confederate states, Texas seems to me (and to others, including Texans themselves) simply Texas—a state of almost unbelievable vastness with a stubborn and individual history of its own, with terrains utterly unlike anywhere else in the South, and with a very strong sense of its own unique identity. Indeed today there is a supposedly "separatist" movement inside Texas, as many car stickers testify. Texas' northern neighbor, Arkansas, is also geographically and culturally distinct from the other Southern states. The pattern of its settlement differs from that of its nearest Southern neighbors Mississippi and Louisiana, and the Mississippi River would appear to constitute a real frontier. Geography has also resulted in the development of Florida along very different lines from the other Southern states. The playground of eastern America and a favorite place for people from all over the country to retire to, Florida is distinguished by its unusual urban–rural ratio—80 percent urban to 20 percent rural. Louisiana comes next highest of the once Confederate states with a 66 percent urban population, and in North Carolina, South Carolina and Mississippi more people live in the country than in towns.

As for the two "government-in-exile" states, Missouri would, for geographical and cultural reasons, make no claim to be part of the South. But Kentucky is a different matter. Traveling through the mountains from Tennessee into Kentucky one feels no sense of passing from one region into another. The wooded ravines continue.

36

Kentuckians have always felt close cultural and emotional ties with other Southerners, and some of the most distinguished Southerners, including Jefferson Davis himself, came from this state. There is a saying that Kentucky seceded from the Union after the Civil War was over. Certainly some of the finest celebrants of the Confederate past—Allen Tate, Robert Penn Warren and Caroline Gordon—are from Kentucky.

On the west side of the capitol stands a huge memorial to Confederate dead. It is ugly, though by no means without dramatic effect. I read after I visited Montgomery that it is crowned by a symbol of peace, a figure of a woman laying down a sword and lifting up a flag. I did not notice her, and certainly peace is not what this flamboyant monument suggests. In fact, I was more interested in the pedestal than in the swirl of forms it supports. The cornerstone was laid in 1886 by Jefferson Davis himself. One cannot help wondering what his emotions must have been as, twenty-one years after the defeat of the nation over which he had presided, he laid this stone. A man of great integrity, he had little cause for guilt but much for sorrow: an ideal and vision collapsed, thousands of men killed, whole cities burned, great tracts of countryside laid waste, and every Southern state harrowed and punished by the exploitation of the Reconstruction. Davis himself had known the anguishes of imprisonment, demands for his death from his former enemies, and blame from his former followers.

Yet the monument suggests defeat and regret even less than peace. On each of the four sides of the pedestal a verse is engraved. With interest I copied these stanzas down:

> *The Knightliest of the Knightly Race*
> *Who, since the days of old,*
> *Have kept the lamp of Chivalry*
> *Alight in hearts of gold.*

> *The seamen of Confederate fame*
> *Startled the wondering world*
> *For braver fight was never fought,*
> *And fairer flag was never furled.*

> *When this historic shaft shall crumbling lie*
> *In ages hence, in woman's heart will be,*
> *A folded flag, a thrilling page unrolled,*
> *A deathless song of Southern chivalry.*

37

> *Fame's temple boasts no higher name*
> *No king is grander on his throne,*
> *No glory shines with brighter gleam,*
> *The name of Patriot stands alone.*

These sentiments are to be found—better expressed—in novel after novel dealing with the Civil War written by Southerners, from works of fine literary quality like Ellen Glasgow's *The Battleground* to popular bestsellers like Margaret Mitchell's *Gone with the Wind*. Many are the work of women—and do not the verses say "in woman's heart will be . . . a deathless song of Southern chivalry"?

Inevitably a counterreaction surfaces, prompted by the late-twentieth-century distrust of public heroics. For surely, without in any way detracting from the undoubted bravery and idealism of many of the fighting Southerners, there was a great deal of self-interest in their stand; indeed, we know there was—in their desire to keep the South a prosperous agrarian economy. The South had no monopoly on courage and honor, contrary to what it often suggests; there were probably as many Northerners with these qualities, many of whom (though much Southern writing scarcely admits the possibility) really did fight inspired by their detestation of the "peculiar institution" of slavery.

But there is something soul-stirring in a nation of nine million (almost half of whom were slaves and over a third of whom were not soldiers) taking on in combat a greatly richer nation of twenty-two million. The histories of the Southern leaders—Stonewall Jackson, Robert E. Lee, Jeb Stuart, P. G. T. Beauregard, and Jefferson Davis himself—make inspiring reading; there *was* a heroic stature about these men. And the terrible losses the South suffered also demand sympathy. Professor Roland, in his book *The Confederacy*, makes such a demand:

> Her resistance was so determined that it was overcome only after four years of prodigious strife and after immense regions of the Confederacy were laid waste through total war. Out of approximately 1,000,000 Southern men enrolled in the Confederate ranks during the conflict, more than one-fourth died of wounds and disease. Almost 100,000 were killed in battle. In relation to the number of Southern white people, these service casualties were as great as those endured by major European participants in the wars of the twentieth century. If the North

during the Civil War had suffered commensurately she would have lost more than 1,000,000 men instead of 360,000. The American Colonies in revolt against England would have lost 94,000 men instead of 12,000. The United States in World War II would have lost well over 6,000,000 men instead of somewhat more than 300,000. The Confederacy rendered the heaviest sacrifice in lives and substance ever made by Americans.[7]

Perhaps no impersonal public monument—either in stone or in words—ever really touches one. Certainly Allen Tate's wonderful poem "Ode to the Confederate Dead" moved me to serious realization of Southern valor and defeat far more than this towering affair in Montgomery:

> *Turn your eyes to the immoderate past,*
> *Turn to the inscrutable infantry rising*
> *Demons out of the earth—they will not last.*
> *Stonewall, Stonewall, and the sunken fields of hemp,*
> *Shiloh, Antietam, Malvern Hill, Bull Run.*
> *Lost in that orient of the thick-and-fast*
> *You will curse the setting sun.*
> *(Cursing only the leaves crying*
> *Like an old man in a storm) . . .*[8]

I was also moved by reading what a Southern soldier toward the end of the Civil War wrote on the back of a Confederate note, which was worthless.

> *Representing nothing on God's earth now,*
> *And nought in the waters below it,*
> *As the pledge of a nation that passed away,*
> *Keep it, dear friend, and show it,*
> *Show it to those who will lend an ear,*
> *To the tale this paper will tell,*
> *Of liberty born of a patriot's dream,*
> *Of a storm-cradled nation that fell.*

"A nation that fell." Perhaps it is too little remembered outside the South that the Confederacy had wanted to be a separate nation at peace with its greater neighbor. Jefferson Davis stated these wishes in his inaugural address. "But," he continued, "if this be denied to us, and the integrity and jurisdiction be assailed, it will but remain for us, with firm resolve, to appeal to arms and invoke the blessings of Providence on a just cause." The necessity to appeal to arms was felt only three months later, and for the next four years the South fought for nationhood.

The Confederacy had its own president, its own permanent government, its own very powerful armed forces, and its own constitution which—like its capitol building—was closely modeled on the original federal one. The Confederates had no real quarrel with the U.S. Constitution; they viewed themselves faithful to its spirit. All the same, there were interesting differences between the two constitutions. Slavery was named and approved as such: no law could be passed denying or weakening a man's right to hold slaves; foreign slave trade was prohibited but not trade in slaves between North and South. Protective tariffs for industry were forbidden and exports could be taxed by authorization of Congress. All this was designed to endorse the South's authenticity and give it strength as an agrarian society. A curious feature of the Confederate constitution was its silence on the subject of secession. "States' rights" was a determining factor in the breakaway from the Union, but their right to break away from the South was not touched on in this binding document. The writers of the Confederate constitution were anxious to promote a strong sense of Southern nationalism and unity.

The tourist in Montgomery can visit the first White House of the Confederacy (with its charming contrasts of dark oak against white walls, its many fine portraits of Jefferson Davis, and its pretty garden); the Archives and History building (where I had the good luck to tag along behind a visiting guided party of mostly black schoolchildren, who appeared a little bewildered by the significance of what they saw: one boy asked why there were slaves in the first place); and such antebellum houses as the Ordeman–Shaw house, now an admirably laid out museum where one can hear a somewhat propagandist film about life in pre-1861 Alabama. He or she can also look around the capitol itself, and here misgivings may begin to arise.

Around the inside of the capitol's grandiose dome are eight murals painted by Roderick Mackenzie in 1927–30, each depicting scenes from Alabama's past. "Here," said the guidebook I was given by a capitol official, "the heroes and happenings from four centuries live again." But they don't: they are instead given a frozen and phoney idealization. An Indian chief surrenders to Andrew Jackson with a look of dazed admiration on his face while that stern-expressioned general delivers himself of a Nazi-looking salute. A simpering woman and her beau, both resembling musical comedy stars, ride out from a mansion of gracious design and setting, she on a white horse and he on a black one. My postcard reproduction of the painting entitles it: "One phase of social life in antebellum Alabama," and one longs to underline that first word. Blacks make no appearance in the murals until over halfway through the sequence, where they are pictured smilingly toiling in front of an industrial plant, presumably in Birmingham. This, we are told, is a "symbolic picture of Commerce and Industry in Alabama." Perhaps by an unfortunate oversight of the painter's, no *white* person appears in this particular tableau of heavy labor.

I was a little surprised to find that the governor of Alabama, in addition to being sworn into office on the very spot on which Jefferson Davis stood to proclaim the Confederacy, also sits—in the handsome hexagonal Senate chamber—under a plaque which pays Davis further homage. At the time of writing Alabama's governor is the once controversial George Wallace; it is his third term of office. His wife, commemorated by a statue in the central hall, also held the governorship, but only for a year before she died after a long and brave fight against cancer.

My guidebook was laudatory on the subject of both George and Lurleen Wallace, and some of its praise was probably justified. I was told in other parts of the South that Governor Wallace had instigated in Alabama various progressive educational measures that set exemplary precedents; he had personally encouraged cultural and artistic activities by introducing subsidies; and much of Alabama's often vaunted but nonetheless genuine industrial expansion can be attributed to his leadership. But his behavior and attitudes, especially in the bitter years of the Civil Rights movement, cannot be forgotten either, and on this aspect the guidebook is so evasive as to be nearly incomprehensible. Here are some short quotations from it:

> Four years later (1962) Wallace breezed to victory, receiving the largest vote ever given a candidate for governor in Alabama, and on January 14, 1963, became the 46th governor of Alabama. During his term he continued his fight for states' rights and law and order.

The Wallace family has the distinction of being the only family in modern times that can boast of two governors, and one of the few families in history to have the distinction of two members named among the ten "Most Admired People in the World." Continuing his fight for the right of states to govern their own affairs, Wallace decided to enter the presidential campaign for 1968. He ran as a third party and jolted American political history by obtaining ballot position in all fifty states.

Not a word about what issue the fight over states' rights involved. Admittedly it would be difficult to suggest how the matter should be expressed, but perhaps better silence than such imprecise, flattering, and—to me—dishonest diction.

The dramas Montgomery has witnessed are not confined to the Civil War period. In 1955 was the famous bus boycott led by Rev. Martin Luther King. In 1965 almost 30,000 antisegregationists marched from Selma to Montgomery and were abused and threatened by an angry mob as "niggers" and "nigger-lovers." Things now, a decade later, seem somewhat different, and many must sincerely regret their former views, words, and actions and wish they would recede into the past. These people should not forget that the spiritual wounds they inflicted may last a lifetime, but to persist in resentment might be destructive. What must not be allowed to happen is that people tell themselves falsehoods about the past or distort it through false perspectives. Pleasant though Montgomery is and agreeable though my time there was, I cannot altogether acquit it of this failing.

The tediousness of the bus journey from Montgomery to Mobile, most of which took place after dark, was compensated for by the theatrical impressiveness of the approach to the port. You enter Mobile via a complicated serpent's knot of overpasses that thread over and across one another above an expanse of water. At night the knot of roads shines with street lights and the headlights of cars, while the water below is a glittering black, and in the distance are the lights of huge ships in dock and of the town's buildings. Downtown Mobile looked seedy and abandoned. I found a hotel in which to stay that was stuccoed and shabby—an old Spanish townhouse. A grand social function was taking place inside it—a banquet for the Alabama Antiquarian Society. This meant that the dining room was not serving dinner to ordinary people and that I had to find a restaurant further down the street at which to eat. A police car honked outside and an ambulance hastened down the road, and I saw the waitresses looking tense. There had been a shooting just outside the diner only an hour ago, they explained; did this commotion mean another? I was to hear more agitated honking three times before getting to sleep that night.

I got up early the next morning to walk around Mobile, for I could tell the day was going to be hot. Spanish in its distant origins, Mobile actually derives from the French settlement founded by Sieur de Bienville in 1702, and it is of Mediterranean coastal cities that one is most often reminded when walking through it. Straight, dusty streets march toward little squares with trees and water fountains, and the anchored ships can be seen from many angles. Radiating out from the heart of the port are wide, gracious avenues with Spanish-style houses and gardens vaunting more spectacular azaleas; indeed, there is an "Azalea Trail" that extends beyond the limits of the town itself and can be followed on foot, by car or in a buggy. My polaroid camera attracted much attention from a group of black boys playing football around a church, on which was posted a notice beseeching us all to repent, for the day of judgment was at hand.

An amiable, talkative student bound for Austin, Texas, was sitting next to me on the bus between Mobile and New Orleans. His home, he told me, was on one of the islands in Mobile Bay in a small community that was half Catholic, half Baptist. This division was continued inside his own family—his mother was Catholic and his father Baptist. As for himself, on the whole he followed his mother's religion. He was fond of his island home but often found it claustrophobic; for example, he had once dated a black girl but had so dreaded the scenes that he knew would follow that he had backed out of the relationship. The interstate highway to New Orleans was somewhat dull, although I did get my first fascinated glimpse of swampland, with which I was to become rather more familiar later.

New Orleans! How often had songs and tunes invited me there. When I was in my adolescence a raucous song by Freddie Cannon had proclaimed:

> *Way down yonder in New Orleans,*
> *In the land of the dreamy scenes,*
> *It's the Garden of Eden,*
> *Well, you know what I mean!*

And there had also been Fats Domino's "I'm Walking to New Orleans," the words and minor-key melody of which evoke an almost desperate longing. There are many stomps and rags named after New Orleans streets. I thought to myself, not for the first time and by no means for the last, how unimaginable the world's popular music would be without the South's contribution. Ragtime, jazz, the blues, jugband, soul, bluegrass, rock 'n roll, country —these have all originated in the South as the expression of its various peoples and yet have since spoken to millions upon millions of people across the globe. The "genres" of course overlap at many points; one tune can be treated in several forms, and even the distinction between sacred and secular music is blurred. New Orleans is one of the most significant cradles of music in the world.

It is also rich in literary associations. George Washington Cable lived there and wrote his touching stories of Creole life until 1886, when local unpopularity drove him northward. Walt Whitman worked in the city on a newspaper; Sherwood Anderson escaped to it; William Faulkner led a *"vie de bohème"* there and wrote a volume entitled *New Orleans Sketches*. The boy hero of Truman Capote's *Other Voices, Other Rooms* set out on his strange quest from New Orleans; and one of the finest American novels of our time, Walker Percy's *The Moviegoer*, is set there. Above all, as far as the general reader is concerned, there is the work of Tennessee Williams, who though not a native either of New Orleans or indeed of the South has made himself a sort of dramatist-laureate of the place. His latest play at the time of writing is named after the most famous part of New Orleans—the *Vieux Carré*.

A jagged line of many-storied buildings on the opposite side of wide, muddy water announced this fabled city, and I felt a moment's pang not so much of disappointment as of unfulfilled anticipation. These skyscrapers were colorless, ugly and undistinguished. Was New Orleans going to be just another large, hectic modern city that contained a few carefully preserved old streets and self-consciously quaint institutions for tourists to photograph? (This is the fate of too many American towns, in particular that old steamboat capital, Louisville, Kentucky.) The bridge over which I passed and the glimpses of overpasses and factories it afforded seemed to confirm this possibility. However, I need not have worried. New Orleans seems to need those predictable tall modern buildings—first to complete its amazing jumble of architectural, cultural and human styles and secondly to offset the exotic nature of so much of the city. Certainly no city is more *sui generis* than New Orleans. I was not to leave until nine days later, although this period included trips out from it to the Bayou country, to Covington on the far side of Lake Pontchartrain, and to Baton Rouge, Louisiana's capital.

I stayed in a large, crumbling, peeling mansion of a hotel on St. Charles Street. It was very cheap. Its stuccoed ceilings, the brass rails of its staircase, and the bird cage nature of its elevator all suggested *belle époque* grandeur. The building was not air-conditioned; instead each bedroom had an old-fashioned fan shaped like a huge moth, which gyrated at different speeds according to which rope you pulled. The nights were clammily warm, so the maximum speed was needed to insure comfortable sleep, but I found it strange to wake up at times during the night and to see this whirring wooden insect above me sending down overlocalized coldness on the large and uncomfortable bed. When I first took the room none of its light bulbs worked; for two nights the telephones both internal and external were out of order; and once—worst of all—the fan failed. The people who ran the hotel were very charming and rather indolent, and I only saw them roused into any animation once— when I returned to the hotel late on Sunday afternoon. I had missed something, the receptionist told me: a man had been stabbed yards from the front door by a band of youths (white, she stressed). The youths had run off and the man had been dragged into this very foyer by some passersby. He'd then been rushed to the hospital, and they'd heard only a few minutes ago that he was not in any serious danger. But things like that happened too often. Though white herself she didn't like it when people blamed violence on black youths. In her view the white boys were worse.

My days in New Orleans tended to follow a certain pattern. Mornings and afternoons I would work in the fine city library, testimony to New Orleans' considerable civic pride. The table at which I worked was next to the Foreign Language Service desk, which was in constant demand; from opening time to the hour when I packed up my books I heard Spanish conversation. I had already been amazed at the amount of French I had heard on New Orleans streets; many of the speakers, I gathered later, were visitors from French Canada.

I could walk to the library from my hotel via either Tulane

45

Avenue or Canal Street, but I preferred the latter route. Canal Street is downtown New Orleans' main artery, separating the French Quarter from the rest and containing the largest stores. It is, I think, appropriately named—straight and long, its width emphasized by the narrowness of the streets that lead off it, it resembles a broad, busy waterway; the garish, neon-signed shops that line it form its "banks," and for craft there are the clanking street cars. It was with a feeling almost of shock that I saw one of these bearing as its destination the name "Desire." "They told me," says Blanche Dubois, the central character of Tennessee Williams' play, "to take a streetcar named Desire, and then transfer to one called Cemeteries and ride six blocks and get off at Elysian Fields."

At midday and in the evening I invariably went into the French Quarter. For despite the grandeur of the Garden District, despite the interesting contrasts of bustle and squalor of the waterfront areas (New Orleans is the third biggest port in the world—surpassed only by Rotterdam and New York—and the quays along the Mississippi, dominated by a World Trade Center, are impressive), the *Vieux Carré* contains the essence of the city and is the lodestar for those who know and love it. At midday I could do justice to the cheerful, harmonious blend of colors presented by the lines of old houses along Bourbon and Royal Streets and admire the almost musical beauty of the patterns in the elaborate wrought-iron tracery that festoons these houses like some sturdy creeping plant. I could look into patios and walled gardens and see wisteria rampant over sun-baked walls and azaleas framed by arched doorways. I could browse in the old bookshops on Royal Street; I could take photographs—of sunshine and shadow in the alley where William Faulkner lived, of an old donkey pulling a cart and wearing a straw bonnet, of the Spanish forms of the Cabilde (where in 1803 the ceremony to mark the Louisiana Purchase was held), and of the towers of the cool and solemn-interiored St. Louis Cathedral. But it is after dark that the French Quarter appears at its most individual and extraordinary. Without exception, the nights of my stay in New Orleans were warm and balmy, and I was able, one of strolling hundreds, to wander about the streets until the small hours.

But dinner first, for New Orleans is one of the great gastronomic capitals of the world. Galatoire's, Brennan's, Antoine's—these restaurants have rightly acquired an almost mythological reputation, as the long patient lines to enter them show. Later the poet

James Dickey said how he thought peoples revealed their essential qualities in their national cuisine. The British betrayed their basic puritanism in the monotony and waterloggedness of their dishes, whereas Southerners showed their sense of *douceur de vivre* in theirs. New Orleans cooking is of course distinct from that of the rest of the South—Spanish, French and Creole tastes have formed it together just as they have its architecture. I only have to hear mentioned Vichyssoise, eggs Benedict, the gumbos that possess so many forms, jambalayas and "Cajun Lost Bread" (French toast with raisins, cherries and syrup) to see again those fragrant courtyards at night and to hear, beyond the talk and laughter of fellow-diners, the sounds of jam sessions in nearby streets, bars and clubs. And the character to which these dishes testify—a love of the luxurious, the ripe, the colorful, of the unexpected bringing together of piquant sensations, is the New Orleans personality.

Not all the people on the streets were ambling tourists like myself or local citizens out for a good evening; there were many prostitutes standing in doorways, leaning against walls or simply walking up and down. So many girls offering themselves, but . . . I looked again and doubts about their sex assailed me. Never have I seen so many transvestites as in the *Vieux Carré*; the more pointed the breasts, the longer the eyelashes, and the more winsome the walk and gestures, the more likely it was that the person was male. There were many touts trying to entice one into entertainments—one house on Bourbon Street kindly provided heterosexual and homosexual revues on alternate nights. Next to such establishments were stores whose windows were stuffed with pornography, and not only in the form of books and magazines. Edible underwear was a speciality of one store—("He eats hers, she eats his"), and the garments came in a variety of flavors—raspberry, banana, chocolate, etc.

The sale of such fatuous obscenities seemed at first a sad fate for these pretty old houses; but then I realized that from its earliest days the *Vieux Carré* has been the home of the disreputable, a place where you could indulge yourself with easy amorality. New Orleans is a big port of a particularly cosmopolitan kind and has been obliged to provide a big port's amenities. It is also a racial mélange made up of people who have in common a remarkable difference in outlook, ancestry and lifestyle from the average white Southerner. Add to this its curiously enervating climate; its inheritance of old Spanish and French architecture indicative of a softer, Old World culture; and the result is the city of license that New Orleans has become. It was famous as such throughout the mid to late nineteenth century. You could buy cocaine on almost any street corner in the French Quarter for a matter of a few cents along with the ever-present honky-tonk women and honky-tonk music.

Bourbon and Royal Streets are still places where you can hear, any evening, scores of jazz musicians of varying quality. Some play in the middle of the street surrounded by admiring passersby; some play in bars, the doors of which are flung open so that one can not only enjoy their sounds but the sight of them as you walk past— intent, sweaty faces and eyes shining and bulging with loving effort. People dance and caper in the street to the strains of the trumpets and saxophones, some out of a sudden, spontaneous burst of *élan*, others for money. To this latter group belonged a black man and his small son, aged about ten, whom I watched on several consecutive evenings. They tap-danced with great skill and relentless energy, particularly the child, who at times had to be restrained by his father. Periodically the boy even turned upside down and danced on his hands.

Much of the music that assailed us as midnight walkers was lively and full of individual displays of bravura. Yet I must confess that jazz always suggests to me the dissipated search for happiness rather than happiness itself; in its melancholy aspects the indulgent and the maudlin are, I feel, never far away. Even the classics of jazz bespeak the city that, long past its age of innocence, has become self-mocking and jaded.

Something of what I feel about jazz I feel toward the art of the French Quarter's best-known celebrant, Tennessee Williams. I have been reading his work since my midteens, and some of his plays (in particular the heart-rending *The Glass Menagerie* and the still powerful *Cat on a Hot Tin Roof*) have become part of the literary furniture of my mind, as they have for many of my generation. Tennessee Williams is a poet of the theater; all his plays possess a distinctive unity of atmosphere that is a fusion of their setting, their imaginative symbolism, and their use of emotional encounters that echo and anticipate one another. Tennessee Williams' name is one that most readily occurs to the non-Southerner when the South, and New Orleans in particular, are mentioned. Certainly it would be hard to imagine his dramas without their

Southern settings such as the claustrophobic Mississippi mansion of *Cat on a Hot Tin Roof* or the drygoods store in *Orpheus Descending*, and their most intense emotional exchanges depend in part for their power on Williams' command of the Southern idiom. In only one play, however, is he explicitly concerned with the South as such—*A Streetcar Named Desire*. The playwright has himself admitted that in the plight of Blanche Dubois we are to read the plight of the South itself, which is not to say that Blanche, her sister and brother-in-law are not interesting in themselves.

The story this play tells is a terrible one. Blanche Dubois, her life in ruins and her family home, *Belle Rêve*, compulsorily sold and the profits from it frittered away, arrives in the Elysian Fields district of New Orleans where live her sister Stella and brother-in-law Stanley. Their home is in a poor street and their lifestyle totally lacks refinement. The coarseness of Stanley and his pals is something that Blanche finds hard to accept—they are of Polish descent, and she views them as peasants, animals. But nevertheless Blanche stays on in Stanley's house, for where else has she to go? In fact, there is dishonesty in her fastidious disdain for Stanley and his circle, for she has left behind her in Mississippi a promiscuous past. Stanley finds out about this and disabuses his friend Mitch of the illusions he has built up around Blanche, thus destroying an incipient relationship that could have burgeoned into a saving marriage. He then forces himself upon her sexually with the words, "We've had this date with each other from the beginning!" and finally arranges for her commitment to a lunatic asylum. Stella, distressed at her sister's departure, is nevertheless consoled by her husband's physical attentions. Her sobs cease as his fingers find the opening of her blouse.

Tennessee Williams' conscious intentions are clear. Blanche represents the backward-looking aspect of the South, at once degenerate and refined, proud yet whorish; faced with the crude energy of such a man as Stanley how can she do other than go under? How fair an analog Blanche is to the South may well be questioned; in literary terms however there is a consistency of vision. But there is not this consistency in Williams' portrait of her violator Stanley. His impatience and cruelty where Blanche are concerned are feasible, but not his ultimate acts of destruction. It is not just that his acts seem symbolic rather than psychologically convincing; it is that they are portrayed with a distorting and morbid relish that is also fascination, which vitiates the author's purpose.

The play is indeed a deeply morbid document: Blanche had once been married but her marriage ended in a sudden and tragic way:

> There was something different about the boy, a nervousness, a softness and tenderness which wasn't like a man's, although he wasn't the least bit effeminate-looking—still—that thing was there. . . . He came to me for help. I didn't know that. . . . I didn't know anything except I loved him unendurably but without being able to help him or help myself. Then I found out. In the worst of all possible ways. By coming suddenly into a room that I thought was empty—which wasn't empty, but had two people in it. . . . Afterward we pretended that nothing had been discovered. Yes, the three of us drove out to Moon Lake Casino, very drunk and laughing all the way. . . . We danced the Varsouviana! Suddenly in the middle of the dance the boy I had married broke away from me and ran out of the casino. A few moments later—a shot! . . . I ran out— all did—all ran and gathered about the terrible thing at the edge of the lake! I couldn't get near for the crowding. Then somebody caught my arm. "Don't go near any closer! Come back! You don't want to see!" See! See what? Then I heard voices say—Allan! Allan! The Grey boy! He'd stuck the revolver into his mouth, and fired—so that the back of his head had been—blown away. . . . It was because—on the dance-floor—unable to stop myself—I'd suddenly said—"I know! I know! You disgust me. . . ." And then the searchlight which had been turned on the world was turned off again and never for one moment since has there been any light that's stronger than this—kitchen candle. . . .[9]

This is moving history movingly related. But it is also an intrusion into the play that brings confusion with it. Blanche— the sensitive but debauched Southern sensibility—is shown as having been unresponsive and unkind in her treatment of a homosexual. The South may be as unresponsive and unkind, but in a different way. Personal emotions have imposed themselves on artistic purpose, unless we take it that the dreadful and continuous punishment Blanche suffers results partly from this earlier failure with her maladjusted boy-husband. If this is the case then Tennessee

Williams is guilty of an emotional cruelty as great as Stanley's.

One cannot help thinking that in this play—powerful though it is, and imaginatively evocative of New Orleans' sights, smells and music—Tennessee Williams is using the myth of the South for complex personal reasons of his own. Anyway, the South is too complicated to be reduced to the status of one neurotic woman. And New Orleans, of whose moods Tennessee Williams shows such understanding, is not the South but an intriguing entity within it, and to think and suggest otherwise is surely mistaken.

I also went to Baton Rouge to see the novelist, critic and editor David Madden, who teaches creative writing at Louisiana State University. I spent an afternoon and evening with David Madden in his charming house in Baton Rouge's Garden District—as elegant and sequestered as its more famous namesake in New Orleans. In the evening his wife and son joined us for a meal of crayfish, which we ate outside in the garden. His son said that one reason he would always want to live in the South was crayfish, and as I ate the delicious meal I could see his point.

The journey to Baton Rouge had taken me through swamp and bayou country. Beyond the road groves of trees were standing in water, their bases some way below its still, fetid surface; periodically dark overhung inlets appeared in this watery woodland. There was something at once enticing and fearful about these jungle creeks! At Baton Rouge one is mindful above all of two things—the wide Mississippi rolling muddily past, spanned by an enormous bridge; and the gaunt, thirty-four-story capitol, put up when Huey Long was governor of Louisiana. That notorious, powerful and unscrupulous man was assassinated in this building, and his grave and monument now face it. (Only slightly disguised, Long's history provided the subject for Robert Penn Warren's *All the King's Men*.) Otherwise, apart from the Garden District and the extensive, handsome grounds of Louisiana State University, Baton Rouge is a dull sort of town, resembling a hundred others with its featureless banks and stores. *Ode to Billy Joe* was showing here, too, and the music of the awful ballad floated out into the hot street from the cinema as an enticement to passersby.

I do not include David Madden among the fuller interviews because, energetic and adventurous writer though he is, I do not think that he has yet—with one possible exception—produced a

51

book that satisfactorily brings together his abundant talents into a shapely, artistically unified whole. Born in 1933, he will I feel, succeed in doing so in the near future. He has behind him a rich, colorful, utterly nonbourgeois background upon which he has drawn in his fiction. Both his elder brothers have spent time in prison, one serving in a chain gang, a punishment from which David personally obtained his release. Their plights—and the dreams that led to them—are recorded in his novel *Brothers in Confidence*. Autobiographical, too, is the novel *Bijou*, which depicts the burgeoning sensibility of a small boy in David Madden's native Knoxville during World War II. What is most impressive is the author's demonstration of how the creations of certain major genres of popular culture—the movies, comic books and popular romances —become translated in the mind of the small boy into beings and events of almost religious significance. Knoxville is well evoked, and there is interest (and a certain pathos) in the book's ending which has the young man setting out for Asheville, North Carolina where his new hero, Thomas Wolfe, lived. *Bijou* suffers, however, from overlength and a subsequent diffuseness, and at times the author seems too close to his material, resulting in a glut of detail.

David Madden's most successful novel seems to me *Cassandra Singing*, which was thirteen years in the making. It is not autobiographical; Knoxville does not feature in it, and the novel is instead set in the strange, forlorn mining hill country of eastern Kentucky, a region to which the author felt strongly drawn. It is a somber tale with three protagonists—the passionate but innocent and essentially noble youth, Lone; his invalid sister, the Cassandra of the title, whose dreams and stories have a significant influence on those around her; and Boyd, a wild youth to whom they both are drawn. Boyd's charm and sexual vitality conceal a lust for cruelty, and other peoples' discovery of this provides one of the principal tensions of the novel. A summary of the novel's situations cannot give an indication of its balladlike power and its poetic apprehension of the longings for emotional and actual adventure that assail all of us. Not the least of the novel's triumphs is David Madden's capturing of the spiritual side of small-town machismo—the yearnings of the soul that lie behind the motorcycle-and-leather-jacket culture celebrated in such works as the Marlon Brando film *The Wild One*, which are still strong today in Britain and America. *Cassandra Singing* deserves to be better known than it is.

David Madden talked about the South; he thought a distinction could be drawn between Appalachia and the lowland South : eastern North Carolina and Mississippi possess certain cultural features in common that would not be found in, for example, western North Carolina or eastern Kentucky. He also thought that the role each Southern state played in the Civil War had determined its consequent attitudes and ways of life. For instance, his own state of Tennessee had been divided, and eastern Tennessee had been largely pro-Union. This ambivalence is reflected he feels, in the richness of Tennessee's literature, and certainly his state has the best claim to be the South's literary giant. Nevertheless, David Madden did believe in the South as an entity, and as a literary entity. He felt that Baton Rouge, Louisiana, was an appropriate place for him, a Tennesseean, to live and work.

He said that for him the strength of the Southern literary tradition derived from the strength of the Southern oral tradition. Southerners loved to tell and hear stories about people, and the people, not the actual events that befell them, were the central objects of their interest. Southerners would not mind hearing the same story told over and over again : indeed, repetition built up a relationship between teller, listener and subject. He had often been asked to tell the story of how he got his brother off the chain gang, and the hearers of the story felt each time a renewed sense of kinship with both him and his brother.

The night was hot and the sky like velvet when I traveled back from Baton Rouge to New Orleans. In the near-deserted Greyhound bus station at Baton Rouge I met Tony, a black chiropractic student. As we sat next to each other on the bus traveling the flat dark miles to New Orleans, he asked me what I thought of the States, of the South, and of the position of black people here as opposed to Britain. My answers were vague and evasive; it would· be presumptuous of me to give an opinion, I said. He asked where I had been. I told him, among other places, that I had visited Montgomery, Alabama. Had I? Did I remember Governor Wallace's barring the door of the University to black students? I said I did— that at the time it happened the deed had shocked and distressed me.

Tony told me he had studied for his first degree at a Baptist college in Mississippi; he was, he said, "learned" in the Bible and was still, he supposed, a believer, but he could not accept the traditional Christian division between the adherent and the doubter. Surely it was only human to doubt, and doubt seemed to come so involuntarily; it was cruel of a religion to prohibit intellectual speculation. The Baptist faith held tremendous sway over Southerners, both white and black, he felt. His own family was black middle class—his father was a professor, his sister a psychologist, and one of his brothers was a doctor. He began to tell me of a girl he had fallen in love with, a Lebanese girl whom he had been visiting at Baton Rouge, but the lights of New Orleans came into view, and soon we were passing the city's gigantic, brilliantly illuminated superdome.

I returned to New Orleans with a feeling that I knew it far better than in fact I did. Perhaps this is the spell this strange city casts over all its visitors. The next day I had lunch with a very sympathetic man I had met. Lowell Kelly owns and runs the Old Mint Bookshop in Royal Street, a treasure trove for anyone interested in Southern literature and history, and though it was only a matter of days since I had arrived for the first time in New Orleans I had a feeling of coming back to some sort of home.

The other expedition I made from New Orleans was by paddle steamer, a beautiful old boat called the "Cotton Blossom," down the Mississippi and into the Bayou/Cajun country. The day was scorching and the sunlight was cruel on the brown waters; the atmosphere was tense as with impending storm, but it never broke. The name Cajun is a contraction of Acadian, and refers to the French-speakers who, expelled from Nova Scotia by the British in 1755, settled in southern Louisiana. They have evolved a curiously haunting musical style of their own, though their often melancholy falls and modulations show a distinct cousinship to the rest of Southern folk music. Though there is superb Cajun fiddle music, it is the accordion that this culture has most imaginatively exploited, its protracted swellings of sound, somehow suggesting deep nostalgia for a land that can never be regained—a nostalgia that transcends the original Acadians' longing for Canada or France and sets one thinking of the lost paradise for which we all pine. "*Hip et Taiaut*," "*Jolie Blonde*," "*Allons Danser Colinda*," and "*Allons à Lafayette*" are some of the most captivating of all folk tunes.

I had hoped all that Sunday afternoon on board the "Cotton Blossom" to catch a glimpse of an alligator swimming in the waters of the river; passengers were told that it was quite likely that we would see one. The boat left the Mississippi proper for other waterways and chugged past bayou after bayou for hot hours, but no alligator did we see. Then we stopped at a little Cajun village. Here, close by the levee, a crowd had gathered around a netted enclosure and, curious, I went to see what had drawn them. There, in a little artificial pool, were two alligators, one supposedly caught that very morning. A local boy jumped over the netting and seized the bigger of the two alligators by the tail. A woman asked whether alligators were intelligent. "No, ma'am," the boy replied, "Their brains ain't no bigger than golf balls." Around and around he swung it, four feet of snarling savagery.

This episode brought to my mind one of Eudora Welty's finest stories, "No Place for You, My Love." A man and woman meet by chance in the New Orleans restaurant, Galatoire's. Obeying an impulse that neither quite understands, the man takes the woman on a car journey south of the city ("South!" the nameless woman thinks, "How can there be any South from here! Does it just go on and on?") They come to a ferry in bayou country:

> The boys had a surprise—an alligator on board. One of them pulled it by a chain around the deck, between the cars and trucks like a toy—a hide that could walk. He thought, well, they had to catch one some time. It's Sunday afternoon. So they have him on board now, riding him across the Mississippi River. . . . The playfulness of it beset everybody on the ferry. The hoarseness of the boat whistle, commenting briefly, seemed part of the general appreciation.
>
> "Who want to rassle him? Who want to, eh?" the boys cried, looking up. A boy with shrimp-colored arms capered from side to side, pretending to have been bitten.
>
> What were there so hilarious about jaws that could bite? And what danger was there once in this repulsiveness—so that the last wordly evidence of some heroic horror of the dragon had to be paraded in capture before the eyes of country clowns?[10]

Wherever you travel in the South, it would seem, its writers have anticipated you, have already memorably captured the typical sights, sounds, happenings and situations. Like the woman in Eudora Welty's story, I was surprised at how much country lay south of New Orleans. Did it just go on and on? But perhaps the term *south* is as much an imaginative as a geographical term, always suggesting some ultimate that can never be reached. The lushness and languor of the southern countryside through which I was traveling heralded some Platonic country of supreme lushness and languor. Perhaps it was the same with the literary-cultural notion of a South?

Night had fallen as I mounted the bus that was to take me hundreds of miles back to my base in Charlottesville, Virginia. We looked back at the skyline of New Orleans as a symbol of the commercial and industrial renaissance of the South, perhaps not fully acknowledged yet by the rest of the world. According to one of my companions, companies were all the time moving southward; investment was being poured on a huge scale into Southern concerns; the growth figures for Georgia, Tennessee and Alabama were amazing; soon there'd be hardly anyone bothering to stay up North, the balance would transfer south of the Mason–Dixon line to that once-despised area. As he spoke I looked out of the window where along the Gulf coast the beaches were gleaming, magically white. The moon was full and the southward-stretching water was still, black and virginal.

2: THE WRITERS

Madison Jones

AMES GLENN, the young man at the center of Madison Jones' most ambitious novel to date, *A Cry of Absence* (1971), is in a terrible predicament. He has found out that Cam, his handsome, secretive younger brother and the apple of their mother's eye, has with another boy killed a young black civil rights agitator in a particularly brutal murder. He also knows that their mother, though in possession of all the salient facts, refuses to face up to Cam's guilt.

"How was he killed?"

"Say they figures he was rocked!"

"Rocked?"

"Yes'm. Had the marks all over him. Say somebody had just kept on busting him with rocks. Knocked one eye plumb out."

Ames comes from a long-respected upper-class Southern family, and he wishes to honor his heritage. At the same time he is a natural humanitarian with an instinctive belief in justice. The novel is set during the bitterest period of the civil rights movement in the South. One evening, as an antidote to his personal troubles, Ames applies himself to his history books. This is what he reads:

> Seen thus objectively, in the unbiased light of modern statistical and other research, these facts necessarily explode virtually all the romantic illusions about the Old South. That such a society, based squarely upon a crushing exploitation of the Negro, with its largely rude, oppressive and antidemocratic characteristics, should give rise to so many dearly cherished fairy tales is a classic illustration of the hollowness of most of our myths. It scarcely needs saying that the persistence of myths like these, playing havoc as they do with the rational conduct of life, gravely reduces the chances for the achievement of truly free and just societies.[11]

57

These are disturbing words for someone in Ames' situation. And indeed *A Cry of Absence* is a profoundly disturbing novel, so much so that I must confess I felt a certain awe at the prospect of meeting its author.

In fact Madison Jones is a gentle, amiable and kindly man to whom I found it extremely easy to talk, both personally and about his work; he was moreover very hospitable. His intense eyes, however, suggest a searching vision troubled by what it finds. It is his eyes, I feel, which have guided his pen.

He was born in Nashville in 1925 and reared in and near that city. He attended Vanderbilt University, where he was taught by, among others, Donald Davidson, the Fugitive poet. Madison Jones calls him a man of so fine a spirit that "you felt as though you could die for him." Then and later Madison Jones consorted with other Southern intellectuals of the Fugitive generation, with Allen Tate and Andrew Lytle, for instance, both of whom were later to speak to me of him and his work with admiration.

After leaving the university Madison Jones lived and worked on a farm in Cheatham County, Tennessee, for some years. He eventually resolved the conflict between literature and farming in favor of literature, and since 1956 he has been writer-in-residence at Auburn University, in Alabama. His home is in Kuderna Acres, a few miles outside Auburn. We drove past the azalea-laden gardens of the town's residential streets and out through woodland to the farmhouse where Madison Jones and his large family live. It stands in land that they work. Madison Jones told me he was at present wondering whether to install some exotic animals in the pastures, zebras perhaps. The atmosphere inside the house was much to my liking. His charming wife is herself a perceptive judge of literature and they have five children, three sons and two daughters. Three are attending Auburn University at the time of writing. There was a nice sense of the coming and going of young people: his eldest son talked to me about his father's books, the South and boxing; his second son spoke of his interest in philosophy and about how I should visit the historic Southern towns of Natchez and Eufala. In the house were representations of grotesque heads sculpted by Madison Jones himself, which recalled Dürer or Grunewald.

As I have already related, the weather during my stay in Auburn was uncertain; I had arrived there in torrential rain but on the day of my visit to Madison Jones it was warm and calm enough for us to sit out after lunch in a sequestered corner of the garden close to the swimming pool. I began by questioning him about his first two novels, *The Innocent* (1957) and *Forest of the Night* (1960). Though these seem to me apprenticeship for his later writing, they are early work of a peculiarly individual and accomplished kind.

A young man returns after seven years in a distant city to his old country home. Determined to live the life of his forefathers, he devotes himself to the restoration of the farm and particularly to the breeding of a horse from a once-famous and now almost extinct bloodline. From the start the horse bears a strange resemblance to Duncan himself. It also displays a streak of wanton viciousness that increases with maturity. This the proud young master refuses to acknowledge. His interest in the colt comes to isolate Duncan from his community, and as a consequence he becomes involved with the only man in the vicinity as reclusive as himself, a depraved moonshiner. This association leads eventually to the young man's acquiescence and assistance in acts of viciousness as unmitigated as those of his horse and to an early, cruel and futile death. Such is the plot of *The Innocent*.

Forest of the Night is kin to it. A young man in the opening years of the nineteenth century rides into the Tennessee wilderness from civilized Virginia. Brought up by an idealistic father who admired Rousseau, he feels he has a mission—to establish a school in these backwoods. Of the backwoods people's nature and life he is, however, profoundly ignorant. He knows nothing of the ways of Indians or wild animals, the mores of pioneer settlements, or the existence of outlaws such as the notorious Harpe brothers (historical persons). Soon after his arrival he succumbs to his desire for a girl who lives in isolation with a crazed old father. The young man does not realize until tragically too late that she has been the lover of both the Harpes and that for a time she had joined in their evil exploits. (The girl too has historical ancestry.) Still less does he realize that he himself bears an uncanny resemblance to the younger of the two Harpes. This resemblance has attracted the girl to him in the first place, and it leads in the end to his being cruelly harrassed by the very people he has set out to educate.

Both these fictional young men, Madison Jones told me, can be seen as ideological Yankees. Their shared ideology stems in his view from Jean-Jacques Rousseau and the French Enlightenment and entered the American mind through Jefferson and Thomas Paine. Madison Jones says elsewhere, "Simply, it held that man in the state of nature is good, that evil is not a positive thing or force but simply a negation of good caused by the corrupt institutions of civilization and the dead hand of the past." Madison Jones' heroes come to grief precisely because of their adherence to such a philosophy; in particular, it blinds them to the dark forces that govern and propel men like the moonshiner in the first book and the outlaws in the second.

Interesting though they are, these novels seem to me so shot with ambiguities and authorial tensions as to be bewildering both in detail and overall vision. Where they are most alive is also where they are most confused. *The Innocent* derives in part from Madison Jones' own years of young manhood on the Tennessee farm, and there is much beauty in its evocation of the lush Tennessee landscape, the kinesthetic pleasures of farm work, and the perils and rewards of dealing with animals. Nor are the more domestic sides of Southern country life forgotten—there are marvelous descriptions of Duncan's family home with its old portraits and log fires and of playing traditional music on the guitar. It would, of course, be foolish for anyone through enthusiasm for such a life, to attempt to shut out existence's harsher aspects. But Madison Jones sees this in a much darker and more metaphysical light:

> Adam ate of the tree of the knowledge of good and evil and was cast out for ever; and we all share his condition. Evil is a prime fact of our existence: we may be forgiven for it, but we cannot escape it. *The Innocent* who reenters the garden is destined to find that it is not God but Satan who walks there now. So with my hero. His flaw leads him into the hands of the Enemy who destroys him.[12]

The destruction is nightmarishly rendered; I use the word deliberately, for the fates of the young men suggest those terrible moments in dreams when one feels caught in a trap from which there is no escape. Their horrible nature compels me to doubt their alleged justice. One has an uncomfortable feeling that the author turns against his heroes not so much because of their limited vision but because of their adherence to that other Jeffersonian ideal—the pursuit of happiness. It is for this that they must pay, and significantly in both books an erotically evoked sexual relationship contributes to their fall. Tacitly, of course, Madison Jones opposes against the ideology of his two heroes the Southern religion that stresses the reality of evil and the necessity of God's deliverance from it.

Since these two novels Madison Jones has published *A Buried Land* (1963), *An Exile* (1967), *A Cry of Absence* (1971) and *Passage through Gehenna* (1978). All are distinguished by an extraordinarily clear and pure style. James Dickey declared of Madison Jones' latest book: "Madison Jones is one of the great prose stylists of our time."

Today Madison Jones does not speak warmly of *A Buried Land*. He does not like the cold callousness of Percy, its central character, and consequently this is the dimmest in his mind of all his novels. Nevertheless, with this work he came of age as a novelist. It is a strong and frightening work, executed with considerable assurance.

He told me how the novel started life. He had been angered by the Tennessee Valley Authority's (TVA) widespread flooding of large, inhabited areas of Tennessee and northern Alabama. Valleys, farms and entire communities, as well as much rare wildlife, were destroyed. He wanted to write a novel in which destruction by flood (TVA-authorized) played a key part. The question that particularly exercised him was this: to what extent would the physical destruction of a place entail its spiritual destruction, i.e., of the life, joy, guilt and relationships created within it.

As he was pondering this theme a friend's story came into his mind about a youth who got a girl pregnant and then arranged an abortion for her which killed the girl. The two ideas united and fused. In *A Buried Land*, the youth Percy's first sexual experience is with Cora, a simple, uneducated girl. She becomes pregnant. He and his best friend take her to the backstreets of Nashville for an abortion, but hours after the operation Cora dies. Percy and his friend Jesse bury her in an old graveyard which is soon to be covered by TVA flooding.

Percy is a clever, ambitious, self-seeking young man who has set his sights on rising high in the legal profession. When we next meet him he seems to be doing just that in the small town of his youth. But can he leave the ugly past behind? His former friend is now a pathetic, shiftless person who fills him with snobbish repulsion, but he knows the truth. Moreover, Cora's fanatical brother ceaselessly broods on her tragic disappearance. Nor can Percy wholly stifle his memories, and at the bottom of the reservoir is the graveyard in which her body still rests.

The situation is the perfect metaphor for Madison Jones' belief in the consequences of sin. But, it may be asked, wherein does Percy's sin lie? Most boys of Percy's age experiment with sexual relations; his insistence on the abortion is a graver matter, but he does not want Cora to die. Surely his sin lies not in these acts, morally dubious though they may be, but in his dishonesty in not confronting them, in pretending a false virtue. Readers may look into their hearts and memories and realize that they are no better than Percy, but maybe they have the saving grace of admitting their fallibilities. In order to shut out his crime against Cora, Percy turns against all he had once known—his friend and his family. This is what brings about his downfall, demonstrated by Madison Jones with far greater control and understanding than in earlier books. It is therefore far more horrifying than the fates of his earlier heroes.

Few things in the novel impress me more than Madison Jones' treatment of Percy's erstwhile best friend Jesse. He is a subtler version of those *doppelganger* figures in the first two books. He urges his buddy on to sexual experimentation, and he is therefore an accomplice in Percy's loss of innocence. This is surely very true to life, for most young males seem to feel the need for conspiratorial solidarity with their own sex when first establishing relations with the opposite one. Jesse can thus be seen as the voice of the cerebral Percy's libido. He shares in Percy's crime—the death of Cora and her secret burial.

> In a low sullen voice Jesse said: "It was your baby."
>
> "Yeah." The shock of rage darkened [Percy's] eyes, fastened like cramp his grip on the wheel. He had an impulse to throw himself on Jesse. "Yeah, try that! That's why you came, isn't it—just to help an old buddy out? God damn you, you're in it like me. God—damn —you."[13]

The relationship informing this dialogue is ironically reversed eight years later, when it is Percy who wishes to forget what they did together and penitent ne'er-do-well Jesse who insists on their common past.

Madison Jones' next book, *An Exile*, was his most successful to date. It was made by Johnnie Frankenheimer into a film called *I Walk the Line*, starring Gregory Peck and Johnny Cash (whose insistent country-style title song suggests something of the atmosphere of both book and film). *Carmen* was, according to Madison Jones, a starting point for this shortest and most beautifully constructed of his novels. Its story, of a fat failure of a sheriff brought down through his physical passion for the daughter of a moonshining family, is a moving one. As in the previous books, we receive a sense of a man helplessly caught in a web, devised in part by his deeds (over which he has some control) and in part by his nature (over which he has but little). As also in the previous books one man acts as an agent of destruction for the central figure, in this case the sheriff's deputy Hunnicut, who is a disturbing figure with his "bottle-green eyes . . . with little seeds of hatred glimmering in their depths" and his constant perusal of obscene magazines.

Drops of rain splashed on bushes, the pool and the lawn, though it was still warm and windless. Madison Jones and I moved back into the house. He showed me a photograph of an elegant Southern country house which had belonged to his family and had sadly been burned down. He told me of his grandfather, a Southern gentleman who was born in 1856 and remembered the Civil War. He had become a scholar on the subject of the war, and Madison Jones had loved to listen to his conversation. There were also other Confederate champions in the family. Indeed, he had grown up in an atmosphere in which the Southern past was cherished and discussed. Madison Jones' own interest in it received further encouragement at Vanderbilt from Davidson's lectures. Davidson and his fervent faith in the abiding merit of Southern culture had further endorsed my companion's own belief in certain aspects of it. Madison Jones lamented that the history taught to young people in schools, Southern as much as others, was presented from such an indefatigably Yankee point of view; young Southerners were taught to feel an almost exclusive guilt over their society's past, and he could not help thinking that this was not only sad but dangerous. He regretted that "Dixie" was not playable any more. Madison Jones talked about Southern resistance to the civil rights changes of the 1960s. By no means all the resistance, he said, derived from racist or economic motives. One powerful factor, he continued, was the Southerner's impulse to hold on to his old identity, racial segregation being the last fleshly survivor of a world now nearly gone, the last living expression of his link with the past, the one thing that preserved his Southernness.

This conversation had the strongest bearing on Madison Jones' most explicitly Southern novel, *A Cry of Absence*. It seems to me both a major work of art and a major statement about the South. It is set in a small town in an unspecified area of the South, probably Tennessee. The central character, Ames, is divided in conscience and loyalties. He by no means repudiates his Southern inheritance, and its patriarchal, paternalistic ideals are still dear to him. The Roman notions of duty and sacrifice of self to a larger cause are paid rich homage in the novel, as is the idea of the veneration of illustrious dead. Not to remember the past is to contribute to the shallowness of a society, and the upholders of traditional Southernness are certainly not guilty of this contemporary failing. They acknowledge man's spiritual obligations. They resist with every fiber of their controlled but passionate beings the commercial values and glib materialism of the self-appointed social reformers who advocate a carpetbagger's world in the name of enlightenment.

There is no more devout follower of the beliefs that animated the great Confederate dead than Hester, Ames' mother. Proud, nobleminded, gracious in manner and inflexible but desirous of being good, she reminded me of Volumnia in Shakespeare's *Coriolanus*, and I was interested to find out that Madison Jones had reread this play while working on the book. Hester possesses the fatal flaw that, in the author's view, runs through all diehard Southern idealists and which is curiously related to Percy's crime in *A Buried Land*—she refuses to acknowledge the ills of the past and thus wilfully blinds herself to the ills of the present. For though they are a much more complex matter than some civil rights advocates would have allowed, there is absolutely no doubt that the offences of white Southerners against black Southerners were many and extremely heinous. What should have happened, Madison Jones suggests, was a working through of the predicaments, an admission of wrongs, and a restitution and a growth toward friendship and neighborliness on the basis of equality and mutual respect. Instead there was enforcement and polarization. Hester is a victim of this, and her consequent suffering is terrible.

She loves no one more than her second son Cam, so athletic, so good looking; in him she sees all the grace of the young Southern male aristocrat, and so she educates him to be proud and aware of his Southernness. It is this person who brutally stones a young black to death. When she finally faces this fact her grief and horror know few bounds, and in one of the most heart-rending passages in modern fiction she contemplates killing him.

In fact, Cam kills himself. Afterward Ames speaks to his mother about the tragedy:

"He was what you taught him to be." Ames' eyes, cold gray, did not even blink.

She said, "I taught him decency. And respect. Always. And he perverted it."

Ames' lips parted, then shut hard against something already in his mouth—thin lips, clamped together like halves of a shell. She saw them open again, releasing a voice that was unexpectedly hushed:

"You taught him drivel. Old South drivel."[14]

Madison Jones was insistent that this remark must be taken in context. Nevertheless there is a point being made here. It was made earlier in the novel in the fine scene in which Hester and Cam at last talk about his murder:

"Mama," he said again, dimly, "I guess you hate me, don't you?"

"No," she barely murmured.

"You act like you do." When he got not answer, he added, "I think you wish there wasn't any me. . . . Then he said, "I never did like anybody but you. I don't even like Ames. Or anybody. Except you. You won't believe me, but I always did like I thought you wanted. As much as I could."

"And you did this," she said in a hoarse murmur.

After a moment, "You know you hated him, Mama. And all those people."

"Please go away from me." She shut her eyes.

"I've always tried to be the best, like you wanted me to. And I am the best." His tone brightened a little, with pride. "You know I am. I'm the best at sports and school and everything. Everybody knows it."

Hearing his disembodied voice say these things in the darkness behind her shut lids, she thought it was like a dream, and she opened her eyes again. . . . "I never made anything but A's at school. And I was all-state pitcher this season. They were even scouting me, all the colleges were, and I was just a junior.

And I'm good to look at, too—you know I am."

"You really think these are the things I wanted?"

"You acted like you did," he said sullenly.

"And not the other things? The things I tried to teach you? Goodness and honor and respect. And loyalty."

"I never have been disloyal. I want the same things you want. And I've got respect, too. Most boys don't respect their grand-fathers, and all the old things, like I do. Like you taught me."

"And you did this," she breathed.

He paused. After a moment, "If those old people were still alive, you know they'd be glad it happened."

She drew a breath but never tried to put it into words. Closing her eyes she waited with a kind of dread for him to continue, imagining again that his voice would come from a shape barely visible against the gray daylight. She waited a long while.

"Are you going to keep on being this way? There's nothing to do about it. Why can't we go back being like we were?"[15]

Cam's bemusement and Hester's horror are harrowingly caught, but what is truly frightening about the passage is its suggestion of a covert complicity in and approval of the ghastly deed by the Southern *ancien régime*. Ames in the novel and perhaps also the author are obsessed by the idea that Cam was merely acting out, in strong and vile deed, the dark subterranean desire of his community. In a society in which there are repeated eruptions of violence, they wonder if those eruptions reflect its will. The murkiness of the question derives above all from the society's refusal to be honest about what it considers good and evil. The implications of the novel are severe and alarming enough solely in reference to the South, but of course they have a universal relevance.

Madison Jones had told me earlier that he saw comparatively little diminution of the power of Protestant Fundamentalism in the South, especially the rural South. Many of his students believed strongly in their faith, and he was glad that this was so. He was a fellow-traveler of their religion, rather than an adherent, but he was pleased that this spiritual sense is still alive among Southern young people. Societies were worse where there was none.

The uneasy relationship between extreme Protestantism and sexuality is the subject of Madison Jones' most recent book, *Passage through Gehenna*. In its haunted presentation of the individual trapped by partially involuntary events it resembles the author's previous novels. Violent events are a recurring feature in all Madison Jones' work. Here they are the novel's very essence, which is to say that it is not strictly a realistic novel but a symbolic tale which, for all its vivid rendering of place, purports to present a spiritual truth about existence. It is surely significant that during the novel's gestation period Madison Jones was imaginatively engaged with that curious masterpiece of Calvinist Scotland, James Hogg's *Confessions of a Justified Sinner*, and with the works of Flannery O'Connor. He knew the latter and had carried on an extensive correspondence with her, and her pared style was an influence on his book.

The novel's very opening paragraph suggests its almost parable nature and also hints at its theme:

> His name was Jud, Judson Rivers. When he was growing up, in the Bethel hills ten or twelve miles from town, the religion still had a great deal of starch left in it. So this fact is some part of an explanation for Jud's turn of mind at so young an age. At least there was nothing much in the air around to weaken his grip on the ambition he had got hold of—or that had got hold of him. The ambition was to become a man of God, a preacher.[16]

What weakens the grip of his ambition is, in fact, Jud's sexual desire for a beautiful "witch" of a woman called Lily who, without gratifying his desire, takes delight in encouraging him and rejoices in the havoc this plays with his faith, of which she is a declared enemy. In particular she incites him to carry out a test of the religious man's immunity to sexual temptation: Jud persuades a prostitute to offer herself to an eccentric but fervent preacher and healer. The man succumbs to her charm and then, in anger and alarm at his fall, he kills her!

Passage through Gehenna is an obsessive novel; the assumptions of its milieu, strange to more metropolitan readers, must be accepted if one is to respond to its dramatization of a debate. Though stilled somewhat now, this debate has exercised many peoples in many periods. Certainly the novel's sense of horror is as acute as that in any of Madison Jones' previous works. When reading it I was reminded not only of Hogg and O'Connor but of the fiction of certain French masters—François Mauriac, Georges Bernanos and Julien Green. Here were the same rural communities in the same hot countryside, the same dangerous juxtaposition of primitive passion and puritanical religion, the same suspicion of the modern and rational, and the same sultry brooding.

The day after my visit to his house I saw Madison Jones in his office at the top of the one tall building on the Auburn campus. I tried to take photographs of him against a background of the window, from which such a good view of the university and the countryside beyond was to be seen. Four attempts resulted in not one decent photograph. Madison Jones was very patient and very amused. I again thought of the contrast between his gentle, ironic manner and the turbulent darkness of his fiction. *Passage through Gehenna* ends, however, on a note of hope for the tormented hero. It is interesting to speculate whether there will be a louder note of cautious optimism in the novel on which Madison Jones is now at work, which is set for the first time specifically in Alabama itself.

Walker Percy

"FOR SOUTHERN WRITERS," Walker Percy claimed, "Faulkner may have been a blessing but he has also been a curse." We were talking by the edge of what he said would have been called a bayou had it been in another part of Louisiana. It flowed at the far end of the backyard of his tranquilly handsome house. The morning was warm and windless, without a ripple on the surface of the water nor any stirring of the dense overhanging trees. Walker Percy in his youth actually knew Faulkner, who used to play tennis at the house of his uncle, who brought him up. He said that his own fiction began approximately four thousand miles away from Faulkner—in the Paris of the Existentialists. Certainly the relation between his first novel *The Moviegoer* (1962) and Camus' *L'Etranger* (*The Outsider*) is a very real one. Its hero, Binx Bolling, like Camus' narrator, feels himself to be detached from the hot tangle of desires, aspirations and activities, social and business, of those around him.

Binx is the first of the reluctant, confessed outsiders whose often tormented consciousnesses receive Walker Percy's sympathetic and intense consideration. Will Barrett in *The Last Gentleman* (1966) also stands apart from his fellow-men, in his case because of his nervous condition. He suffers from curious amnesiac attacks, "fugues" in which he is unable to identify either places or people and can summon only fragmentary memories of himself with which to carry himself through them. This affliction, attributable in part to his father's suicide, prevents both integration with the working world and any sustained relationship with the opposite sex. Lancelot Lamar, in Walker Percy's most recent book *Lancelot* (1977), is doubly apart from ordinary humanity. The novel takes the form of his confessions to a friend (priest) in the cell of a lunatic asylum to which he has been confined. His memory is shaky, and it takes him some time even to place the man he is addressing. So much for the present. But in the past, before he was committed, he was an outsider too, usually as a recluse by choice. He had been a stranger in his own home and community, living alone with only Civil War histories, the Mary Tyler Moore television show and the whisky bottle as his solaces. (I am omitting from this short survey the novel *Love in the Ruins*, 1971. Though in some ways the apotheosis of Walker Percy's vision, it is set in an unlikely future and its events, though fictionally credible, seem to belong to a different genre than that of the conventional novels which are my usual subject in this book.)

The reader may already have noticed an essential paradox—these characters, though detached, are tormented too. Here is the central tension of Walker Percy's novels. Binx, Lance, Will and Sutter (Will's curious mentor, almost as important a character in *The Last Gentleman* as Will himself) may stand aside from human life, but the reason is not that they do not feel. On the contrary, as becomes both subtly and dramatically apparent in the course of the novels they feel strongly—but life as it is conventionally lived cannot satisfy them.

Binx Bolling, as the title of the novel suggests, is a keen movie-goer and television watcher. His reason is partly to conquer the ever-present ennui inside him. The idiocies of his chosen recreation are sharply and humorously conveyed:

> A play comes on with Dick Powell. He is a cynical financier who is trying to get control of a small town newspaper. But he is baffled by the kindliness and sincerity of the town folk. Even the editor whom he is trying to ruin is nice to him. And even when he swindles the editor and causes him to have a heart attack from which he later dies, the editor is as friendly as ever and takes the occasion to give Powell a sample of his home-spun philosophy. "We're no great shakes as a town," says the editor on his deathbed, teetering on the very brink of eternity. "But we're friendly." In the end Powell is converted by these good folk, and instead of trying to control the paper, applies to the editor's daughter for the job of reporter so he can fight against political corruption.[17]

We probably laugh at this because it is so exact and devastating a summary of the sort of drivel with which we have all wasted too much of our own time. But it is not very comfortable laughter, because it suggests the phonyness of the feelings society deploys to protect itself from pain. What is frightening is that we need these celluloid lies. Though the ludicrous sequence of events described is impossible, all over the Western world people insist that this kind of art is acceptable "entertainment." Worse, the phonyness is not confined to the art which modern civilization has produced in order to console itself. It is also to be found in the very stuff of everyday life and social intercourse, including sexual intercourse. This is why Binx (and Sutter and Lance) cannot join in.

But some things do stir their emotions. Binx has a deep affection for his fourteen-year-old crippled younger brother Lonnie, with whom he enjoys easy conversation, based on common tastes. Lonnie is a religious boy:

> After I kiss him goodbye, Lonnie calls me back. But he doesn't really have anything to say.
> "Wait."
> "What?"
> He searches the swamp, smiling.
> "Do you think that Eucharist—"
> "Yes?"
> He forgets and is obliged to say straight out: "I am still offering my communion for you."
> "I know you are."
> "Wait."
> "What?"
> "Do you love me?"
> "Yes."
> "How much?"
> "Quite a bit."
> "I love you too."

But Lonnie dies, and this has a profound effect on Binx's subsequent life. Walker Percy himself directed my attention to the key passage here, one which had much moved me when reading it. Lonnie's brothers and sisters question Binx after the boy's death.

> Donice casts about. "Binx," he says and then appears to forget. "When Our Lord raises us up on the last day, will Lonnie still be in a wheelchair or will he be like us?"
> "He'll be like you."
> "You mean he'll be able to ski?" The children cock their heads and listen like old men.
> "Yes."
> "Hurray!" cry the twins.[18]

Whatever Binx's faults, according to Walker Percy, he cannot lie; he always tells people the truth. So in answering his half-brothers and sisters he almost takes himself by surprise, because unknown to himself he had discovered the knowledge of a metaphysical truth. It is this truth that enables him to marry his psychologically disturbed cousin Kate and, it is presumed, to build with her a fulfilling and giving life.

Suffering and death stalk through all of Walker Percy's work in the form of intimations of mortality that should show the proper dimension in which to live. Will Barrett in *The Last Gentleman* is hired by a rich Southern family, the Voights, to be a companion to their mortally ill son Jamie, whose death is horrifyingly and movingly rendered at the close of the novel. This death alters the lives both of the bemused Will and of the despairing, mocking, divided agnostic Sutter.

Walker Percy is a Roman Catholic. The uncle who brought him up was the poet William Alexander Percy, author of a fine Southern autobiography called *Lanterns on the Levee*. The older man began life as a Roman Catholic but, as his book records, lost his faith. He lived, so his nephew says, according to a Greco-Roman code which he himself feels played a strong part in the culture of the Old South, particularly of the upper classes. Walker Percy's own writing seems to me to be informed by a very high regard for the Greek philosophy of stoicism. Indeed, this is what his central characters live by when we meet them prior to their conversions. Nonetheless, though he would not describe himself as a very good Catholic, Walker Percy's faith is the determining force in his fiction. It is this that brings his work back from the Paris of the Existentialists to Louisiana, a predominantly Catholic state, divided into parishes rather than counties. And his Catholicism does not cut him off from certain strongly Southern preoccupations and imaginative traditions. I have mentioned the frightening yet purifying omnipresence of death in his books. The Southerner does not forget death as easily as members of most Western societies. In *The Last Gentleman* Percy says that nobody understands and deals with death and the dying like Southern women. He praises Southern blacks in the same novel for treating death as "the oldest joke of all."

Walker Percy talked to me about his religion. He asked me if I had any religion, and I said that I supposed the answer was no; I had never been able to make up my mind whether I wanted one or not, since the terror of believing seemed as great, if not greater, than the terror of death as extinction. He said he understood, and I shall never forget the way he said it. He showed an almost involuntary empathy, for the terror of being alive is captured in his novels. Yet he does pose resolutions and give intimations of a sweet immortality as well as of a cruel mortality. Born in 1916, Percy did not become a Catholic until 1946. He trained as a doctor and only left medicine when he contracted tuberculosis and had to spend a protracted time in hospitals and sanitoria. During this period he read philosophy, particularly Kierkegaard and Heidegger, and studied and thought his way, so to speak, to the Catholic faith. At this time his interests changed in direction from science—though his novels, particularly *The Last Gentleman*, teem with medical references—to philosophy and literature. He told me that he regretted that Thomas Mann with *The Magic Mountain* had preempted writing about a tuberculosis sanatorium; he thought it so rich a situation for fictional treatment.

Walker Percy has a thoughtful face and manner; he is grave, kind and courteous. I met his wife and daughter, and we had a delightfully relaxed lunch of crayfish on the veranda of his house. Covington, where the house stands, is as picturesque a village as can be imagined. Old houses seem to have been dropped into a world of flowers and trees where nature is benevolent, and only the South, one feels, could contain it. The interior of the house was ordered, peaceful and cool in contrast to the heat which covered the yard, the bayou and the woods; Walker Percy spoke a little about the Civil Rights period, in which he played an active and determined part—a Southern scene. Yet Walker Percy repudiates certain concepts of himself as a Southern writer, thinking no doubt of his literary and philosophic affiliations and his obsession with contemporary, particularly American, civilization, its limitation, blindnesses and follies. He diagnoses certain of our civilization's manifestations in its art and entertainment and depicts thoughtful, aloof and asocial men; he avoids any kind of local color or descriptions of particular varieties of Southern life. He belongs to a universal church. He owes, he says, nothing to the Southern oral tradition, and stories told on porches played no part in his life. Southern gossip may or may not have interested him, but he cannot see its fruits in his fiction. Neither can I. True, the South is the setting of his work. New Orleans is vividly evoked in *The Moviegoer* and Mardi Gras even features in the novel, though his hero refuses to live in the picturesque French Quarter and despises Royal Street. *The Last Gentleman* opens in New York, in Central Park, but the pulse of the book quickens when the hero begins picaresquely to move southward. The book contains a vivid re-creation of the hero's home, Ithaca. *Lancelot* takes place in Feliciana Parish (now no more), River Road and New Orleans. But though these settings are described as only someone who knows them intimately from from the inside could, this fact in itself is not enough to make Walker Percy a Southern writer in any deeper sense of the word.

All the same Walker Percy thinks he probably is one. Through-out all his novels, but particularly loud, throbbing and violent in his last (and possibly finest) novel, *Lancelot,* is a consistent hatred of the rapacity, selfishness, self-indulgence, false gods and cowardice of modern culture, the centers of which (no figment of Percy's imagination, this) are New York and California. To attack this culture Walker Percy uses not the Catholic faith, for this transcends American culture, but some residual Southern culture which, it seems, has conditioned his troubled heroes to feel the profound malaise they do toward modern life. It can surely be no accident that all three of his main characters come from old Southern families which are guided by values deeper and tougher than those of the soft urban society around them. Significantly Lancelot's greatest interest before his crime, mental breakdown and punish-ment was the Civil War; later he fights a sort of spiritual Civil War.

Lancelot seems to me Walker Percy's most Southern and most compelling novel, though I have more personal affection for the kindlier and more wry *Moviegoer. The Last Gentleman*, the most original and quirky, is spoiled for me by its diffuseness; I cannot help thinking its picaresque structure is a mistake, for it renders it uneven; the novel is strong only at its dramatic beginning and its equally dramatic and harrowing close.

Lancelot Lamar's actress wife Margot is unfaithful. Her lover and friends are engaged in making a movie in *Belle Isle* (his Southern home) and its environs. His wife, limited though her talents are, will have a star role. The film is a contemporary Southern romance, a ridiculous hodgepodge of clichés about Southern life which is very loosely based on reality. The absurdity of these clichés is com-pounded by others peculiar to West Coast culture which have been grafted onto the Southern romance to give it a false topicality. A Christ-figure is introduced, bringing an indulgent kind of peace to everyone in the story, black and white. Clearly Percy means for us to realize the truths behind these media distortions—the strength and hardness of the Old South and of Christ, and *genuine* kindness and mercy.

There are other symbols, too. Margot, Lancelot's wife, has devoted much of her life to an uncomprehending restoration of *Belle Isle*, thus emasculating it. Her friends cannot accept the reality of a hurricane which threatens Louisiana and thus show themselves unable even to entertain honest fear. Margot's circle has protected itself from reality by secondhand and imported fantasies.

I do not myself accept a lot of the thinking behind *Lancelot*. I find in it, as elsewhere in Walker Percy's work, an almost hysterical denunciation of sexual promiscuity that strikes me as misplaced. I think the correlation between overt genital indulgence (which can certainly have repellent features) and the weakness of modern society is greatly overstressed (and not only by Percy). Few societies have been conspicuous for sexual restraint, but in their semblance of it they created worlds of shame and cruelty like the Victorian underworld and the tormented Victorian psyche. To indulge in Lancelot's rantings against American pornography, with his particular disgust for male homosexual acts, a very Southern prejudice, is to overplay the role of sex in both private and public life. Even Lancelot admits that orthodox Catholicism does not see sex and religion in some sort of perpetual antithesis. And the fructifying myth of Lancelot and the Holy Grail, used as if it were an actual spiritual truth, must be seen as ultimately a literary creation. Human frailty and limitation must be recognized by any philosophy which attempts to prescribe to people how to live, and Lancelot's does not recognize them. Lancelot's terrible deed—he set fire to *Belle Isle* in order to kill his wife and the others of whom he disapproves—is a virtual sanctification of violence and murder as a demonstration of righteous anger against the falsity and vice of the world. This I find unacceptable.

All the same, I respect *Lancelot* precisely for its intransigence. Whatever its faults, it presents people as spiritual beings and advocates a society in which they are so seen. The book thus seems to me the work of a good man.

Among Lancelot's many obsessions is one of a new society in the Blue Ridge Mountains of Virginia, in which the original pioneers first proved their strength and godliness:

Yes, don't you see? Virginia is where it will begin. And it is where there are men who will do it. Just as it was Virginia where it all began in the beginning, or at least where the men were to conceive it, the great Revolution, fought it, won it and saw it on its way. They began the Second Revolution and we lost it. Perhaps the Third Revolution will end differently.[19]

At the end of the novel Lancelot and the woman he loves, a victim like himself of modern stupidity and cruelty, set off to begin a fresh and good life in those Blue Ridge Mountains. It was there that I was going at the end of my journey out of the Deep South.

3: THE TRAVELS

Virginia, Tennessee, Kentucky and North Carolina

Early in the April of 1798, according to appointment, all bade adieu to their old and kind friends, the scenes of early life, some of the graves of their fathers, and many objects besides around which memory will linger, and turned their faces toward the setting sun. It was a time of great tenderness of feeling; many, in taking leave, would not venture to speak; a tender embrace, a silent tear, a pressure of the hand in many cases would be all. But few of the aged men and women now living do not remember such parting scenes. In those early times the emigrants that left Carolina and Virginia to settle in Kentucky or Tennessee hardly expected ever again to see those from whom they parted, nor was there any hope in those who were advanced in years. They parted much as do those who part at the grave.

The children and the Negroes kept up their spirits by thinking and talking about Cumberland—the name of the beautiful new world we were to find at the end of our journey. ... Some days after ... I loitered behind the wagons, and upon catching them up, I found them all stopped on an elevated stretch of road. I asked the cause, and was shown what seemed to be a light blue cloud lying far and away to the west on the verge of the horizon. It was to our young eyes a vision of beauty. In its vast outline not a rent or a fissure could be seen.

I gazed at it with mingled wonder and fear. So this, then, was the famous Blue Ridge about which we had heard so many tales and beyond which lay the land of our homes forever. Could wagons and teams ascend perpendicular walls or scale the clouds?[20]

The above comes from Allen Tate's short story "The Migration," a superb account of pioneer life, and I know of no better presentation of the effect of the Blue Ridge upon someone seeing it for the first time. I did so myself in October, 1975; I will always remember standing in the grounds of Jefferson's Monticello, looking over toward the ridge of mountains—azure haze hanging over a high wall of autumnal colors—and feeling that sense of wonder which Allen Tate's narrator describes. And I felt the same emotion again, standing in the same spot, two and a half years later, on a cold but clear March day, a month before my journey through the Deep South. Again the Blue Ridge could truthfully be called blue; this time, though, the blue was augmented by the blue–gray proper to winter. Its thick woods were quite bare and there were large patches of snow here and there on its precipitous slope. To look at the Blue Ridge is to desire to discover what lies behind so lovely, so dramatic a wall. "Desire" seems to me the appropriate word, for the reasons behind the pioneers' decision to explore and cross it cannot have been wholly economic. I felt excited at the prospect of following in their footsteps in the not too distant future, and indeed the route I was to take from Charlottesville over the mountains to Knoxville and Nashville follows almost exactly the course of the pioneers in Allen Tate's story.

From Monticello, which imparts a great sense of repose and domestic order, you cannot but be mindful of the mountains beyond. Jefferson chose to be buried out on the hillside of his own "little mountain," just a little way below the house he had designed with such obsessive love, care and ingenuity. If you stand at the western extremity of the gardens of Monticello, where the steep downward slope begins, and put a hand in front of your face in such a way as to blot out the small town of Charlottesville below you, you can see virtually what Jefferson and his contemporaries could see—a landscape of hills, woodland, and pasture and, rising sharply out of and above all this, giving away nothing about what lies behind it, the Blue Ridge.

If you walk to the opposite side of the Monticello gardens you do not need this gesture. Unsullied flattish forest land extends as far as you can see.

Travel eastward through it and you will come to Virginia's capital, Richmond, the capital also, one year after its proclamation, of the Confederacy itself. Richmond suffered hideous destruction in the Civil War when fleeing Confederates set it afire, but Jefferson's Capitol still stands, surrounded by dismal buildings of our own time.

Jefferson's mountainside tomb honors him, according to his wishes, as governor of Virginia and founder of the University of Virginia. One would not know from its inscription that he had been president of the United States. Virginia's vision of itself (the Old Dominion State) begets such an attitude. In the Civil War Robert E. Lee was offered command of the Union armies but wished instead to serve Virginia, which, after painful deliberation joined the Confederacy.

It was Virginia which established—in Jamestown in 1619—the first legislative body in the New World, the House of Burgesses. It was a Virginian, Dr. Thomas Walker, who in 1770 discovered the Cumberland Gap in the mountains, thus making it possible for thousands of pioneers to move westward. And in Virginia in 1831 took place one of the explosions of violence that foreshadowed the Civil War: a slave, Nat Turner, led what he believed to be a divinely inspired revolt against the white masters, in which fifty people were murdered. It seems only appropriate then that it was Virginia which produced the first major Southern novelist, Ellen Glasgow (1874–1945).

Ellen Glasgow was born in Richmond and died there; she came, on both sides, from old established Virginian families, and from her novels much can be learned about Virginian history and topography. Her intellectual inclinations were cosmopolitan however, and her literary models were Balzac, George Eliot and Thomas Hardy. It is indeed her literary internationalism that enabled her to achieve her important position in Southern literary history. Her mind sharpened by her intelligent reading of the European realists and determinists, she was the first discoverer of the immense fictional potential of the South as a separate country with its own culture, its own history of struggle and defeat, its own hard and uncertain future.

Ellen Glasgow's ambition was Balzacian in scope; taken together her novels add up to a comprehensive survey of the South and its people from the antebellum days to the comparative prosperity of her own middle age, when Yankee commercial values were rampant. She explores the lives of poor, stubborn Scottish–Irish smallholders living in the countryside below the Blue Ridge as well as those of the great aristocratic families of Virginia, both in their pre-1861 heyday and in their later decadence. She charts the histories of "plain men," of social agitators, self-made careerists rising from poverty to important posts in government or industry, intellectuals, professional men, and—above all—women. The Old South had treated its women with a troubadour reverence; the commerce-dominated society of early twentieth century America virtually excluded women from its jungle warfare of free enterprise. In both cases a singular determination, a lonely sense of self, was called for from women.

Ellen Glasgow depicts her characters for the most part as being quite helpless in the face of the ravages of fate, their own psychological and physiological make-ups, the pressures of their environment and society, and the forces of history. She is, in other words, a social Darwinist. The antebellum Southern gentry may indeed have possessed all the virtues that have been claimed for them—and in *The Battleground* she portrays, completely convincingly, the kind and Christian treatment of both slaves and freed black families by white landowners—but they were undoubtedly devoted to an obsolescent tradition, to agrarian values in a world increasingly dominated by industrial and commercial values. And so they had to go under. This does not mean that Ellen Glasgow does not value nobility and goodness. Rather it makes her peculiarly sympathetic to it, and the beauty she depicts in her frustrated lives is considerable.

For four or five years I collected the novels of Ellen Glasgow and now possess them all, many of them first editions with splendid bindings, charmingly decorated flyleaves and a nice smell. I was helped in my task by the proprietor of the Dedalus bookstore in Charlottesville, whom I encountered on my first visit there; his shop is a cornucopia for those interested in Southern literature. (This enterprising man also runs the town's best restaurant, the C & O, in an imaginatively converted railroad building.) There seems to me a greater interest in Ellen Glasgow's work in the United States now, especially in the South and particularly in her native Virginia, than when I first began my collection; a few of her novels are, happily, back in print. More and more she is being recognized as the first writer to see both the uniqueness and the universal relevance of Southern experience and to bring to the presentation of Southern matters a literary craft and intellectual understanding refined by her contact with the leading minds of other cultures.

Yet I have found that her fiction does not wholly satisfy. This is why, I suppose, it has fallen into comparative oblivion as far as the general novel-reading public is concerned. She herself—once again emulating Balzac—divided her novels into three groups: the "Novels of the Commonwealth" (about the Virginian past, from antebellum to Reconstruction), the "Novels of the Country," and the "Novels of the City." The novels in this last category have earned praise from critics for their wit, and indeed their picture of life among the professional classes of Richmond, here called Queenborough, is sharp and amusing. But I find them sour in tone and lacking in charity. Ellen Glasgow was not a happy woman; a tragic love affair made her attempt suicide, and she was later troubled by a yearly worsening deafness for which she sought cure after cure. Frustration is overdominant in too many of the novels, to their detriment, I think. In many scenes it robs them of any different emotional power they might have otherwise possessed.

I would advise the reader who does not know Ellen Glasgow's work to begin with *The Battleground* (1902), for me the best fictional rendering of what one might term the arcadian idyll of antebellum patrician life in the South. Ellen Glasgow sees behind and beyond the idyll, of course; she does not share the assumptions or the ideals of her main characters. But she empathizes with them, and the result is that this novel conveys the Southern gentry's noble vision of life and of their own roles in it as few others do. This makes its depiction of the ravages of the Civil War even more harrowing. Ellen Glasgow's account of the burning of Richmond, which sends the young woman Virginia mad and thus kills her, is both terrifying and heartrending, and ranks for me among the finest passages in twentieth century literature for conveying the bewildering effect of war upon ordinary people.

Subtler and richer, respectively, are *Virginia* (1913) and *The Miller of Old Church* (1911). *Virginia* is a compassionate and absorbing psychological study of a woman who fulfills the demands of the Southern ideal of womanhood and is consequently overly innocent and vulnerable. Its moving close is not spoiled by Ellen Glasgow's otherwise frequent habit of obsessively hammering nails into the coffins of her characters' destinies. As for *The Miller of Old Church*, one of the "Novels of the Country," its vigorous and poetic rendering of the lives of a handful of people of differing social backgrounds in a pocket of the Virginian countryside deserves comparison with its models, George Eliot's *Adam Bede* and Thomas Hardy's *Far from the Madding Crowd*. It deserves, too, something of their popularity.

The gentry who appear in Ellen Glasgow's novels are very mindful of what they consider the proper behavior and attitudes for gentlemen and ladies, the rules of the *ancien régime* English culture to which they feel themselves heirs. It is often said that Virginia resembles England. Certainly the countryside to the north of Charlottesville bears a recognizable kinship to the English landscape of perhaps the seventeenth and eighteenth centuries. Here are pretty villages, large country houses, pastureland where fine horses graze, lovingly tended gardens and thick woods. I remember a golden October afternoon, in 1975, when a picnic on the grounds of a large neoclassical mansion while watching a steeplechase around its fields made up a scene resembling the tournament in Allen Tate's Virginian-set *The Fathers*. The fearless and fast riders were wearing English hunting pink. Yet I myself did not feel the atmosphere was much like the England I knew; there was a vein of wildness in it that would not have been evident at a comparable occasion in, say, the Cotswold country. Yet it is true that English people take to Virginia very readily, perhaps finding in it something that may have belonged to a pre-Victorian England, and certainly I myself could live in Charlottesville without much sense of being severed from my own land.

The young men in *The Battleground* attend the University of Virginia at Charlottesville; they do so accompanied by retinues of slaves, horses and dogs, and they lead the lives of rich young bucks there; playing cards, frequenting inns, and wenching with girls in the town. To stand on the steps of the university rotunda and look down at the two lines of columns on either side of the lawn below is an inspiring experience. The beauty of Ash Lawn, the center of the university, never wanes. Spring had come to Charlottesville when I returned there from the Deep South, and, though it was known to me in a variety of weather, the new season seemed to have transformed it. The dogwood was in flower everywhere, and I found it pleasant to work outside. Sometimes I would sit among the university students on the lawn itself. The blue of the sky, the white of the colonnades, the tender green of the trees that stand on the lawn, and the mellowed red of the brick—this symphony of colors enhanced my work rather than distracted me from it. Both colonnaded lines include five pavilions, each different and possessing individuality of curve, form or feature yet offsetting the others and contributing to the total, harmonious effect. In the pavilions live professors or university officials, and in the pleasantly proportioned rooms behind the colonnades live students; Jefferson described his design as an "academical village," as good a phrase as any. Sometimes I would sit in one of the little gardens behind Ash Lawn, gardens at once urbane and arcane in their charm and stocked with trees all in blossom, protected by serpentine, self-buttressing walls a single brick thick that Jefferson himself had designed. The pavilions and students' quarters seemed even prettier viewed from the back.

Only a year after the opening of the university, when Ash Lawn's delights were still something new, Edgar Allan Poe enrolled there. Smartly dressed, with a retinue of servants and horses, he led the life of a young Virginian aristocrat, resembling that of the young men in Ellen Glasgow's *The Battleground*. His own background was actually very different from those of the rich youths with whom he consorted. Poe was the son of actors, with a charming but hopeless father and a mother who had trudged up and down the eastern seaboard from theater to theater playing in worthless melodramas. Poe had been rescued from poverty by an immensely rich merchant in Richmond and his aristocratic wife and so had spent his youth surrounded by elegance and luxury. He arrived at the University of Virginia as a handsome, hard-working, robust young man, always well turned out and good-mannered and distinguished by his large, tender gray eyes. But already he had suffered a mental breakdown, and his career at the university was to be attended by unhappiness. Mr. Allan, his benefactor, had never officially made him his son and now quarreled with him, refusing to pay his bills and forcing Poe to take to card-playing for support. And his knowledge of the real difference between himself and his comrades endorsed Poe's already developed sense of insecurity. He was after all still a very young man when he wrote:

You are not wrong, who deem
That my days have been a dream;
Yet if hope has flown away
In a night, or in a day,
In a vision, or in none,
Is it therefore the less gone?
All that we see or seem
Is but a dream within a dream.

Of Poe's art I shall speak briefly when I describe my visit to South Carolina. But here I would like to note a paradox. The first famous product of Jefferson's university became the best known of all those who charted the murky seas of the subconscious. He was a writer who, far from imposing order on life, sought to break the orderly surface formed by the conscious mind to discover what terrible things lie beneath.

Interest in culture, history and literature is a noticeable feature of Charlottesville. Two women writers of note, the West Virginian Mary Lee Settle and the young and promising Ann Beattie, live here; Paul Gaston, the eminent historian of the South and in particular of the New South, teaches at the university. So does one of America's most accomplished short story writers, Peter Taylor, my meeting with whom is described in the next chapter. During my visit a new literary review, the *Blue Ridge* was being launched. The University Press, housed in a building that is an attractive counterpart of those that make up the university and run by the charming Walker Cowan, shows a particular interest in books on Virginian history and topography and on Jefferson. Like all university towns it has a somewhat cosmopolitan flavor, too, yet some of its outer areas partake of the nature of a mountain town. The Blue Ridge seems ever imminent in Charlottesville.

"As we approached the Blue Ridge," says Allen Tate's pioneer narrator, "it seemed to rise higher and higher toward its zenith like a gathering storm."

And after making the first ascent of the Ridge, what does one see but another ridge, and what beyond that but a further one? A ridge, especially a ridge blue with the haze of dense woods, excites longing for something unspecifiable. So, in the Southern Appalachians one is constantly in a state of half-gratified longing, an emotion that evidences itself in the sweeps, and scraped, plucked and strummed melodies of the region's greatest cultural achievement, bluegrass music. I have been an ardent lover of bluegrass since my mid-teens. Though geographically the term refers to the horse-raising districts of Kentucky, musically it can be legitimately used for the style of singing and playing found all over this mountain area. I was excited to be at last in its land of origin.

It was a fair, sunny May day when I traveled over the Blue Ridge and through the mountains of Virginia and East Tennessee to Nashville, where I was to live for seven weeks. I had in fact made the journey as far as Knoxville a few weeks prior to my Deep South trip. The weather then had been inclement, though it had given a strange dimension to the wildness of the country. Of this earlier journey I shall speak a little later. Now those dense woods, bare in March, were luxuriant almost beyond dreaming. I felt, on a high stretch of road, that one could throw oneself down upon the dense treetops below and bounce on them as on some natural green trampoline. Dogwood and judas were liberal with their blossoms in valley after valley.

The bus made its southwesterly journey slowly. (From their original trek the Scottish–Irish settlers of Tennessee and Kentucky were sometimes known simply as "Southwesterners.") Charlottesville soon became unimaginable. Long before dusk I felt almost drunk on the prolixity of wooded valleys and wooded mountains. Towns were small and exuded a near-tangible quietness; they seemed pleasant punctuation marks in a virgin, verdant page. We passed through Abingdon, Virginia, mentioned by Allen Tate's "ancestor" in his account of his migration to Tennessee: "We made for the town of Abingdon which nestled between high ranges running northeast and southwest—the gateway to the Western States for the early ministries of Christianity bearing the word to the new country."

Appropriately enough it was at Abingdon that a pretty girl in her late teens got on the bus. She took the seat next to mine, but throughout her journey—she got off at Johnson City, Tennessee— she was immersed in some pamphlets. She left one of these behind on her seat. It was a tract written by one minister to another declaring that to pretend that any instrument other than the organ was suited to God's house was to be guilty of blasphemy. This upset me—partly because it seemed such gloomily contentious reading for so pleasant-expressioned a girl, and partly because I knew that the area through which we were passing had evolved very haunting sacred music in which fiddles and banjos played memorable parts.

Halfway through the somewhat ramshackle town of Bristol a large sign boldly proclaimed: "THE GREATEST STATE OF TENNESSEE." Beyond this signboard I could see wilder, higher hills magically illuminated by the declining sun. Allen Tate's pioneer spoke of "turning their faces toward the setting sun." The faces of us bus travelers seemed to be continually toward the setting sun, too. A valley would grow dusky, a hill blurred in evening shadow, but beyond was always a ridge touched with the rose light of the sun in retreat.

The eminent English ethnomusicologist Cecil Sharp journeyed throughout the Southern Appalachians at the turn of the century, collecting songs, ballads and dance tunes from the mountain people just as he had done in his own English countryside. He found amazingly preserved many songs and airs from long-ago rural Britain. Some of the ballads he collected are achingly lovely in both melody and words. This song from Tennessee, for instance, is "The False Young Man":

> *Come in, come in, my old true love,*
> *And chat awhile with me,*
> *For it's been three-quarters of one long year or more*
> *Since I spoke one word to thee.*
>
> *When your heart was mine, my old true love,*
> *And your head lay on my breast,*
> *You could make me believe by the falling of your arm,*
> *That the sun rose up in the West.*
>
> *There's many a girl can go all round about,*
> *And hear the small birds sing,*
> *And many a girl that stays at home alone,*
> *And rocks the cradle and spins.*
>
> *There's many a star that shall jingle in the West,*
> *There's many a leaf below,*
> *There's many a damn will light upon a man*
> *For serving a poor girl so.*

It is interesting to note the recurrence of the word "West," that which lies beyond the singer's own ridge-country.

But the settlers in the Appalachians did not only preserve, they developed. Bluegrass—dance and song, sacred and secular—may derive from English, Scottish and Irish music, and this may explain why it is often much liked by British people. (I have found it easier to buy bluegrass records in London than in Washington, D.C., or Boston.) But the Appalachian settlers have in fact evolved something original. The wildness of the mountains, the freedom and adventure that characterized the early colonists, are perhaps responsible for the element, the dimension in bluegrass music that distinguishes it from its precursors—passion. There is passion for the loved one, passion for God and Jesus, passion for liberty, and a passionate approach to everyday life. I looked forward to hearing bluegrass music when I got to Nashville.

It was dark when we reached Knoxville, a city I had spent a night in earlier and was to pass through on several more occasions, so that its Trailways bus station, with its cafe and its jukebox playing Johnny Cash's "There Ain't No Good Chain Gang," is one of the first places that comes to my mind when I think of my Southern journey. On subsequent trips I was able to enjoy the moment when the mountains fall away to reveal fecund land watered by the Tennessee and Clinch Rivers. But not on this occasion.

Between Knoxville and Nashville the country is mostly undulating and wooded and was bitterly fought for by the Indians. The last stretch of any long journey always seems the most protracted, and the hours spent traveling between the main city of East Tennessee and the main city of middle Tennessee seemed slow to me. In the seat behind me a white woman and a black woman, not hitherto known to one another, gossiped—a little too audibly for my liking—about illnesses and deaths in their respective families. Coincidentally, it turned out that both women were married to preachers.

Allen Tate's narrator gives two accounts of old Nashville that are authentic in tone. Of the city in 1798 he writes:

> . . . as we came to the south bank of the Cumberland and I looked across that deep, slow-moving stream, I saw some twenty or thirty houses, mostly log houses but a few of them clapboarded and perhaps one or two of brick, straggling away from the waterfront as if they had been set up at random in a great hurry and only for a few days.

And of Nashville as it was in 1808:

> In the ten years that had gone by since I had been there, the
> town had changed wonderfully. There were not more than
> six thousand people, but the constant bustle, the coming and
> going, the sudden appearance and disappearance of strangers,
> who had tarried there a few days, gave the town an air of being
> a city. The new brick buildings along the waterfront, which
> was piled high with barrels of salt pork and lard, of whiskey
> and corn, and smaller quantities of tobacco, tended to give the
> scene a stability that impressed me greatly.[21]

Nashville, now a city of over half a million, has a curiously complex composite identity: manufacturing town, university city,
"Music City U.S.A." and state capital, it contains some of the
richest residential roads in the whole United States in addition to
districts that are scruffy and seedy. Nowhere has better claim to be
the seminal center of Southern culture, yet it is also a raunchy
stopping-place for travelers. It was in this latter capacity that it
first presented itself to me.

"This is Nashville, Tennessee," said the Trailways driver. "That's
the original Grand Ol' Opry House on your right." Passengers
turned their heads to look at a dark, abandoned-looking brick
building, and then we were pulling in to the bus station. I took a
taxi from there to a motel where I had booked a room. The driver
seemed a little surprised at my choice. "You're wanting to stay
somewhere adult," he said cryptically, and I supposed I was. Downtown Nashville stands on a hill around the base of which the taxi
proceeded to take me. The highrise buildings, uninteresting in
themselves, looked impressive lit up above the rest of the city and
against a backcloth of night sky. The Nashville skyline deserves its
fame (it provided the name for an album of Bob Dylan's), though
unlike Atlanta's it holds out false promise.

Then we drew up at the motel. Signs outside proclaimed its
"adult" status. I met an English friend of mine there with whom I
had arranged to spend the weekend. I asked her about the strange
designation of the motel, and she thought perhaps it referred to
evening cabaret. In fact it referred to pornographic channels on the
television sets in each room. They gave me and my friend no
pleasure, but it cannot be denied that others appreciated them.
Wild whoops of enjoyment came from the room on our left; this

had been taken by seven boys, most of them, I learned, recent recruits to the army, and all from Virginia Beach. They had a whale of a time watching slow-motion technicolor sexual acrobatics. The room on our right had only one occupant; glances from the balcony revealed him unswervingly intent on the blue movie, sitting on the bed in only his underpants with a can of beer in his hand. Louder than life coital sighs could be heard through the thin walls until late into the night. The motel was also too close to the railroad for comfort, and at frequent intervals freight trains of great length clanked and rattled past, announcing themselves, of course, with penetrating melancholy whistles. I stayed in the motel for one night without my friend, and perhaps it was my unattended condition that attracted three black girls in succession to tap on my window after midnight to ask me if I'd like a date.

I then took rooms in an establishment as different from this seedy motel as could be: a college which specialized in training teachers of religion. It was built in a mock English manorial style. During my first weeks there the students were still in residence; then it was taken over by conferences and discussion groups. One morning I woke up to hear a conversation in the adjoining bathroom I shared with the occupants of the next room. "God's just been talking to me this morning," said a young man. "God talks to me the whole day," said the other, just a little smugly. Such easy relationships with the deity were enjoyed by many of the other students and visitors. I heard a girl call out from a tree where she was pruning some branches: "I don't know how I shall be spending this summer —apart from praying, of course!" Repeated encounters with these young believers disabused me of my tendency to think that Fundamentalism by its very nature encouraged fearfulness and repression. For there could be no denying that here were happy, well-adjusted people who, far from cherishing their exclusiveness, earnestly longed for everybody to share their faith. It did seem to me, both from their conversation and from such evidence as notices in the common room and the books being read that they were very little interested in social concerns. But then how many students who claim to be actually do more than pay lip service to the existence of injustices? And I was struck by the pleasant, easy relationship that existed in this college between black and white both on a staff and student level.

From the college I could walk to Vanderbilt University where I used the library. Vanderbilt, perhaps the premier Southern university, was chartered in 1872 and built, as a notice proudly proclaims, with money made from the railroad, a nice matching of symbols in consequence of Vanderbilt's key role in Southern culture. The campus consists of plum-colored brick buildings set among lawns with large trees. A carillon plays at certain hours synthetic folksy melodies. I worked in the library at a table above which two students had scribbled grafitti on the wall. One was a piece of undergraduate ribaldry:

Jockstraps
(i) prevent your nuts from getting caught in your zipper.
(ii) prevent noticeable bulges when sexy girls walk by.

The other was, I recognized, a quotation from an old bluegrass song:

> *Just as far as I can remember,*
> *She'll remain the rose of my heart,*
> *Mom took sick along in December,*
> *February brought us broken hearts . . .*

The walk back in the evening from Vanderbilt to my rooms came to seem something I'd been doing all my life. Those Nashville nights were heavy, warm and humid; lightning bugs and fireflies patterned the thick and fragrant darkness with their darting lights.

During that first weekend in the city I did swift justice to Nashville's sights, for instance, to the reconstruction of the 1790 Fort Nashborough down by the Cumberland River. Interesting though it was to walk around those log blockhouses, cabins and stockades, my attention wandered to the great warehouses of dirty brick that tower above the fort, evidence of Nashville's comparatively early mercantile prosperity. The Hermitage, the orderly country house of Andrew Jackson, deserves visitors to admire the classical proportions of its facade and the charm of its rose garden, but of all its attractions the barren humbleness of the slave quarters made the greatest impression on me. The Upper Room, where Leonardo's *Last Supper* is reproduced in wood, appalled me. Nearby I saw one of Elvis Presley's gold-plated Cadillacs enshrined in a little museum like a sacred totem.

Greek Revival is everywhere in Nashville, most prominently in the 1855 Capitol which, perhaps because of the undistinguished highrise buildings so close to it, failed to move me. Then there is the Parthenon, known to many moviegoers now for the dramatic event that took place there in Robert Altman's lively and malicious film *Nashville*. I could never think of the building as other than "ersatz." But then so it has seemed to many Nashville people:

> *Why do they come? What do they seek*
> *Who build but never read their Greek?*

The Tennessee poet Donald Davidson continues:

> *The golden years are come too late.*
> *Pursue not wisdom or virtue here,*
> *But what blind motion, what dim last*
> *Regret of men who slew their past*
> *Raised up this bribe against their fate?*[22]

But Davidson, I think speaks too harshly. Nashville was the center of an intellectual movement so vigorous that its claim to be the "Athens of the South" is not without justification. And anyway, the merits of Nashville are not to be found among its public buildings. The movement of which Davidson was a key member is the Fugitives and their offshoot the Agrarians. Of them Allen Tate, who returned in his old age to live in Nashville, said in a memoir: "I think I may disregard the claims of propriety, and say quite plainly that, so far as I know, there was never so much talent, knowledge and character accidentally brought together in one American place in our time."

I believe he speaks truly. The cradle and center of this movement was Vanderbilt University.

Its origin was friendships, and its productions have their roots in the delight that friends take in talking at length on subjects of mutually burning interest. A group of men of literary and philosophical turn of mind developed the habit of meeting every other Saturday at the homes of a Nashville businessman, James Frank, and his rich, eccentric, learned brother-in-law, Sidney Mttron Hirsch. Eminent among this group were two professors at Vanderbilt who had moreover graduated from the university, John Crowe Ransom (1888–1974) and Donald Davidson (1893–1968). Hirsch was the creator of "the most artistic and ambitious spectacle ever given in the South," a Greek Revival pageant with a gigantic cast,

91

called "The Fire Regained." He would dominate meetings; re-
clining on a chaise longue he delivered himself of opinions at once
erudite and wayward. He was an invalid who wore a shining pince-
nez, and his hair was curled in Assyrian fashion.

These meetings had acquired regularity by the summer of 1915.
The food was good and lavish, and there was a stimulating coming
and going of clever people. Then in November 1921 Donald
Davidson invited the brilliant young student Allen Tate to attend
one of the Saturdays. And with this invitation, it is generally agreed,
the major phase of the Fugitives began. Allen Tate, in his *Memories
and Essays: Old and New* (1976), remembers:

> By February or early March of 1922, the original "Fugitive
> Group" was formed although it had no name.... Uppermost in
> my mind are Donald Davidson, who, for me, at that early
> stage, meant just about everything.... John Ransom always
> appeared at the Fugitive meetings with a poem (some of us
> didn't), and when his turn came he read it in a dry tone of
> understatement. I can only describe his manner in those days as
> irony which was both brisk and bland.... We all knew that
> John was far better than we were, and although he never assert-
> ed his leadership we looked to him for advice.[23]

It was Hirsch who proposed that the group should issue a
magazine; its title, *The Fugitive*, was bestowed on it by a lesser-
known poet-member, Alec Brock Stevenson. "The name," Allen
Tate continues, "turned out to be a good one because it invited
ridicule. What were we fleeing from? Or toward? . . . a Fugitive
was quite simply a Poet: the Wanderer, or even the Wandering
Jew, the Outcast, the man who carries the secret wisdom around
the world." The first issue of the magazine came out in April 1922.
Other young men of distinction gravitated toward the circle.
Robert Penn Warren joined in February 1923, Andrew Lytle
and Cleanth Brooks toward the end of the magazine's life. Its last
issue was in December 1925.

All these men were Southerners, their sensibilities shaped by their
Southern experience. From Tennessee came John Crowe Ransom,
Donald Davidson and Andrew Lytle; from Kentucky, Allen Tate
and Robert Penn Warren. Yet at first the South, though of very
considerable interest to them, was not the ideological focus it was
so strongly to become later. What brought about this change?

Partly it was the dispersal of the group, which forced each man to look at what common bonds they had possessed, and partly the attack on the South from the progressive intelligentsia of the rest of the country brought forth by the Scopes trial. Tennessee had banned the teaching of Darwinist evolution in schools; a young teacher called Scopes was prosecuted in Dayton and found guilty, though his fine was never imposed on him. Many Southerners found themselves inclined to defend their society's values in the face of Northern asperity. And indeed the teaching of evolution was to remain illegal in Tennessee until 1967; in 1973 a new law was passed which required that the biblical and the Darwinian theories of man's evolution be given equal emphasis in the state's schools. Another factor for the Fugitives was the general increase in urbanization of the South. All these developed what was already deep within these writers—a veneration for the Southern past. But now they came to see the old Southern culture as a remedy or source of remedy for the sicknesses of contemporary American society.

It was at this stage of their intellectual development that they earned the name "Agrarian." For in 1930, under the guiding light of Donald Davidson, "twelve Southerners" contributed one essay each to a volume entitled *I'll Take My Stand: The South and the Agrarian Tradition*. The derivation of the title should be at once apparent:

> *In Dixieland I'll take my stand*
> *To live and die in Dixie.*

Of the twelve Donald Davidson, Allen Tate, Andrew Lytle, John Crowe Ransom and Robert Penn Warren had been true "Fugitives." *I'll Take My Stand* can thus be seen as a product of Vanderbilt University.

The book's ideological purpose cannot be better indicated than by some quotations from the introduction in which all twelve voices speak in unison:

> The authors contributing to this book are Southerners, well acquainted with one another and of similar tastes, though not necessarily living in the same physical community, and perhaps only at this moment aware of themselves as a single group of men. . . . All the articles bear in the same sense upon the

book's title-subject: all tend to support a Southern way of life against what may be called the American or prevailing way; and all as much as agree that the best terms in which to represent the distinction are contained in the phrase, Agrarian versus Industrial.

Nobody now proposes for the South, or for any other community in this country, an independent political destiny. That idea is thought to have been finished in 1865. But how far shall the South surrender its moral, social, and economic autonomy to the victorious principle of Union? That question remains open. The South is a minority section that has hitherto been jealous of its minority right to live its own kind of life. The South scarcely hopes to determine the other sections, but it does propose to determine itself, within the utmost limits of legal action. Of late, however, there is the melancholy fact that the South itself has wavered a little and shown signs of wanting to join up behind the common or American industrial ideal. It is against that tendency that this book is written. The younger Southerners, who are being converted frequently to the industrial gospel, must come back to the support of the Southern tradition. They must be persuaded to look very critically at the advantages of becoming a "new South" which will be only an undistinguished replica of the usual industrial community.[24]

It seems to all the contributors that the old rural Southern society possessed three invaluable assets; stability; the means of giving people creative work satisfaction; and the paternalism that provides opportunities for continuing neighborly and familial unselfishness. Thus, it is argued, it catered for the whole person rather than the modern, fragmented, compartmentalized human being. The search for wholeness and the insistence on its importance permeate the book.

Each man—as is testified in the diversity and range of the essays—found of interest different facets of Southern culture and the fate that threatened it. For John Crowe Ransom the defeat and break-up of the Old South was but a dramatic (and for him personally significant) symptom of the worldwide destruction of organic civilization by the forces of material progress. For Donald Davidson the South was in itself something wonderfully unique that must be treasured and protected; he of all the Fugitive/Agrarians was the most aware of its folklore, music and topography and was consequently the most impassioned in defense of it against all onslaughts by so-called reformers. For Robert Penn Warren the richness of the Southern experience provided literary material in never-failing supply, abundant matter to engage the heart, intellect and talent. For Allen Tate the South's past yielded a usable myth, a series of specific images embodying universally relevant ideas that could fructify not only its present self but other Western cultures. For Andrew Lytle—who had spent time farming—it was the amplitude and goodness of the rural way of life that was so valuable.

The book—and the works of the individual writers that were produced later—has had far-reaching consequences. For here, the world could see, were men of obviously first-rate minds and sensitivities who, far from repudiating the castigated land they had grown up in, cherished it and indeed wished certain of its ways to be emulated elsewhere. Not only could the world see this, but ordinary bewildered Southerners, too, who were in need of encouragement in the midst of their conflict between their love for the society that had reared them and the constant attacks and sneers of the outside world.

As for their Agrarianism, which seemed to some critics merely the cranky espousal of literary men, without empirical significance, time has surely vindicated the twelve Southerners. Dominant among the issues of the 1960s and 1970s have been these related questions: how can Western society break free from its self-perpetuating materialism? how can a meaningful return to nature be made? how best can we restore the organic community? To say that these things are easier said than done is a truism and not very helpful. For changes which can be gradual as well as of revolutionary abruptness occur precisely because of the emotions and acknowledged deep desires of people; even now I believe that the comparative pleasantness of life in late-seventies America and Britain can partly be attributed to this diffused popular reaction, of which the Agrarians can be seen as a doctrinaire (and intellectually impressive) vanguard. And they never intended to provide a practical manual, anyway. They were creative writers, not economists or sociologists.

As I write these lines I think of my visit—made in chilly March— to the Kentucky poet and novelist, Wendell Berry (born in 1934).

If anyone can be said to be living out the ideals of *I'll Take my Stand* it is he. Indeed, he fully and generously acknowledges his debt to the book and its contributors. A handsome and healthy-looking man with kind, boyish, thoughtful eyes, he and his family farm in the countryside he has known since his boyhood—the lovely hilly country of northern Kentucky. His farm stands halfway between Covington and Louisville. The rounded wooded hills slope down to the wide Ohio River, that frontier of the South. The villages here are singularly attractive, and to me they are timber-built cousins of those I love in England. Wendell Berry relates the Agrarian ideology to Thomas Jefferson's; was not Jefferson's ideal that every man should have his own plot of land? Madison Jones, I remember, opposes the Jeffersonian vision of man and nature with the Southern religious conception. Wendell Berry sees no real contradictions in following both. He certainly cannot be accused of being unmindful of the pain and suffering that are part of the experience of every living thing. His poems and his fiction alike have these as insistent themes, and a growing mind's realization of them is a major element in his early sensitive and robust novel, *Nathan Coulter*. For all his recent absorption in the religious culture of the Indians, particularly those of Kentucky, his is a Christian vision. "And," he reminded me as we ate dinner at a delightful hillside restaurant, "St. Paul says that all creation is to be saved." Therefore it is to be peculiarly revered in all its manifestations, and a life spent working in harmony with it must surely bring the greatest satisfaction. Wendell Berry's recent writings have mostly been about agricultural and ecological matters. One hopes that he will eventually return to the quiet penetrations of such poems as those in *Openings* and *Findings*, (both 1969) and of his earlier fiction.

But the South as examplar for the rest of the world? That is a far more difficult matter to deal with, and I must confess that I shrink from judgment of the complex and often inconsistent eulogizing vision of their native land that the writers present. In honesty, however, I feel I should make three objections: first, that to hold up a society for the admiration of the rest of the world (and of itself) is inevitably to deny its many-sidedness, a dangerous denial; second, that the "pastness" of the past is something that must be acknowledged; the past can certainly fertilize the present, and in the end that is perhaps all the Agrarians desired. But their tone often suggests a desire to reinstate the past, something that no one has ever been able to do. And third, it can surely not be denied that what they say may have been true for the *white* Southerner, but for the black it was a different story, and there are many people, including most blacks (and myself), for whom even the most benevolent paternalism is an insufferable notion.

Of the Fugitive/Agrarians I was soon to see Allen Tate (living, as I have said, in Nashville itself) and Andrew Lytle (whose home is in Monteagle in the Tennessee mountains). Robert Penn Warren, who has given so much to American literature—both long and short fiction, poetry, and splendid seminal criticism—I regretfully decided not to contact, for he has made his home near Yale in Connecticut, and I had restricted the authors I would visit to those whose home was still the South.

Vanderbilt still honors its talented sons. Thomas Daniel Young, among other achievements biographer of both Ransom and Davidson, teaches there. No man imparts a greater love, a livelier commonsense on the subject of Southern literature than he. Of rugged appearance and enthusiastic manner, he showed me the greatest friendliness and helpfulness when I called on him in his rooms at the university. Perhaps because of his presence at Vanderbilt, thus perpetuating those of Ransom and Davidson, I feel I should say a little about these last two men, though in this book novelists rather than poets are my primary concern.

John Crowe Ransom's manner is restrained, ironic, metaphysical and learned. Yet his heart is as significant as his head in his work. There is no more moving poem of his than his Southern elegy "Antique Harvesters," and in particular these stanzas:

> *We pluck the spindling ears and gather the corn.*
> *One spot has special yield? "On this spot stood*
> *Heroes and drenched it with their only blood."*
> *And talk meets talk, as echoes from the horn*
> *Of the hunter—echoes are the old man's arts,*
> *Here come the hunters, keepers of a rite;*
> *The horn, the hounds, the lank mares coursing by*
> *Straddled with archetypes of chivalry;*
> *And the fox, lovely ritualist, in flight*
> *Offering his unearthly ghost to quarry;*
> *And the fields, themselves to harry.*
> *Resume, harvesters. The treasure is full bronze*

Which you will garner for the Lady, and the moon
Could tinge it no yellower than does this moon;
But gray will quench it shortly—the field, men, stones,
Pluck fast, dreamers; prove as you amble slowly
Not less than men, not wholly.[25]

Very applicable to Donald Davidson are the words that Robert Louis Stevenson used to describe his father—"passionately prejudiced, passionately attached." His ideology becomes untenable with its frighteningly consistent fixation on the Old South *in toto,* but he has a nobility of vision—did not Madison Jones tell me you felt you could die for him? And I believe his poetry has not had its full recognition outside the South. (In the recent *New Oxford Book of American Verse*, for instance, he is not represented at all.) Yet "Lee in the Mountains," "Randall, My Son," "Sanctuary," and "Sequel of Appomattox" have, it seems to me, a beauty of feeling finely complemented by their musical yet precise language. The plight of the old man in "Randall, My Son" is the plight of the South itself:

Randall, my son, before you came just now
I saw the lean vine fingering at the latch,
And through the rain I heard the poplar bough
Thrash at the blinds it never used to touch,
And I was old and troubled overmuch,
And called in the deep night, but there was none
To comfort me or answer, Randall, my son . . .
Randall, my son, I cannot hear the cries
That lure beyond the familiar fields, or see
The glitter of the world that draws your eyes.
Cold is the mistress that beckons you from me.
I wish her sleek hunting might never come to be—
For in our woods where deer and fox still run
An old horn blows at daybreak, Randall, my son.

And tell me then, will you some day bequeath
To your own son not born or yet begotten
The luster of a sword that sticks in sheath,
A house that crumbles and a fence that's rotten?
Take, what I leave, your own land unforgotten;
Hear, what I hear, in a far chase new begun
An old horn's husky music, Randall, my son.[26]

I was told of an inn where bluegrass concerts were held nightly. I had been having dinner in downtown Nashville, and I hired a taxi to take me there. The driver told me the inn was situated in a rather rough part of the town. "Let me put it in the language of your own country," he said, "there are streets nearby which would frighten the Kray brothers." This did indeed present an alarming picture, but inwardly I smiled in a superior fashion. The streets down which we were now driving were rather dingy—lined with small, shabby-porched wooden houses built too close together. But then I began to recognize certain street names. Why, we were very near the college in which I had taken rooms. How absurd to imagine crime in such a context! The driver, who was about forty, now began talking about himself. He had been raised in Nashville, studied theology and philosophy at a college there, and then joined an insurance firm. But at this point—confronted, I suppose, with so many claims of other kinds—he realized that what he wanted to do most of all in life was sleep with as many women as possible, and therefore he had given up any idea of a professional career. And so we came to the inn.

This was a pleasant old white-painted affair, and you had to drive around to the back to enter the part in which the bluegrass concerts were held. As the taxi drew up I did hear two shots, but I failed to interpret them for what they were. I opened the cab door. Across the yard, dark except for the lights of the inn, came two flashes, then more—now unmistakeable—shots. The taxi driver told me to shut the door and duck my head. He said there was no need for worry. "They ain't fixing to shoot at us. They're just dumb people back yonder." This, I suppose, was true. Two youths (invisible) were firing at another two who were just discernible in the shadows by the far wall of the yard. But somehow the fact that we were not their desired targets was scant comfort.

It must have been only a few minutes later that the driver said he thought it would be safe for me to run to the entrance of the inn, though it seemed far longer. The man taking money at the door—he had retreated during the shooting—apologized for the incident; such things happened from time to time, but he hoped I would enjoy the music. And indeed I did. Fears that those armed young men might burst in on us soon receded as the room filled up with cheerful-looking people. The room itself was like a cross between a speakeasy and a chapel. Huge kegs of beer and the sound of rough laughter suggested the former, while notices about having God as a friend, on the otherwise bare white walls, reminded me of the latter. In the audience all ages were represented, but there were many more men than women. I cannot remember seeing any black people in the audience, but then, having originated in almost exclusively white rural areas, bluegrass seems to lack appeal to black communities. The people on the whole seemed clean-limbed and healthy; a number wore semicomic hats. The beer, served in large quantities, was very good, very cold and was liberally drunk. There were five musicians playing fiddle, banjo, mandolin, guitar and bass; the mandolin player sometimes played the guitar instead and both he and the lead guitarist provided vocals. They played with immense gusto. I have heard subtler players, but these musicians concentrated on the vibrant, driving and fast aspects of bluegrass rather than the lyrical or tender. They gave us "Black Mountain Rag," "Cotton Blossom Special," "Raggerty Annie," the lovely "I'll Roll in My Baby's Arms," and "Holston Valley Breakdown" —tunes that I had known and loved for years. At a later stage in the evening they played bluegrass renderings of "Rocky Top, Tennessee" and "Dixie." The reaction to these of the audience, who had already shown their rowdy tendencies—in the way they made their requests when young men bawled out titles of favorite numbers one against the other—was extraordinary to me. The first song obviously had local significance; it was greeted by audibly expressed rapture. But "Dixie," proclaimed by the bluegrass lead singer as the true anthem of the South, produced a response which, if it had not been so charged with happiness, could well have been described as hysterical. Men shouted, stamped their feet and waved their arms. Through this I sat quietly as an onlooker. Then up to my table swaggered one of the rougher men in the room. What was wrong with me, he demanded, that I didn't show my feelings like everybody else when the song of the South was played. I answered —with only partial truth—that I was English and didn't understand the issue. This seemed to satisfy him; at any rate he walked away. Madison Jones, I reflected, had been wrong about the playing of "Dixie."

As I listened to the more traditional bluegrass numbers that followed—the concert, I was glad to find, was protracted beyond its advertised limit of midnight—I thought what a complete expression they were of the wild Appalachians that I had met and was shortly to meet again. I also thought what a perfect fusion blue-grass constitutes of the excitements of the psyche with those of everyday life.

I was to return to the inn many times. And there I met—by one of those strange, seeming strokes of fate—the friend, as he became, to whom I have dedicated this book. To think of him and of the people he introduced me to is to realize what is ever in my mind as I write now—the dangers and inadequacies of calling people "Southerners," "Americans," "English," and so on. People are themselves before all else, and temperamental compatibilities are stronger and much more important than cultural affiliations. I hope the reader will realize, in any future generalizations I offer, that not only do I think these things but they are articles of faith with me, born of deep personal experience, not least this friendship which began in Nashville.

It is, of course, for its country music that Nashville enjoys popular fame and has earned its much-proclaimed nickname of "Music City U.S.A." The curious phenomenon of Opryland, pleasure-park child of the Grand Ol' Opry, is perhaps the first feature of the city that comes to the ordinary person's mind. I cannot do better than quote from a tourist brochure on the subject of country music Nashville:

> You will see the homes of the immortals of Country Music such as Minnie Pearl, Eddy Arnold, Webb Pierce, Porter Waggoner, Tammy Wynette, the late Tex Ritter and Hank Williams. A highlight will be a guided tour through either the Country Music Wax Museum or the Country Music Hall of Fame. . . . Country music fans will be thrilled when our experienced lecturer takes you to the home of Johnny Cash and June Carter. Also see the homes of Roy Orbison, Kitty Wells, Bob Luman, Hank Snow, Jimmy Snow, Johnny Wright, Col. Tom Parker, Charley Lovin, Wesley Rose and Conway Twitty.

To enjoy immortality when still alive is a rare feat, as is having your house venerated and visited while you are still living in it. So much for Tours One and Three. Tour Seven has a rather more active entertainment in store for the visitor.

> Can you imagine yourself surrounded by beautiful Tennessee woodlands in a rustic atmosphere? Enjoy the finest in country

101

fun, country food and country music. It all begins with croquet, checkers, horseshoes and bingo. When you've worked up an appetite, we'll ring the dinner bell and you'll sit yourself down to a mighty fine picnic supper. Then it's time for some good ole country music. Join in—clap your hands and tap your feet to the finest and most colorful entertainment. We will wind up the evening gathered around a campfire roasting marshmallows and singing some of your favorite songs. It will be the best three-and-a-half hours you will spend. Just come dressed casual and expect to have a great time—a wonderful time that you will remember.

But country music, though so often a sentimentalization and debasement of real traditional music, has kept alive certain folk idioms. It has also given a great deal of pleasure. Back in England there is a popular weekly radio program which usually includes an interview straight from Nashville. There is something absurd about its loving chronicles of country meals and about the contrived pathos of so many of the songs. But sweetness, homeliness, romantic love and happiness are not to be decried, even if the manner of their expression is not always to one's taste, and this is another pervasive art form given to the world by the South. The Lovin' Spoonful song tells us, "There's thirteen hundred and fifty-two guitar pickers in Nashville, and they can pick more notes than the number of ants on a Tennessee anthill," and this is, if anything, an underestimation. Certainly the plucking of banjos and the strumming of guitars float out over the balmy air of Nashville streets in the evening.

I have pleasant memories of Nashville, and I find it strange that until as recently as 1966 it was the capital of a state in which there was limited suffrage, with most of its black population disenfranchized.

From Nashville I made two eastward journeys. East Tennessee was largely pro-Union in the Civil War, sending about thirty thousand soldiers to the Northern armies. Tennessee's divisions— it was also a bitter fighting ground—have been seen by some (David Madden, for instance) as the reason for the richness and strength of its literary productions.

Knoxville, a large industrial city with mountains in tantalizing but invisible proximity, has little real individuality but is not an

102

inhospitable, barren place like so many American cities. I walked around one of its older residential quarters which commands a view over the downtown area and over the undulations beyond. Houses were a little down-at-heel but charming, with their cluttered porches and blistered white weatherboarding. I visited these streets because James Agee (1909–1955) had lovingly acclaimed them in his famous novel *Death in the Family* (1957). The house where Agee lived has now been pulled down, but the atmosphere he evokes in the much-quoted opening to his novel still remains.

Agee was clearly, in the literal sense of the word, a fascinating personality; he seems to have cast a spell on all who knew him. Precocious as a youth, he was in fact late coming to literary maturity; he turned to the South, the society he knew best, only toward the end of his tragically short life. Hauntingly handsome, talented in many directions, tormented and emotional, he has become one of the saints of Southern (and indeed American) literature. I heard him praised by Allen Tate, James Dickey and David Madden; the latter indeed has edited a volume of commemorative essays on Agee. I can only say that on this subject I must part company with these men I so respect. Agee seems to me, even in *Death in the Family*, by far his strongest work, to fall too easily into uncontrolled (and derivative) rhetoric and sentimentality. It is as if he clutched at a Southern tradition of manner and matter for literary support; he certainly brings little of his own to it. I know, of course, that *A Death in the Family* is rooted in Agee's own experience. And as a result there are vivid and moving passages in the novel—the character of the small boy's father, too, is well and shrewdly done. But even its good things are not allowed to stand for themselves; they are drowned in a tide of verbosity and emotionalism that finally banishes sympathy. The Southern and American reader, reminded of extraliterary matters by pages in this novel, has come to have a regard for it that is disproportionate, I think, to what is actually articulated. In this book I have tried to empathize with Southern sentiments but always to retain a detachment of literary judgment. I have praised novels from a conviction that they are independently successful works of art with valuable perceptions about people, society and existence. Agee's work does not for me come into this category.

Nevertheless I had found the rendering of places in *A Death in the Family* sufficiently vivid to want to see them for myself. So on my trip northwestward from Knoxville I deliberately stayed near La Follette where the boy hero's grandparents lived. I even passed, I think, the very spot where the central fatal accident occurs. The motel I stayed in was all but deserted; it stood in a small, shabby village. Hills rose above it, with higher ones looking over their shoulders. The slopes were bare of foliage in March, and so quiet was everything that the hills and the little lake beneath them seemed almost to breathe. The next day I embarked on a bus journey through the mountains of Kentucky.

Kentucky means "land of tomorrow" in the Wyandot Indian language. It is a sadly ironic name in an Indian context, for nowhere was the fighting between white and red more intense and brutal than here. Indeed, the state became known as the "dark and bloody ground" of the Indian. The history of Kentucky should arouse shame in an Englishman; during the time of the American Revolution the British supplied the Indians with arms and encouraged them to attack and kill settlers, exacerbating the tensions between the races for several decades. Perhaps because of the harsh weather in which I made the greater part of my journey, I found something brooding and tragic in the Kentucky mountain country. Rain scoured the narrow valleys; somber hills, with rounded summits, reared their heads at unexpected twists of the road; swollen streams coursed through rocky ravines. Sometimes the road climbed out of the valleys on to plateaus from which we could see more wild hills tumbling until they were lost in the heavily clouded skyscape. The few villages we passed through are among the poorest I have seen, and I have traveled quite extensively on two continents. The fronts of cabins were made of insubstantial-looking wooden boards, but the backs and sides were constructed from an amazing accumulation of boxes, baby carriages, crudely tacked sheets of corrugated iron or canvas, and scrap metal. Walking up and down unpaved village lanes in chilly spring rain, I could think of few places more forlorn and uncomfortable in which to live. Yet Kentucky seems to evoke a deep love in its people; song after song sings its praises, and the sweetest of them come from the country beyond the mountains.

Just before the lovely old town of Danville a great change comes over the landscape. Within a few miles the wild cousin of the Scottish Highlands—which has treasured, like its relation, old songs, feuds, an intense sense of kinship, a proud veneration of the fighting spirit and the gun—has been exchanged for a more luxuriant cousin of the English Midlands. As in Virginia, villages and small towns have the prettiness, the repose, the obvious care for their old features that one associates more with the Old World than the New. This is horse-breeding land; white palings stretch over rich tinted grasslands, the famous blue grass; farms stand in a kindly paternal relation to the countryside and each small town is in harmony with the land around it. I saw Harrodsburg, Lawrenceburg and George-town briefly, and they left a harmonious impression upon me, as did Frankfort. This last town, the capital of Kentucky, differs from the others in being dramatically situated on steep banks above the Kentucky River.

The strange murder trial that inspired Robert Penn Warren to write his famous *World Enough and Time* (1950) took place in Frank-fort in 1826. The defendant appeared to have killed out of pure chivalry to avenge an abandoned girl. As I have said, Robert Penn Warren falls outside the scope of my book, but in mentioning my visit to Kentucky I cannot but salute his diverse yet ultimately uni-fied achievement. He is much more impressive, I myself feel, in his poetry and shorter prose (such as the marvelous short story "Black-berry Winter") than in his immensely ambitious but often diffuse longer novels. And in these can be detected something of the brooding force of the Kentucky scenery:

> *We live in time so little time*
> *And we learn all so painfully,*
> *That we may spare this hour's term*
> *To practice for eternity.* [27]

How different were these squally March days from the weather of my journey via Knoxville to Asheville, North Carolina. On hillside meadows honeysuckles lay spread out like carpets; never have I seen their equal. The air was heady with their delectable fragrance. Sun illuminated the thick green woods so that the high hills themselves seemed to be lighting up the trees.

The mountains of East Tennessee are TVA country. The TVA was created in the economically straitened year of 1933; since then, my guidebook tells me proudly, the TVA has been responsible for making dams, reservoirs, etc., which amount to ten thousand miles of shoreline, more than that of all the Great Lakes put together. Of course, construction on this scale has meant irretrievable losses in wild life, communities and natural scenery. I remembered Madison Jones' *A Buried Land.* I hope that the process of flooding valleys all over the Appalachians is now severely regulated. Nevertheless one has to remember that the TVA brought industry and employment to an area of great hardship. Those dreadful Kentucky mountain villages were not unique. Also the lakes created by the TVA are often stunning in their contexts.

On and on went the roads through the mountain passes of the Great Smokies. And on and on too goes one's response to them—I came to feel almost translated by them, or perhaps received into their lofty, forested, mysterious and prolific forms.

> The mountains were our masters; they went home to our eyes and our heart before we came to five. Whatever we can do or say must be forever hillbound. Our senses have been fed by our terrific land . . .[28]

These are the words of the Great Smokies' most famous literary son, Thomas Wolfe, born in Asheville, North Carolina, in 1900. He died, still a young man, in 1938. The very titles of his works, *Look Homeward, Angel, The Web and the Rock, The Hills Beyond* and *You Can't Go Home Again* betray the anguish of his relationship to the country of his origin; on the one hand he wanted to free himself from the imprisonment of life in a mountain town, to breathe the ampler intellectual and emotional air of more sophisticated places. But on the other hand he knew he was a child of wild North Carolina, and that creatively he would always remain a part of it.

I came to Asheville as the sun of a fine day was setting. The town was red, the dull red of its ugly old brick, the mountaintops, which encircle it (for the town stands high) blue, the sky as I looked behind me suffused with fiery gold. I shall never forget this sight, nor the sensation of being wrapped around by untamed country.

Is or is not Thomas Wolfe a Southern writer? It is a question much debated, but the debate can so easily run into pointless sophistry. He spent most of his adult life away from the South—in New York and Europe; he associated with virtually none of his distinguished Southern literary contemporaries. His central characters, Eugene Gant in *Look Homeward, Angel* and *Of Time and the River* and George Webber in *The Web and the Rock* and *You Can't Go Home Again*—both based on himself—are engaged in an agonizing quest for self-fulfillment which will take them—they

106

believe irrevocably—beyond the Carolina mountains, and the other people in the novel are seen primarily in their relationships to these searching heroes. Louis Rubin, always a percipient authority on Southern literature, argues persuasively in his essay in *Southern Renaissance* for Wolfe's inclusion among the ranks of Southern writers. He draws attention to the Southern nature of his rhetoric with its incantatory magnificences, of his preoccupation with passion and death, and of his rendering of people as independent beings. All this is true.

Yet I feel that, in this context, Wolfe is best described as a great Southern expatriate. An expatriate can never shake off those early influences, especially if he or she chooses in writing to explore the world he or she has left. Doubtless if we enumerate Thomas Wolfe's various qualities we shall come across some that are very properly Southern, as are his people and his places. But these are always fixed in a constant relationship to himself; so it is with D.H. Lawrence and the English East Midlands, and so it is, largely, with Joyce and Ireland. Writers who have stayed at home can more easily liberate their characters from the tether of their own predicaments, and the place in which they grew up cannot seem the personal emotional property that it does to the expatriate.

I trust this does not sound censorious. I am not suggesting that Wolfe would have been a finer novelist had he remained in Asheville, North Carolina. Indeed, had he stayed he would not be the Wolfe we know and admire. He is a writer for whom the word "genius" is not misused; wonderfully unlike anybody else, he possessed a splendor of language unrivaled by any English-speaking writer this century, even by Faulkner, Joyce or Lawrence. He created scenes of power that stay in the mind forever. I will always remember my first reading in adolescence of the scene (in *Look Homeward, Angel*) of the death of the hero's brother Ben, and how very moved I was. And the motto of the novel "O lost and by the wind grieved, ghost, come back again!" encapsulates lyrically a sentiment of universally poignant truth.

But all the same I cannot think of Wolfe as a Southern writer in the same way that I do Faulkner, Allen Tate or Eudora Welty. And what is more, I do not think he would have thought of himself so either.

Southeast of Nashville is lush farming country, and its center is the town of Murfreesboro, site of a bloody Civil War battle and the old capital of Tennessee. The pastures and the low wooded hills reminded me of the English counties of Herefordshire and Shropshire, and I imagined the atavistic emotions they must have aroused in certain of the earlier settlers. One Sunday I passed through a little village and saw the people coming out of a chapel; the congregation was almost entirely black. But for the most part the inhabitants of southeast Tennessee seem to be white. By chance, traveling through this countryside I came upon a large market; it seemed in the middle of nowhere. Table after table was laden with what elsewhere might have been termed Victoriana—souvenir jugs, plates with mottoes and crests of arms, paperweights, statuettes of children and pets, birdcages, ashtrays of fancy design. And around these walked not antique sellers and young intelligentsia, but tanned countrymen with wide-brimmed hats on their heads and often a can of beer or Dr. Pepper in their hands.

And then the Appalachians begin again. It was hot, very hot, when I traveled from Murfreesboro to Monteagle. The mountains shimmered in the heat. Soon I could feast my eyes once more on bank upon high bank of woods, utterly still and silent under the intense afternoon sun. The road now corkscrewed upward; green precipices plunged below. The road made further twists in its ascent. And we came to Monteagle, home of the novelist, critic and former Fugitive Andrew Lytle (born 1902).

His house is so romantic that I must describe it. It stands in an elevated enclosed wooded area, a little apart from the rest of Monteagle, and was built about a hundred years ago. It is in log cabin style and a veranda runs along no less than three of its sides. On the veranda are a plethora of hammocks and swings of different sizes and elevations from the floor. For the greater part of my visit Andrew Lytle and I sat out on the veranda gazing over a tangled and aromatic garden, from time to time drinking iced tea, which was constantly welcome on those steamy days. Inside, the house amply fulfills its exterior promise. Imagine a Red Cross flag: the cross is an open hall, each end leading outside. The white parts of the flag, so to speak, are taken up with square-shaped rooms. The cross-shaped hall, the walls of which are also of log, is imaginatively furnished. Old pictures hang on the walls, some of them portraits of local Indians about whom Andrew Lytle is knowledgeable, and in bookcases are many rare editions of American and English novels and verse. I can think of no house I myself would like to live in more.

In this very house Andrew Lytle wrote, in 1930, his first significant piece of prose—the essay "The Hind Tit" in *I'll Take My Stand*. (This is for me the most durable of the Agrarian essays from a purely literary point of view.) It is a portrait of the joys, merits and rewards of old-style rural life in Tennessee, and an articulate and morally incisive one, too. Here he speaks of Southern folk dances:

> At the square dances, unlike round dancing, the stage is set for each individual to show the particularity of his art. Each couple is "out" in turn, swinging every other couple separately, ending up at "home" when the whole line swings "partners," then "corners." In this way a very fine balance is reached between group and individual action. Everybody is a part of the dance all the time, but a very particular part some of the time. There are no wallflowers, no duty dances, no agonizing over popularity, and the scores of such things which detract from free enjoyment at the round dances.... And the prompter ... is an artist and wit whose disappearance will leave the world much the poorer. Such calls as:
>
> > "Swing the gal you love best:
> > Now cheat and swing . . .
> > Women swing hard, men swing harder
> > Swing that gal with the buckskin garter."
>
> are metaphors and imperatives with full connotation for the dancers, and in an agrarian society will be as applicable a hundred years hence. But so will the fiddlers' tunes, "Leather Breeches," "Rats in the Meat Barrel," "Frog Mouth," "Guinea in the Pea Patch," "Arkansas Traveler," "Cotton-eyed Joe," "No Supper Tonight," "Hell among the Yearlings," "Got a Chaw of Tobaccy from a Nigger," "All my Candy's Gone," and "Katy, Bar the Door." With a list of such dances as a skeleton, if all other records were lost, some future scholar could reconstruct with a common historical accuracy the culture of this people.

The essay is not a mere chronicle of the beauties of the past, but a clarion call to action, action of what I would term dynamic conservatism:

> ... to maintain a farming life in an industrial imperialism, there

seems to be only one thing left for the farmer to do, and particularly for the small farmer. Until he and the agrarian West and all the conservative communities throughout the United States can unite on some common political action, he must deny himself the articles the industrialists offer for sale. It is not so impossible as it may seem at first. . . . Do what we did after the War and the Reconstruction: return to our looms, our handcrafts, our reproducing stock. Throw out the radio and take the fiddle from the wall. Forsake the movies for the play parties and the square dances. And turn away from the liberal capons who fill the pulpits as preachers. Seek a priesthood that may manifest the will and intelligence to renounce science and search out the Word in the authorities.[29]

Contemporary man, Andrew Lytle declares, has "been turned into the runt pig in the sow's litter. Squeezed and tricked out of the best places at the side, he is forced to take the little hind tit for nourishment . . ."

Like the younger Madison Jones, whom indeed he knows, and whose career bears distinct resemblances to his own, Andrew Lytle farmed for a time, at Cornsilk in northern Alabama. Like Madison Jones, too, he is dubious about both the wisdom and the ethics of a deliberate retreat into the rural past, and his powerful little novella, *A Name for Evil* (1947), a sort of Southern *Turn of the Screw* and to my mind more frightening than that rather overrated work, suggests that he no longer adheres to the remedy for the diseases of industrialism that he advocates in the stirring passage I have quoted above.

Like his fellow-Fugitive Donald Davidson, Andrew Lytle is preoccupied with the unique cultural and historical features of the South. This is shown in the nature of his *oeuvre*. His first prose work, *Bedford Forrest and His Critter Company* (1931), was a biography of the colorful Confederate cavalry leader Nathan Bedford Forrest, who has enjoyed posthumous notoriety as the founder of the dreadful Ku Klux Klan. His first novel *The Long Night* (1936) is set in its latter section during the Civil War itself; it empathizes moreover with a distinctly Southern notion of vendetta—the altruistic avenging of wrong done to a loved member of one's family. Andrew Lytle was most interesting about the genesis of this novel, which is as exciting as any thriller. A friend had told him a story of his family in which a relation who lived at the time of the Civil War killed thirty men as an act of revenge. Andrew Lytle and he decided to write this up together in novel form, but in the end it was Andrew Lytle who carried the task out.

Andrew Lytle sees the South, however, not only for itself but as a culture capable of giving the insider and the outsider a peculiar illumination of the human condition:

> Now the South was a mixed society, and it was a defeated society; and the defeated are self-conscious. They hold to the traditional ways, since these ways not only tell them what they are but tell them with a fresh sense of themselves. Only defeat can do this. It is this very self-consciousness which makes for the sharpened contemplation of self. It is comparable to euphoria. The sudden illumination made life fuller and keener, as it made life tragic. But it stopped action. The very heightening of self-awareness made for a sudden withdrawal of the life force. What was left of it remained in the surface forms. The forms were shattered, but because of this force they held their shape briefly. The shed skin for a while shines with life, but the force of life is already on its night sea journey.[30]

These words come from an essay on his own novel *The Velvet Horn* (1957), which he spoke of repeatedly as his finest achievement. It is a complex novel, not least in its intricate narrative presentation. Set in rural Tennessee in the mid-nineteenth century, it is partly an account of a boy's initiation into manhood, and partly a study of an incestuous relationship and its consequences. Both aspects are seen symbolically as metaphors for man's nature and destiny; incest— too common in the old rural South—is the perpetual search of a man, for instance, for his feminine half. Andrew Lytle is deeply versed in mythological and religious matters, and each section of the novel refers to mythological and religious archetypes. This does not make for easy reading or comprehension, and there are times when I feel that this strange and poetic work is in danger of drowning in the waters of esoteric thought. Particularly as Andrew Lytle, an Episcopalian, often seems to demand acceptance of Christian myth as fact.

Lytle is a man of deep and wide knowledge of literature and the history of ideas. After he forsook both farming and an attempt to write for the New York stage he became a university teacher; for two long periods he taught at the University of the South at Sewanee, which is not very far from Monteagle. For some years he edited that distinguished journal of Southern literature, *The Sewanee Review*. He spoke to me about many writers, both American and otherwise, during our talk on the veranda; he counted Flaubert as the greatest influence on him, but he also talked with feeling about Scott, Emily Bronte, Tolstoy and Henry James.

Yet for all this, I feel that Andrew Lytle's writings are most meaningful to the reader who has immersed him or herself in Southern culture. They do not, for all their imagination and ingenuity, completely transcend their country of origin. I do not think that even *The Velvet Horn* has the universality of reference that we find in the work of the other Fugitives: in the fiction of Allen Tate and Robert Penn Warren for example. That is not to regret its existence in the form that we do have it. At the time of my visit reprints of this novel and of the earlier *The Long Night* were under consideration. They are indeed overdue.

Andrew Lytle is a widower and his daughters are grown up. As a university teacher he obviously won the devotion of his students; one of them was staying, helping him in the house and its grounds, at the time of my visit. He made us a refreshing lunch of a fine salad augmented with herbs culled from the garden. Then he drove me to Monteagle's humble bus station. The bus was late; it came down the burning road like some motor-propelled seal, moving through the quivering heat with a certain difficulty.

The bus took me to Chattanooga and then into Georgia. Chattanooga, not attractive architecturally, has perhaps the most magnificent setting of any town I know. The shining Tennessee river is wide here, flowing through artificial lakes; the mountains (the highest is Lookout Mountain) ring the town but create no claustrophobic effect. Indeed they suggest promise and release. But when I think of Chattanooga I think of approaching it from the other side. I was coming from Rome, Georgia, where I had been to stay with a friend's family. It was the night of the Fourth of July. Descending into Chattanooga we saw below us the lights of the town, but shooting up from them brighter, more exotic lights that rose into the dark sky and eclipsed, so it seemed, the tops of the encircling mountains. These were, of course, the celebratory fireworks.

But now, as the bus pulled into the streets of Chattanooga, I thought back to the conversation with Andrew Lytle. He has known Allen Tate for almost all their mature lifetimes; he knew and encouraged Madison Jones. Peter Taylor had told me that Peter had known him when he himself had been a young man in Nashville; indeed, their fathers had been friends. And this made me travel back in my mind to Charlottesville and my meeting with Peter Taylor himself.

4: THE WRITERS

Peter Taylor

ON THE DAY I went to see Peter Taylor in his office at the University of Virginia, the pleasant, warm spring weather had been temporarily broken by a rainstorm. I hastened along the colonnaded walks while chilly rain harried Ash Lawn. After two or three hours' conversation the rain had intensified; it was that day in Auburn, Alabama, all over again.

Peter Taylor was born in 1917 in Nashville, and he speaks of the city with the greatest affection. Having learned that I was shortly to go there for the first time he recommended with lyrical enthusiasm places I should visit. He returns there quite often and spends part of his summers up in the Tennessee hills. Almost all his major stories are set in Tennessee, most often in Nashville itself or a fictional town he calls Thornton. It is Tennessee's social atmosphere, and its various interrelating "worlds" that preoccupy him. Though he is capable of evoking a place, a view or a house very vividly and economically, he rarely indulges in scene painting as such. His stories often make use of the device that the readers know the places concerned as well as the narrator—or very nearly as well.

The story "Miss Leonora When Last Seen" begins, "Here in Thomasville we are all concerned over the whereabouts of Miss Leonora Logan. She has been missing for two weeks, and though a half dozen postcards have been received from her, stating that she is in good health and that no anxiety should be felt for her safety, still the whole town can talk about nothing else." These words assume that we know all about Thomasville, where and what kind of place it is; the narrator even begs us to keep an eye out for the missing old lady. We are thus brought into the world of the story without further ado. Any detailed description of scene would shatter this illusion.

Often, though, Peter Taylor points out various features of Tennessee life that the outsider would not be likely to know, speaking through one of his characters:

There is an exchange between the two cities of Nashville and Memphis which has been going on forever—for two centuries almost. (That's forever in Tennessee.) It's like this: A young man of good family out at Memphis, for whom something has gone wrong, will often take up residence in Nashville. And of course it works the other way around. A young man in Nashville under similarly unhappy circumstances may pack up and move out to Memphis. This continuing exchange can explain a lot about the identical family names you find among prominent people in the two places, and about the mixup and reversal of names. Henderson Smith in one place, for instance, becomes Smith Henderson in the other. Or a habitual middle name in Nashville, say, may appear as a first or last name in Memphis.[31]

This is the kind of information only a well-informed but analytical and somewhat detached insider could provide, and such is the most frequent narrative stance in Peter Taylor's stories.

His knowledge of Tennessee life must be considerable. His family is long established there and long enjoyed not only association but friendship with his dignitaries and intellectuals. His grandfather, for example, was a close friend of Andrew Lytle's father. Peter Taylor has known Andrew Lytle and Allen Tate since his early years. His was a prosperous family, and it is the Tennessee upper class and *haute bourgeoisie* that he has most consistently portrayed in his fiction—the families of judges, lawyers, important businessmen, country property owners, members of university and college faculties, and the inhabitants of those gracious porched houses that exist in every Tennessee small town or in smart suburbs such as Belle Meade in Nashville.

In one respect his family was not typical of the Southern class to which it belonged. His father was a freethinker who offended certain relatives by his outspoken disrespectful remarks where religion was concerned. On his deathbed, however, he was converted to Catholicism. The difference between the religious attitudes of his own family and those of his friends and acquaintances put Peter Taylor at a remove from them, however close his identification in other ways, and this may have given him the detachment necessary both for becoming a writer of fiction and for becoming the particular kind of writer he is.

I have already mentioned Andrew Lytle and Allen Tate as early influences; Peter Taylor was also taught by John Crowe Ransom himself, not at Vanderbilt but at Kenyon College. He was a close friend of the poets Robert Lowell (who appears in a disguised form in one of his most delightful stories, "1939") and Randall Jarrell. Despite his intimacy with these writers, however, all of whom are quite concerned with metaphysical matters, Peter Taylor has stuck with exemplary sureness to his own literary identity. He concentrates on presenting and assessing the lives of specific but representative individuals in specific but representative societies. His search for the right medium in which to communicate his observations, however, was marked by more temptations. He started out, like Andrew Lytle before him, wanting to be a dramatist. (His *Tennessee Day in St. Louis* is a distinguished work.) He also had aspirations toward poetry, in particular narrative poetry. In this respect he feels the somewhat rigid teaching approach of John Crowe Ransom and his affection and admiration for Robert Lowell may have inhibited him. The short story attracted him, too, and he began to write in this medium with success. But like almost every short story writer, he was haunted by the feeling that sooner or later he should write a long novel.

For some writers the short story is the perfect form to express their imaginative vision of life. And why not? It was for Chekhov and de Maupassant. It is a form which has had a particular attraction for the Southern mind, as Allen Tate and others pointed out to me. Katherine Anne Porter and Flannery O'Connor wrote their best work using the short story form; Eudora Welty's finest stories are certainly the equal of her longer fiction; and the short stories of William Faulkner, Robert Penn Warren, Allen Tate, Carson McCullers, Truman Capote, Reynolds Price and Ernest Gaines cannot be counted as the least of their distinguished productions.

Peter Taylor did, in fact, speak to me of his love for and satisfaction with the short story form. It admits none of what Flaubert spoke of as *remplissage*, the filling up of space with description, rambling conversations and plot devices. Indeed the short story, particularly the type that Peter Taylor writes, does not need much plot. I suspect organized plot is not something that interests him

116

very much, and one can think of many novelists who would probably be much happier not bothering with plot so that they could reserve their energies for the creation of character, mood and social atmosphere. Peter Taylor remains attracted to the narrative poem, and in his last (and in my opinion best) book *In the Miro District and Other Stories* (1977) he has included four in blank verse form. He told me that he is composing stories in this medium more and more often.

Peter Taylor seemed to me in a nonpejorative sense a gossip. Often the mention of a person or a place led him to discourse on interesting details that were not strictly germane to what we had begun talking about, but these sidelines were evidently a delight for him to pursue and deliver and consequently they were a delight to me as the listener. Gossip has a creative and essential part to play in the life of a community; it is one of the best ways of learning not only about our fellow beings but about the values of the world in which they move. But perhaps a society must possess a certain cohesion before its gossip is a valuable reservoir for its writers. Eminent English writers including Anthony Powell, Angus Wilson, Barbara Pym and Kingsley Amis are still able to draw upon it, and so is the Southern writer. He or she can still, it would seem, assume a common bank of knowledge in readers so that anecdotes, selected from those discussed at parties and over dinner tables, have a general as well as an individual interest. No doubt, as Peter Taylor said in our conversation, the older South was the more cohesive society. In his boyhood he had access to many circles which had very clear relationships to one another and to his own, from the family of the state governor to that of the black "mammy" who played so crucial a role in the emotional life of many white children. On this last subject Peter Taylor has written a touching and much-anthologized story, "What Do You Hear from Em?," in which the central figure has both dignity and pathos and yet is never treated sentimentally because she is too much part of the world of the tale to acquire a falsifying or isolating light.

Peter Taylor's method of presenting his subject is very much akin to the gossip's yet its seeming artlessness conceals a careful and sophisticated art. A small incident may be mentioned which involves several people, all of whom may prompt the narrator to compose an anecdote. The reader is thus given an idea of what kind of people they are and the relationships they bear toward one another. Peter Taylor then can concentrate on one or two of them. "There is something about them that should be told," he says; "Perhaps after what I've already said about them you may not be surprised. On the other hand, you may be." For in the end individual vagaries and desires are seen as stronger than social attachments, even though the people involved may not acknowledge this and even though—such is the strength of the society itself—no renunciation of such attachments is ever contemplated.

Peter Taylor's voice in the story is a relaxed and worldly one, and this means that in one sense his work is at a much lower emotional key than we have come to expect from Southern writing. It does not rasp the nerves or bring tears to one's eyes. And yet the world he shows, even in his most urbane and humorous stories, is a world in which the passions are constantly evident; there is love, hatred, envy, remorse, guilt and sexual desire. In dealing with the latter subject, an important one in Peter Taylor's work, his prose can take on a throbbing intensity of diction. But it is essential to Peter Taylor's purpose, which is the illustration of the unpredictability and uniqueness of human beings, even in stratified and code-dominated societies, that we should see the actions of men and women from a detached point of view. If we become too involved, too much a part of the quarrels, tempests and declarations of love, we might lose sight of the prolix nature of human individuality.

I do not want to imply that Peter Taylor's stories do not make an impact on the feelings. One of his finest achievements is the story "The Fancy Woman." At its center is Josie, the fancy woman of the title, who is vulgar and sex-hungry. She is not above malicious exploitation of the men off whom she lives, and she may be guilty of a sordid sexual gesture toward a minor. All the same, we feel the pathos of her situation acutely when she is contemptuously treated by her lover and the Memphis society with which he associates. We see the craving for affection that lies underneath her soft, coarse, wheedling exterior. But this does not mean that we condemn those who exploit her; George, her lover, is certainly far from admirable, with his taste for cockfights and his moral dishonesty, but when he is with his sons we see another side of him. In other words, the story is a fictional realization of the proverb *"Tout comprendre, c'est tout pardonner"* (To understand all is to forgive all). In "Venus, Cupid, Folly and Time," for instance, an eccentric elderly brother and sister give annual decadent parties for the young of the town in order to gratify strange fantasies of their own. They may deserve the high-spirited and ingenious deception played upon them by the young jokers, but they also command our sympathy for their innocence and sweetness.

Peter Taylor has written five volumes of stories, the finest of which are gathered together in *The Collected Stories of Peter Taylor* (1969). They provide many similar experiences which expand our tolerance. All the same, I think Peter Taylor's last volume, *In the Miro District and Other Stories*, is his best. On the whole the mood is darker than in the earlier work, though humor, irony and the gossipy tone are still present. A story like "Daphne's Lover" is wholly characteristic of its author and could not have been written by anyone else. The narrator's relationship with his friend Frank, who is both wilder and more suave, particularly with the opposite sex, is very shrewdly rendered. The story makes the point that part of everyone's sexual development is a vicarious appreciation of someone else's love life. But the two most remarkable pieces in the book are the narrative poem "The Hand of Emmegene" and the long short story that gives the title to the book.

Peter Taylor told me that the horrifying incident that is the heart of the poem derived from an actual occurrence. Near Chattanooga the severed hand of a girl was once found. In Peter Taylor's verse story Emmegene leaves an unsophisticated and rough yet puritanical rural community to stay with her middle-class Nashville relatives. She is attractive to and attracted by young men, yet her own moral code does not permit giving herself fully to any of them:

> *"You know I wouldn't let him do that, Cousin Nan," she said.*
> *"Not really. Not the real thing, Cousin Nan."*
> *"What do you mean?" Nancy asked in genuine bewilderment.*
> *The girl looked down at her hands, which were folded in her lap.*
> *"I mean, it's my hands he likes," she said.*
> *And she quickly put both her hands behind her, out of sight.*
> *"It's what they all like if they can't have it any other way."*

The meaning of these words is lost on Nancy and her husband; it is clear to the reader, however, that Emmegene has been masturbating her boyfriends. This behavior finally so repulses her that she kills herself, cutting off the offending hand first.

> *My first thought was, "Why, that's a human hand."*
> *I suppose it was ten seconds or so before I was enough myself*
> *To own it was Emmegene's hand*
> *She had cut it off with the wood ax.*
> *I did just what you would expect.*
> *I ran out into the driveway, seeing the blood every step,*
> *And then back inside, past the houseman, still retching over the*
>   *bannister,*
> *And telephoned the police on the kitchen telephone.*
> *They were there in no time.*[32]

Somehow the conventionality of the narrator's reaction, saying and doing "just what you would expect," only serves to emphasize the dark, dramatic puritanism that had so ruled the dead girl's mind.

Better still in my opinion is "In the Miro District," in which sexual behavior is again a dominant motif. The imaginative contrast that provides the shape and theme of the story is that between the youthful narrator and his maternal grandfather. The latter, to paraphrase St. Paul, is a Confederate of the Confederates:

> Seeing [him] like that at the wheel of his tan touring car, swinging into our driveway, it wasn't hard to imagine how he had looked riding horseback or muleback through the wilds of West Tennessee when he was a young boy in Forrest's cavalry, or how he had looked, for that matter, in 1912, nearly half a century after he had ridden with General Forrest, at the time when he escaped from a band of hooded nightriders who had kidnapped him then—him and his law partner (and who had murdered his law partner before his eyes, on the banks of Bayou du Chien, near Reelfoot Lake).[33]

Grandfather Manley is always reminiscing about his past, and his grandson comes to resent his ceaseless anecdotes, not just because he is bored by them (though he *is*) but because he dislikes the spirit behind them, their insistent and crippling machismo. ("Likely I'm the onliest man or boy who ever called Bedford Forrest a son-of-a-bitch and lived.")

The old man makes three unheralded eruptions into the narrator's adolescent pleasures. First he finds him drinking and acting wild with some friends; then he finds him and his pals entertaining girls of dubious repute in his parents' absence. Both of these his grandfather finds acceptable. His grandson is, after all, simply being the "hell-of-a-fellow" that W.J. Cash, in his *Mind of the South*, says every young Southern male was expected to be. The third intrusion, however, displeases his grandfather greatly. He discovers the youth when he has just made love to a girl of his own class.

> His life, whether or not it was in any way his fault, had kept him from knowing what love of our sort was. He might know everything else in the world, including every other noble feeling which I could never be able to experience. He might be morally correct about everything else in the world, but he was not morally correct about love between a man and a woman... he turned on me a look cold and fierce and so articulate that I imagined I could hear the words his look expressed: "So this is how bad you really are?" Then he went directly over to the bed, took up his bag and his cane, left the room, and left the house without speaking to me again.
>
> When I had heard the front door close I took the leather ottoman across the room and sat on it, holding hands with that brave and quiet girl who, with the door wide open now, remained crouching inside the wardrobe. When finally we heard him drive out of the driveway we smiled at each other and kissed. And I thought to myself again that his generation and ours were a thousand years apart, or ten thousand.[34]

When I met Professor Thomas Daniel Young at Vanderbilt he asked if I had read "In the Miro District." I had. He said that in his opinion it was one of the finest and most important pieces of fiction to have come out of the South this decade. Certainly it is a splendid crystallization not just of a conflict in sexual ethics but of a deeper cultural conflict in which the liberal and forward-looking element in Southern society (which had, in fact, retained the antebellum Southern belief in sexual passion and chivalry) is struggling against a certain hardness and narrowness in the ways of the Old South.

The girl in this story lives, like many other of Peter Taylor's characters, in Belle Meade, Nashville. As I walked around its prosperous residential streets of splendid houses and gardens I could imagine the kind of life in which social codes and individual passions prompted men to fight duels, make truces and prepare for duels again.

Allen Tate

ALLEN TATE LIVES in the rather pleasant Nashville suburb of West Meade, beyond the grander Belle Meade. Speaking of the original society of the latter he used the term *"arriviste"*; recent wealth rapidly amassed in the late Reconstruction years and after was used to create an upper-class lifestyle of self-conscious and often bogus luxury which helped to undermine the traditional social order of the South. There is certainly nothing *"arriviste"* about Allen Tate. From his early twenties onward he has brought to literature a remarkably sophisticated and civilized mind, and throughout his long life he has striven for what can perhaps best be described as an all-pervading intellectual purity. He has constantly—and frequently with scathing wit—attacked cultural vulgarities, shoddy values and ungenerous attitudes. This does imply a satirical turn of mind.

Allen Tate has not been a prolific writer. Born in 1899, he has produced only one novel, *The Fathers* (1938), and but two short stories. Poetry has been his principal task, but even here he has written comparatively sparingly as the recent *Collected Poems 1919–1976* (1977) shows. He has aimed for perfection and has, I think, been rewarded for his devotion. For *The Fathers* is one of this century's few supreme masterpieces in any language, and his poetry has a classically articulated complexity of thought and feeling that renders it certain to survive. I must say here that I think a short account of his work such as this chapter must perforce contain cannot but be inadequate; I hope that after it the reader will turn again to Tate's own prose and poetry.

Allen Tate and his family—he has two young sons—have returned to Nashville quite recently; he thus is now back in the city where, as a young and brilliant member of the Fugitives, he first embarked on his long career of dedication to literature. In his old age he suffers from severe emphysema. This disease ties him to his bed and means that he becomes easily exhausted. Nevertheless he is a lively, compelling and creative talker, but not a comfortable one. His sharp wit and a certain acerbity of judgment are constantly at play on the subjects under discussion. These qualities are revealed in his refined and intellectual face.

122

When I told Allen Tate of the purpose of my book, and that I had come to see him primarily about *The Fathers* and his two short stories, he said that the Southern literary mind had expressed itself best in fiction. He had never been able to come to any satisfactory explanation of why this should be the case, but thought that the dislocation of society caused by the aftermath of the Civil War was something which lent itself to fictional rather than poetic or dramatic expression. Of his own work, with the exception of *The Fathers*, he valued his poem-sequence "Seasons of the Soul" (1914) and the three autobiographical poems, "The Maimed Man," "The Swimmers" and "The Buried Lake," above all else he had written. Indeed the intense nature of the "Seasons of the Soul" prevented the writing of a projected second novel.

His one novel, however, as his conversation reveals, is very much alive to him. (Some other writers quite sincerely speak of their early work as though it were by someone else.) Recently the Louisiana State University Press brought out a timely new edition of *The Fathers*, and this volume also contains the two short stories. Allen Tate made several revisions to the original text, and as he talked about this operation it was clear that the matter of the book is still very clear in his mind. He spoke of episodes in it that failed to satisfy him even now, that still seemed to demand fuller treatment. And yet what impresses one most about *The Fathers* on several readings (it is a novel for which one reading is quite insufficient) is precisely the sureness of the author's handling of his complicated material. Its tragic and often murky events are transfigured by the book's formal beauty.

In Allen Tate's room hang two silhouettes of members of his family. Their making is described in *The Fathers*, for the novel, as its title indicates, is rooted in family history. This is clear from a preface to the new edition, an earlier poem called "The Dream";

> *The boy-man on the Ox Road walked along*
> *The man he was to be and yet another,*
> *It seemed the grandfather of his mother,*
> *In knee-breeches silver-buckled like a song,*
> *His hair long and a cocked hat on his head,*
> *A straight back and slow dignity for stride.*[35]

This "grandfather of his mother" in the novel is Major Buchan, one of its two main protagonists. The other, George Posey, is Major

Buchan's son-in-law and thus Allen Tate's grandfather, though certain important aspects of his personality came, it seems, from one of his brothers. These two men stand in actual and symbolic contrast to one another, and the differences between them (themselves a complex matter) are central to the author's portrait of a culture in the throes of a profound tension that erupts in violence and destruction. If the people in the book derive from ancestors, if its events follow the course of the Civil War, its personal drama is the author's own invention. It bears resemblances, as critics have pointed out, to Webster's *Duchess of Malfi*, but Tate says that these were originally accidental though they now serve to illuminate the themes.

The Fathers is narrated by an old man, Lacy Buchan, who looks back over the events of a terrible yet determining period of his life which occurred when he was only a youth:

> Is it something to tell, when a score of people whom I knew and loved, people beyond whose lives I could imagine no other life, either out of violence in themselves or the times, or out of some misery or shame, scattered themselves into the new life of the modern age where they cannot even find themselves? Why cannot life change without tangling the lives of innocent persons? Why do innocent persons cease their innocence and become violent and evil in themselves, that such great changes may take place?[36]

Lacy Buchan's narrative tone—quiet, restrained, analytical, perplexed and intelligent—is essential to the book. It is also capable of conveying strong and far from simple emotions: his ardent boyish love for his morally ambiguous brother-in-law George; his adoration of George's sister, Jane; and his hatred of his own brother Semmes when he also falls in love with Jane.

The bare story of the novel is this: George Posey, a young man from a Georgetown family, wins the heart of Susan Buchan, Lacy's sister and daughter of a Virginia land-owning family. Despite the grave and justifiable reservations of Susan's father, Major Buchan, about his integrity, he marries her in 1859. Two years later the Civil War begins. Susan's feelings for George and his family have undergone a dreadful change by this time, and now faced with her husband's continual and ill-explained absences she suspects him of infidelity. This is not in fact the case, for unlike Susan's staunchly pro-Unionist father, George is supporting the Confederates by gunrunning for them.

However, Susan feels so strongly that the connection between the Buchans and the Poseys is a tragic mistake that, knowing her other brother Semmes loves George's sister Jane, she determines to prevent the match. She entices George and Jane's colored half-brother Yellow Jim to enter Jane's bedroom. The results of this deed are appalling. Jane's screams of distress bring about her mother's death, Semmes shoots Yellow Jim, and George, in a moment of love upon seeing his half-brother dead, shoots Semmes. In consequence Jane enters a nunnery and Susan goes mad. And Major Buchan, faced with Confederate soldiers about to burn down his cherished family home (ironically named Pleasant Hill), hangs himself.

As with all major works of literature, in the last analysis the novel's events and actions are beyond analysis, just as human beings themselves are. Nevertheless, out of this somber, Jacobean tangle meaningful and illuminating patterns do emerge.

The nobility (in the sense of both its meanings) of Major Buchan's character, exemplified in his hatred for the disruption caused by the South's secession, in his movingly portrayed love for his old black servant Coriolanus, and in his courageous suicide, has blinded some readers and critics to the weaknesses not so much of his private personality as of his public one (though not Thomas Daniel Young in his perceptive introduction to the new edition). There is dignity, yes, in the many rituals and courtesies of his Virginian aristocratic life, but these are also symptoms of a culture approaching a state of fossilization. By making him not only an aristocrat but an anti-secessionist, Allen Tate shows him as crippled by conservatism. Not only change but any strong action which might result in change is repugnant to him. His daughter Susan hates her husband's family because of their mysteries, things which she abhors.

Placed in contrast to the Buchans is Susan's husband George Posey. "In my boyish delight," says Lacy, "I would have any day followed him over a precipice, just for his bidding. I know distinctly that I thought of him always boldly riding somewhere, and because I couldn't see where, I suppose I thought of a precipice."

George himself doesn't always seem to know where he is riding. He is a man of self-acknowledged contradictions. He is capable of rash, almost daredevil deeds, yet he cannot face up to the rites of death at his own mother-in-law's funeral. He displays generosity, indeed largesse—toward young Lacy, toward Semmes at the beginning and to a beggar woman, but he will sell his colored half-brother to raise money for his own selfish purposes. He blushes at seeing cattle copulate, unlike his Buchan friends who take such matters in their stride, but at the same time he uninhibitedly disregards the shibboleths which govern so much of this circle's conduct. He is a Catholic yet can engage in the ethically dubious practice of gun-smuggling.

The first version of the novel ended with Lacy's words:

He (Brother George) cantered away into the dark. I waited until I heard the change of the hoofbeats on the big road. I kicked the old nag in the sides and headed back into the lane that ran by the south field. I'll go back and finish it. I'll have to finish it because he could not finish it. It won't make any difference if I am killed. If I am killed it will be because I love him more than I love any man.[37]

Allen Tate told me that he had received many letters over the years on the subject of this ending. "I wrote it," he says in a note to the new edition, "very fast, without calculation, because I was convinced it was right. Critics have wondered how Lacy could love a man who had killed his brother, run his sister crazy, and hated the life of Pleasant Hill." So now the novel ends:

As I stood by his grave in Holyrood cemetery fifty years later I remembered how he restored his wife and small daughter and what he did for me. What he became in himself I shall never forget. Because of this I venerate his memory more than the memory of any other man.[38]

Allen Tate told me that he himself still prefers the first ending, and so do I. For George Posey engenders, indeed compels love more than veneration and this fact is surely of supreme importance. Love, that lord of terrible aspect, is at once creative and destructive; it will not tolerate stasis. *The Fathers* speaks of civilization as an arrangement, an acknowledged relationship with the abyss. ("The Abyss" is the title of its third and last section.) To ignore the abyss, which love will not allow one to do, is profoundly dangerous. It is the fault of the overritualized antebellum Southern aristocracy and of the materialistic North alike. But it is certainly not the fault of the postbellum Southern culture as represented by *The Fathers*.

The Fathers takes Southern experience and uses it, among other things, as a metaphor of man's dual relationship to his own civilization and to the forces of history which have determined it. When I think of a parallel among this century's literature for *The Fathers*, it is to Pasternak's *Dr. Zhivago* that I turn. Both are the finely wrought single novels of major poets, both sensitively depict individual predicaments in a time of turmoil, and both see these predicaments in a universal and eternal context. They both also use scenes which, while furthering the dramatic action, are pregnant with symbolic images and meanings. In *The Fathers* there are, outstandingly, the riding tournament and the terrible shootings near the river witnessed by the young Lacy:

> But I was looking at Semmes. Suddenly he looked startled, fell upon his left knee and swaying slightly pitched like a sack of corn over the ledge into the river. Then I heard it, and saw, delayed, the streak of fire from George's pistol. He was saying: "I never had any idea of killing that nigger."
>
> He bent over Jim and felt him, rose and lifted the body with one arm; he dragged it to the edge of the rock and let it fall into the water. He turned around slowly and looked at me. As he came toward me I backed off, step for step. But he stopped. He moved his foot quickly and kicked into the river the pistol that had fallen from my hand. He took no further notice of me. He walked deliberately up the bank through the bushes and disappeared.
>
> I went over and looked at the black water and then I was running and my shins burned from the scratches as I passed the rock house. I was running lightly. . . . "I'm back," I said, and gazed stupidly toward the east and the rising sun. I looked down the river, and kept looking. Then I knew what it was. The Confederate flag over Arlington was gone.[39]

Of Allen Tate's two short stories, "The Migration," an attempt to re-create the pioneer side of Southern experience, has already been quoted extensively in the chapter on the Appalachians and Tennessee. "The Immortal Woman" is a symbolic tale; the old woman who comes every day to look at a house of erstwhile grandeur and present shabbiness is an overt representative device for the South. The doctor she meets in the park is the gentle Lacy

Buchan of *The Fathers* many years later in his life. In the end the old lady is led off by a young man: "He looked like a tower of new brick.... His clothes seemed carefully impersonal and subdued. He must have stepped out of a fashionable hotel. . . . He was leaning over the old lady, kissing her, his arms at his side." He is a symbol of the New South, a fairly benevolent one based on another of Allen Tate's brothers.

Allen Tate's conversation ranged over many topics. He spoke of his admiration for the English poets Louis Macneice and Stephen Spender, about the French writers Julien Green and Paul Valery, and of his feeling for Robert Frost. He talked of academics and publishers in both America and Europe. A Southerner in origin, experience and conviction, he nevertheless cannot be accused of parochialism. Among contemporary Southern writers he was enthusiastic about the late Flannery O'Connor and about Eudora Welty, Madison Jones and Reynolds Price.

He feels that the South did not possess the right religion to sustain its culture. (This idea, though made from a different standpoint, received first expression in his essay in *I'll Take My Stand*.) Catholicism would not only have made the desired appeal to the passions of a passionate people, it would have given them a universal and intellectual frame of reference lacking in the Southerners' particular brand of Protestantism. Had Catholicism been the dominant faith, the racial question would never have arisen in the bitter form it did. Catholicism cannot tolerate notions of the elect and the subsequent sense of apartness as extreme Protestantism can (e.g., the Dutch Reformed Church in South Africa). He drew attention to the fact that the Catholic church had always protected slaves and guaranteed them certain rights. He pointed to the record of the treatment of colored people in Catholic Brazil and Peru.

Of his own Catholicism, which he describes as devout, to say that he once underwent a conversion is less than the truth. Certainly there were years when he was not a Catholic, but in fact his mother's family belonged to this faith and he had been educated at a Catholic prep school, Georgetown. He also said that though he believed in conserving the valuable and the meaningful from older cultures, he was not the political reactionary he had sometimes been called. In fact, a moderate socialism was to his taste, and had he been in England he would most likely have voted for the Labour Party.

He thought the strength of the South—in the separateness of

which he still believed—lay in its access to a common mythology denied to the rest of America. "Any defeated society has this; the defeated remember." There was a parallel between the South and Troy, one that had long preoccupied him (I thought of his poem "Aeneas at Washington," one of his finest). He had not thought of this parallel himself—he thought Robert Penn Warren and the West Virginian John Peale Bishop had. But he believed in it. Of course, from the defeated Troy came Aeneas (bearing his aged father on his shoulders), who went on to found the great Rome. Another parallel could be found with the oppressed Irish. Both Irish and Southern writers have found particular expression in the short story.

He was especially fond of his own poem "The Swimmers," based on an experience in his Kentucky boyhood:

> *Kentucky water, clear springs: a boy fleeing*
> *To water under the dry Kentucky sun . . .*

Though regretfully his poetry is outside the scope of this book, I cannot forebear mentioning this narrative and autobiographical poem of 1953. Young Allen Tate and his friends journey deep into woods to find a clear spring on a hot day. They find something else, too.

> *. . . peering, I heard the hooves come down the hill.*
> *The posse passed, twelve horse; the leader's face*
> *Was worn as limestone on an ancient hill . . .*
>
> *Into a world where sound shaded the sight*
> *Dropped the dull hooves again; the horsemen came*
> *Again, all but the leader: it was night*
>
> *Momently and I feared: eleven same*
> *Jesus-Christers unmembered and unmade,*
> *Whose Corpse had died again in dirty shame.*

The corpse is that of a Negro:

> *The melancholy sheriff slouched beneath*
> *A giant sycamore; shaking his head*
> *He plucked a sassafras twig and picked his teeth:*
> *"We come too late." He spoke to the tired dead*
> *Whose ragged shirt soaked up the viscous flow*
> *Of blood in which It lay discomfited.*[40]

So in the heart of that tranquil Southern scene there lies a murdered black man. And yet the unknown victim has not gone unmourned, and he has been transfigured. The darkness of much of the Southern past can be atoned for by the light of its subsequent art.

Allen Tate's is a mandarin and complex art, not easy of access, and some of the emotional power of its highest point, *The Fathers*, must surely derive from the author's personal connection with the prototypes of his characters. It seems to me likely that Allen Tate, Andrew Lytle and their associates (and perhaps the generation following them) are the last to have stood near enough to people for whom the Civil War and its aftermath were bitter reality to be able to bring genuine personal feeling into their historical novels. For a literature, if it is to be fully relevant to its society, must produce thoughtful and imaginative works of art which refer directly to the world in which the writer and reader both live. Eudora Welty's work amply justifies this description, and it was to see her that I went from Nashville to Jackson, Mississippi.

5: MISSISSIPPI AND EUDORA WELTY

No COUNTRYSIDE HAS ever seemed stranger to me than that of Mississippi as I traveled through it in humid and heavy heat toward its capital Jackson, home of Eudora Welty. Fetid and luxuriant swamps stretched into shimmering distance; when these gave way to farm or woodland the strangeness did not depart. Mountain valleys do not surprise when they turn out to be arcane in atmosphere but one does not expect this quality in flat country. Yet after leaving Memphis I felt I had entered a country that had changed very little this century and had even less intention of doing so in the future. The villages and little towns are rather poor and quite shabby; they impart a feeling of being sunk into the moist woody land. The countryside—unlike the rural areas of neighboring Tennessee—has a large proportion of black inhabitants.

From Nashville to Memphis the journey had been a beautiful one; no one had ever sung the praises—in print or in word—to me of this part of Tennessee. Hilly and carefully farmed, it had a freshness and a secrecy about it that I found wholly captivating, and which were enhanced by its somewhat sleepy and charming towns, so inextricably connected to the surrounding countryside. I relish in memory the moment in my journey when the Tennessee River presented itself to us, broad, fast, strong and handsome, with fine woods on either bank.

Memphis, the largest city in Tennessee, is sometimes spoken of as one of neighboring Mississippi's two real capitals, the other being New Orleans. But despite its splendid setting above the bluffs of the Mississippi River, it is an ugly city, sprawling and barren of charm. As we pulled out of its bus station a fellow-passenger in the seat behind me engaged me in conversation. She was a pretty but somehow rather sad-looking black girl in her mid-twenties. She asked me the all too familiar question "Where are you from?"

"England."

"You made the journey here by bus?"

I was so surprised that for a moment I deliberated as to whether it would be politest to say "Yes." As a matter of fact, because of an antipathy to flying, I had arrived in the United States by an unusual mode of transport for winter—a cargo boat. So I said: "No, by ship." She thought about this for a moment, and then said: "I guess you came to St. Louis." Further elucidation seemed unnecessary.

She asked me if there were any blacks where I lived. I said that in some English cities there were. She hoped that white and black got on with each other, which wasn't the case in her country. It was hard being black, you were always looked down on. And there had been in the past so much suffering imposed on blacks; even in the better present how could they forget it? Her parents—whom she was about to visit—had not only had to contend with poverty most of their lives, but had had to put up with endless insults and slights. Some people would tell you, she went on, that the North was better for black people, some the South. She thought there wasn't all that much to choose between them, because black people had a difficult time wherever they lived. If she had to make a choice she would opt for the South—partly because it was her home country, partly because the blacks were numerically stronger there, and partly because she did really think that Southerners were more friendly and interested in people than Northerners. She also said that she thought Southern white men were friendlier to blacks (of both sexes) than were Southern white women.

I had, of course, no experience to bring to bear on any replies I might make to her remarks. I heard myself deliver a few platitudes of humanist optimism. For how can I, or indeed any non-black, know the miseries and confusion of being despised, rejected, patronized, encouraged and constantly discussed? I am not saying that these have been the experiences of every Southern black; but to know how hard the lot has been of many people to whom one is related either by blood or by culture must surely have a profound effect on one's vision of life. If I thought (as I did) that there was something a little self-pitying about my bus companion, was I not also moved to some very uncomfortable thoughts as I traveled past those steamy woods and pastures, those sluggish rivers and those scruffy but picturesque villages? We—though perhaps it is more honest simply to say "I"—find extreme or dramatic injustices easier to react to than ones more subtle and continuous. Rank discrimination, brutality or aggression—against these one can bring outrage and action (though never as much of either as one would like to think oneself capable of). But nonacceptance of others by a comfortable and exclusive immersion in one's own social group, this too brings pain and it is a crime of which I myself am guilty. When I do seek to remedy the situation it is too often because I like to think of myself as good and kind, not because I have truly confronted the unhappiness of the outcast. Southerners, because of the situation they have inherited, are at least spared the hypocrisy of a person like me. Their words and deeds, both deliberate and unthinking, can have a distinct practical effect upon other people's lives and vision of life. Some feel cause to be heartened by what has been happening in the South in the last decade or so, and of this positive aspect of a tragic inheritance I shall speak more later.

The journey to Jackson seemed interminable. Even inside the bus it was hot. If you got out at one of the stops, it was only to stumble wearily through the clamminess in search of the temporarily ease of a Coke or Sprite.

Eudora Welty met me with her car at the bus station in Jackson. She drove me to the house where she has lived for most of her life, in a quiet tree-lined avenue of an older part of the city. The house inside was cool, comfortable and tasteful, with lovingly accumulated books, photographs and paintings. This was the most refreshing antidote possible to my journey.

I spent the evening with Eudora Welty; I stayed overnight in Jackson and was thus able to spend half of the next day with her as well. I had heard much about her from people, some English and some American, who had met her or heard her speak; all accounts had been touched by a veneration and enthusiasm which I can now fully understand. I felt at the time, and still feel now, that I was in the presence of a truly remarkable person from whom goodness seemed to radiate like some shining force, which lit up people and places and rendered them worthy of more love and interest than one might have ordinarily given. The qualities that impress one so much in life are also in Eudora Welty's work. It holds a special and extremely important place in contemporary Southern literature, for its light has illuminated the way for others.

Mississippi, her native state, was in the grip of the Depression when Eudora Welty returned home from college, and her first full-time job was with the Works Progress Administration (WPA). This meant she was sent all over Mississippi to write up projects, and before long she was taking a camera with her on all her assignments. She was to take several hundred photographs, and she has collected a selection of these into an album, *One Time, One Place* (1971). To look through this book is a moving as well as a fascinating experience. Caught for ever at work and at play, in solitary contemplation and in conversation, her Mississippi people both suggest and defy the transience of life. There is a picture of three white boys watching a hypnotist at the state fair in Jackson; delight, suspicion and incredulity show on their three faces. Where are these boys now? No doubt deep into middle age, yet their boyish re-actions to a long-ago event are eternally preserved for us. Here is a retired black midwife, now dead, proudly contemplating the hands with which she delivered so many babies into the world. Here are two aged Confederate veterans meeting under huge trees in a Jackson park. Here are tomato-packers taking a break while one of their number strums a guitar. Here also are the dithyrambic elations of the black worshipers at Holiness Church when the "unknown tongue" descended on them.

During the course of her journeys around Mississippi Eudora Welty came to realize that she would write stories. Even then she must have made the connection between the impulse that made her take these photographs and her literary urge:

> I learned quickly enough when to click the shutter, but what I was becoming aware of more slowly was a story-writer's truth: the thing to wait on, to reach there in time for, is the moment in which people reveal themselves. You have to be ready, in yourself; you have to know the moment when you see it. The human face and the human body are eloquent in themselves, and stubborn and wayward, and a snapshot is a moment's glimpse (as a story may be a long look, a growing contemplation) into what never stops moving, never ceases to express for itself something of our common feeling. Every feeling waits upon its gesture. Then when it does come, how unpredictable it turns out to be, after all.[41]

These words also apply to the stories Eudora Welty later wrote, particularly to the early ones in which so often she seems to be catching people in the midst of the motion of their lives, and then, in reverent stillness, developing her picture so that more of its subject can be realized and understood.

> It was December—a bright, frozen day in the early morning. Far out in the country there was an old Negro woman with her head tied in a red rag, coming along a path through the pine-woods. Her name was Phoenix Jackson. She was very old and small and she walked slowly in the dark pine shadows, moving a little from side to side in her steps, with the balanced heaviness and lightness of a pendulum in a grandfather clock. She carried a thin, small cane made from an umbrella, and with this she kept tapping the frozen earth in front of her.[42]

Who is this old woman and what is she doing? What sort of journey is she undertaking and for what purpose? What emotions are accompanying her slow trudge? Here, on a Delta road at sunset, is a car slowing down to pick up two hitchhikers. "One of them stood still by the side of the pavement, with his foot stuck out like an old root, but the other was playing a yellow guitar which caught the late sun as it came in a long straight bar across the fields." What kind of man is the driver, what kind of men are the hitchhikers? How will they get along in the car together? What will happen when they reach their destination?

A camera, of course, does not feel; the photographer, the short-story writer, does. "The Key" captures a group of people at a country station waitingroom in the same way as one of the photographs in *One Time, One Place* might. But, says Eudora Welty after describing a young man loitering and smoking there:

> You felt a shock in glancing up at him, and when you looked away from the whole yellow room and closed your eyes, his intensity, as well as that of the room, seemed to have impressed the imagination with a shadow of itself, a blackness together with the light, the negative beside the positive. You felt as though some exact, skillful contact had been made between the surfaces of your hearts to make you aware, in some pattern, of his joy and despair. You could feel the fullness and the emptiness of this stranger's life.[43]

These last sentences are excellent descriptions of the writer's, and consequently of the reader's, approach to the subjects of the stories. Eudora Welty always, so to speak, photographs with the heart.

There are four other connections I would like to make between Eudora Welty the inspired amateur photographer of Depression Mississippi and Eudora Welty the eminent professional writer. In some of her photographs the people confront the camera; they do not pose so much as present themselves. I have already cited perhaps the most striking example of this—the pictures of Ida McToy, the black midwife. But there are others almost as memorable: a proud old woman delegate before the governor's mansion in Jackson; a black yard man with his hat full of roses; a lady bootlegger comically pretending to drive Eudora Welty away with an ice pick; and a black woman in a buttoned sweater, her face a moving testimony to a life of hard endurance. So too in her fiction does Eudora Welty have her people (more often than not women, as in her photographs) turn to the camera and tell their life histories. The photograph parallel should not be overdone, though. These stories would not work if Eudora Welty did not also possess an almost miraculously exact ear for vernacular speech, and they also owe much to the whole Southern tradition of storytelling and gossip. But I cannot help thinking that the genesis as well as the subsequent shapeliness of the stories relate closely to her camera portraits. Here we confront a woman at the local Post Office, which she has made her home:

> But oh, I like it here. It's ideal, as I've been saying. You see, I've got everything cater-cornered, the way I like it. Hear the radio? All the war news. Radio, sewing machine, book ends, ironing boards and that great big piano lamp—peace, that's what I like. Butterbean vines planted all along the front where the strings are.[44]

Her story "Why I live at the P.O." is an explanation of why this particular woman has chosen to make her home in so unorthodox a place.

Story after story can be seen in this way. That comic tour-de-force *The Ponder Heart* makes use of a similar device—Edna Erle looking out at us from her private hotel with her beloved eccentric uncle upstairs somewhere.

136

A number of photographs show occasions, gatherings and meetings, as indeed any private snapshot album might: a pilgrimage to Open Day at a stately home; a political meeting; a state fair; a Sunday School; a church service; and a pageant. Eudora Welty's fictions of more ambitious size she weaves around such events. The last story of *The Golden Apples*, which draws together the diverse strands of the previous stories, is concerned with a funeral as is the all-important second section of *The Optimist's Daughter*. *Delta Wedding*, as its title suggests, revolves around a wedding to which relations from far and near have come; her longest novel, *Losing Battles*, centers on a birthday reunion.

A few photographs are of places without people—a ruined, colonnaded house; two cabins in a ghost river town; some country churches—but in almost all the pictures the setting is of very great importance. Indeed, one could not imagine them without their backgrounds. And so it is with the fiction. Eudora Welty has written the best essay on place in fiction that I have read, (in *The Eye of the Story*):

> Location pertains to feeling; feeling profoundly pertains to place; place in history partakes of feeling as feeling about history partakes of place. Every story would be another story and unrecognizable as art if it took up its characters and plot and happened somewhere else. . . . It is only too easy to conceive that a bomb could destroy all trace of places as we know them, in life and through books, could also destroy all feelings as we know them, so irretrievably and so happily are recognition, memory, history, valor, love, all bound up in place. From the dawn of man's imagination, place has enshrined the spirit; as soon as man stopped wandering and stood still and looked about him, he found a god in that place; and from then on, that was where the god abided and spoke from if ever he spoke.[45]

Eudora Welty's rendering of place is a curious and very individual blend of the objective and the subjective, of the precise and the atmospheric, of the detached and the involved. (After all, the photographer is actually out there, exposed and sensate, taking the pictures.) Her language in some of her descriptive passages often seems a lyrical, elegant stirring; intellectually agile, it seems to point to a state of perception where mere words will not do. She can evoke places very different from her own South: the Ireland of "The Bride of the Innisfallen," for instance, is as vivid as anything in her admired Sean O'Faolain or Elizabeth Bowen. San Francisco is marvelously conveyed in that strange story "Music from Spain" in *The Golden Apples*. But most of her fiction is set in the South, indeed in Mississippi, and it is Southern scenes she describes with the greatest intensity. Many examples spring to mind, but this is Natchez in winter from the beginning of one of her finest stories, "First Love":

> The Mississippi shuddered and lifted from its bed, reaching like a somnambulist driven to go in new places; the ice stretched far out over the waves. Flatboats and rafts continued to float downstream, but with unsignaling passengers submissive and huddled, mere bundles of sticks; bets were laid on shore as to whether they were alive or dead, but it was impossible to prove either way.
>
> The coated moss hung in blue and shining garlands over the trees along the changed streets in the morning. The town of little galleries was all laden roofs and silence. In the fastness of Natchez it began to seem then that the whole world, like itself, must be in transfiguration. The only clamor came from the animals that suffered in their stalls, or from the wildcats that howled in closer rings from the frozen cane. The Indians could be heard from greater distances and in greater numbers than had been guessed, sending up placating but proud messages to the sun in continual ceremonies of dancing. The red percussion of their fires could be seen night and day by those waiting in the dark trance of the frozen town. Men were caught by the cold, they dropped in its snare-like silence. Bands of travelers moved closer together, with intenser caution, through the glassy tunnels of the Trace, for all proportion went away, and they followed one another like insects going at dawn through the heavy grass. Natchez people turned silently to look when a solitary man that no one had ever seen before was found and carried in through the streets, frozen the way he had crouched in a hollow tree, grey and huddled like a squirrel, with a little bundle of goods clasped to him.[46]

Many of Eudora Welty's unusual juxtapositions of words—"the

red percussion of their fires," "all laden galleries and silence"—
have the compression and the imaginative leaps of a poet. She
makes frequent escapes from the literal in pursuit of a deeper
exactitude. She makes use of a pool of human response to a scene
to create its effect for her readers (the townspeople betting on
whether river passengers were alive or dead; the feeling that the
whole world had receded from the town). But while we feel during
the description that we are being held in still contemplation of a
scene, all the time we are moving toward the human being, the
human event that is the dominating feature of the story—in this
case the arrival of the dead man in Natchez. Eudora Welty has herself emphatically said, after all, in "Place in Fiction": "What can
place *not* give? Theme . . . Human life is fiction's only theme."

Sometimes a specific place suggested a specific story to Eudora
Welty. She told me that the colonnaded house as photographed in
One Time, One Place gave rise to the short story "Asphodel," while
out of Rodney's Landing and the Natchez Trace country beyond
came that extraordinary short novel *The Robber Bridegroom.* But
more often than not it is the particular but nonunique—a house, a
village, a cafe, a suburban garden, a fairground, a station waitingroom, a lonely farm, a dancehall ("this shadowless steel-trussed
hall with the roselike posters of Nelson Eddy and the testimonial
for the mind-reading horse in handwriting magnified five hundred
times")—that appeals to her.

Looking through *One Time, One Place* one frequently finds
tributes to a grim life of poverty to which proud resignation is the
only possible attitude. Of course, these photographs were taken
during the worst of the Depression. But then, as Eudora Welty
tartly points out in her introduction to the album, "the Depression
was not in fact a noticeable phenomenon in the poorest state in the
Union." Though things have since improved, Mississippi is still
today one of the poorest states and certainly the poorest of those
described in this book. It has the highest ratio of country to urban
dwellers (56 percent rural) and the highest proportion of blacks to
whites (37 percent). But the blacks who feature so prominently in
Eudora Welty's album have not only suffered economically. No
state has an uglier history of racial conflict than Mississippi. Writing
about the many photographs of hers with poor black subjects,
Eudora Welty had said, "And had I no shame as a white person for
what message might lie in my pictures of black persons? No, I was

too busy imagining myself into their lives to be open to generalities."

This applies to Eudora Welty the writer, too. Like most sensitive Southerners, she was deeply concerned about the racial unhappiness and violence of the Sixties. But as a novelist she refused to write the kind of Civil Rights propaganda—the overt treatment of the Southern problem—that some non-Southern critics thought should come from any and every pen below the Mason–Dixon line. On this subject she has written a trenchant essay, "Must the Novelist Crusade?" Her answer is that in their writing (their private lives are another matter) novelists need not. It is better that they go on with their chosen tasks, which precludes their using the propagandist's approach since as writers they must decline to label one set of actions, one group of people, as always right and another as always wrong. But of course the sensitive artist is a natural democrat. Interested in the life within and respecting all people as its vessel, he or she must eschew all distinctions based on externals. Reading about the black musicians in the short story "Powerhouse" or about Old Phoenix Jackson in "A Worn Path," looking at the queenly face of the retired midwife Ida McToy, is to realize afresh not only how cruel but how stupid, blind and limiting any legal or philosophic system which discriminates against such people must be! But that message was not Eudora Welty's overt object in writing the stories or taking the photographs, which was instead to celebrate in shapely form the lives, looks and natures of certain unique individuals who happened to be black.

Celebration is a significant word for Eudora Welty. In Reynolds Price's interview with her for the *New York Times Review of Books* of May 7, 1978, on the occasion of the publication of her volume of essays *The Eye of the Story*, she replies to his question "Do you have a sense of a single source within yourself from which the stories come?" with these words: "Well, I could answer generally, I think it probably is a lyrical impulse to—I don't know if the word *praise* is right or not . . . I think it's probably that. I imagine again that must be the most common impulse that most of us do share, and I think it's a good one to share . . . I think it presumes that you will be *attentive* to life, not closed to it but open to it."

What other aspects of life is Eudora Welty attentive to? She has an extraordinarily intense rapport with nonhuman living things such as plants, insects, birds and animals. These are never mere background decoration but are seen as separate entities constituting mysteries in themselves which elicit complex responses from us. *Separate* is a term crucial to Eudora Welty's thought, and in this respect a passage from what I consider her most remarkable short story, "A Still Moment," is of importance. In this story (for which no other author could possibly be responsible) three very different men—the naturalist Audubon, the brigand James Murrell and the evangelist Lorenzo Dow converge on a remote part of the Natchez Trace. In the stillness of the forest a solitary snowy heron appears.

> It was as if each detail about the heron happened slowly in time, and only once. He felt again the old stab of wonder—what structure of life bridged the reptile's scale and the heron's feather? That knowledge too had been lost. He watched without moving. The bird was defenseless in the world except for the intensity of its life, and he wondered, how can heat of blood and speed of heart defend it? Then he thought, as always as if it were new and unbelievable, it has nothing in space or time to prevent its flight. And he waited, knowing that some birds will wait for a sense of their presence to travel to men before they will fly away from them.
>
> Fixed in its pure white profile it stood in the precipitous moment, a plumicorn on its head, its breeding dress extending in rays, eating steadily the little water creatures. There was a little space between each man and the others, where they stood overwhelmed. No one could say the three had ever met, or that the moment of intersection had ever come in their lives, or its promise fulfilled. But before them the white heron rested in the grasses with the evening all around it, lighter and more serene than the evening, flight closed in its body, the circuit of its beauty closed, a bird seen and a bird still, its motion calm as if it were offered: Take my flight . . .[47]

Indeed Audubon takes this in a literal and terrible way. He pulls the trigger of his gun "and his eyes went closed. In memory the heron was all its solitude, its total beauty . . . But it was not from memory that he could paint."

The death of the heron makes a somber and frightening impact on the mind of the religious zealot Lorenzo Dow:

> The hair rose on his head and his hands began to shake with cold, and suddenly it seemed to him that God Himself, just

141

now, thought of the Idea of Separateness. For surely He had never thought of it before, when the little white heron was flying down to feed. He could understand God's giving Separateness first and then giving Love to follow and heal in its wonder; but God had reversed this, and given Love first and then Separateness, as though it did not matter to Him which came first. Perhaps it was that God never counted the moments of Time; Lorenzo did that, among his tasks of love. Time did not occur to God. Therefore—did He know of it? How to explain Time and Separateness back to God, Who had never thought of them, Who could let the whole world come to grief in a scattering moment?[48]

The fragility of that one unique heron's existence in time and space differs in no significant way from that of our own existence. This is a terrifying realization, and the ability to communicate metaphysical terror is not the least of Eudora Welty's gifts. We are dreadfully vulnerable in the power of immovable and unknowable forces. Yet beyond this Eudora Welty seems to feel a mystic harmony: all life is part of a whole and bound, from one living creature to another, by deep and subtle bonds. From this fact a certain comfort and joy can be taken.

This attitude to nature suggests the primitive, and indeed Eudora Welty is that paradox of the sophisticated artist who has retained a primitive self. She has in fact written with a rare ease of empathy about primitive peoples, for instance the Natchez Indians in "Some Notes on River Country." Such a mind as hers would seem naturally to tend to the mythic, the mythopoeic. And so it is. Eudora Welty's attitude to myth is an idiosyncratic one and is inextricably connected to her attitude to history, or should I more properly say her attitude to the past.

But not the usual Civil War past. Eudora Welty told me that she hated the Civil War (though she has written one moving and horrifying story about it, "The Burning"). No, her past is to be found further back than that—among the French and Spanish colonists of the Mississippi country and among its early English settlers in the years following the Louisiana Purchase. Real historical persons appear in her pages—the Harpe outlaws, Aaron Burr, Lorenzo Dow, James Murrell and John James Audubon. Yet, her treatment of them is in no way like a historian's or even a historical novelist's. It is far closer to that of a storyteller of folktale and myth.

Eudora Welty and I discussed quite extensively her approach to myth. She reminded me that in its original form the folktale, such as the Brothers Grimm collected, made use of features profoundly familiar to its audience: forest, woodcutter, castle, robber baron, serf, brigand, duke, swineherd, meadow and tollbridge—these were part of the daily landscape of life. Of course, mystery could lurk in the forest, sinister rumors accumulate around the castle, various brigands or daughters of the manor could pass into popular history on account of their vices or virtues. But the properties which have since been crystallized into the tales were at one time the property of a large and mixed audience. Eudora Welty felt that Americans, and most of all Southerners, had access to a similar world, if perhaps at one remove. The Natchez Trace, the forest and the river country, the swamp and the delta, the Indian relic (and indeed Indian descendants), cabins, old houses, landings, plantations are all there to be encountered. And over the years stories have attached themselves to certain real people—to the naturalist Audubon, for example—which have helped them to pass from history into folklore.

Out of all this Eudora Welty has created stories that partake equally of intensely personal visions and universal (though Southern-rooted) myths. I know nothing in literature quite like those two short stories "First Love" and "A Still Moment" or like her short novel *The Robber Bridegroom*. The very opening sentences of this last suggest the folktale:

> It was the close of day when a boat touched Rodney's Landing on the Mississippi River and Clement Musgrove, an innocent planter, with a bag of gold and many presents, disembarked. He had made the voyage from New Orleans in safety and his tobacco had been sold for a fair price to the King's men. In Rodney he had a horse stabled against his return, and he meant to spend the night there at an inn, for the way home through the wilderness was beset with dangers.[49]

The Robber Bridegroom, in part derived from a Grimm folktale, makes use of many traditional folktale devices—a wicked stepmother, a talking bird, a disappearance into the forest and a confusion of identity. Its folktale form provides an apotheosis of the Natchez country and of the wild spirit of its early settlers; its extraordinary sequence of events forms a crystallization of ideas concerning love, sexual fulfillment, the routing of evil in addition to a paradigm of the social history of the area.

What seems to me Eudora Welty's greatest achievement, *The Golden Apples*, is also suffused with the mythic. It is also, of course, drenched with a sense of the real, and the complexity and diversity of human beings and their lives. The apple in most folklores is a love-symbol, and the golden apples, guarded by the Hesperides at the garden at the world's end, are associated with the search for love and the search for the heart's desire. It is this property of the golden apples that was in Yeats' mind as he wrote the poem "The Song of Wandering Aengus," a poem which haunts the girl Cassie Morrison in the book and is indirectly present as a summary and a summons throughout its pages: "I went out to the hazel wood/ Because a fire was in my head," it begins. An apparition of a girl appears to Aengus, one which fades as suddenly as it has come:

> *Though I am old with wandering*
> *Through hollow lands and hilly lands,*
> *I will find out where she has gone,*
> *And kiss her lips and take her hands;*
>
> *And walk among long dappled grass,*
> *And pluck till time and times are done*
> *The silver apples of the moon,*
> *The golden apples of the sun.*[50]

Most of the people of Morgana, Mississippi are shown to be in a permanent state of quest for the fulfillment of emotional yearnings, some acknowledged, some only half guessed at. Into the head of Cassie as she lies awake in her moonlit bed—confronting her own puberty, her unanticipated glimpses of the sadness maturity must bring, and her unguessable future—there "flowed the whole of the poem she had found in that poem. It ran perfectly through her head, vanishing as it went, one line yielding to the next, like a torch race. All of it passed through her head, through her body. She slept, but sat up in bed once and said aloud: *"Because a fire was in my head."* Then she fell back unresisting. She did not see except in dreams that a face looked in; that it was the grave, unappeased and radiant face that was in the poem."

Some find a representative of what they are looking for in the elusive, morally and socially defiant figure of King Maclain, something of a satyr, a vagabond, a Wandering Aengus—and father of more than just the two sons who bear his name. His life is that of the primitive. A society can never contain him; his way is that of the animal in the song quoted about him:

> *In the night time,*
> *At the right time,*
> *So I've understood,*
> *'Tis the habit of Sir Rabbit*
> *To dance in the wood.*

Morgana is on the whole a harmonious community, full of kindly gossip and neighborliness, a place in which the identities of its citizens are secure and defined. Certainly Eugene, King Maclain's son, is unhappy away from his hometown (in San Francisco), in what is perhaps the most extraordinary story in the entire book, "Music from Spain":

> Now, too late when the city opened out so softly in beauty and to such distances, it awoke a longing for that careless, patched land of Mississippi winter, trees in their rusty wrappers, slow-grown trees taking their time, the lost shambles of old cane, the winter swamp where his own twin brother, he supposed, still hunted.[51]

In the deepest and widest sense of the word *The Golden Apples* is a religious book, concerned with nothing less than man's longing for spiritual satisfaction and grace, and it is the stronger for being so firmly and lovingly rooted in Mississippi.

Yet, having singled out for special praise *The Golden Apples,* I feel I must say that the superficially more conventional *The Optimist's Daughter*, with its studied and heartfelt portraits of the bereaved Laurel and her younger stepmother Fay, is fully its equal for subtlety and insight into human behavior.

No account of Eudora Welty would, however, be complete without reference to her humor. Like Mark Twain and William Faulkner she owes much to the Southern tall story ("The Wide Net" is an example of this). Her delight in human variety is revealed in the kindly laughter her innocent and impulsive people arouse. And perhaps the most delightful expression of her humor is in *The Ponder Heart*, which, in its story of a simpleminded and over-generous man who brings about the death of his frail young wife by tickling her, is also a touching revelation of the fragility and lovable nature of mankind.

Leaving Eudora Welty and Jackson on my journey northward, I passed Oxford, Mississippi, hometown of William Faulkner (1897–1962). Any significant American or British bookstore or library has not only copies of many of Faulkner's novels, but a fair number of books about him, too, as a man and as a writer. He is not only the best-known of Southern writers, he is among the best-known writers of this century in any language and deservedly so. His tormented, passionate, exacting novels provide some of the most exciting emotional and intellectual challenges and rewards that twentieth-century literature has to offer.

Yet I must confess myself disinclined to add to the multitude of statements made about his work. What could I say in a space as short as this about such individual and complex creations as *The Sound and the Fury* and *Absalom, Absalom* that has not been said already and better? And yet to leave the matter at that would also be unsatisfactory and a form of intellectual cowardice.

For many Faulkner *is* the South—in literature and in life. Faulkner's use of the Southern myth has meant that it has been disseminated among the educated throughout the world. It has been well summed up by Allen Tate in his essay on Faulkner's *Sanctuary* thus:

> . . . the South, afflicted with the curse of slavery—a curse, like that of Original Sin, for which no single person is responsible— had to be destroyed, the good along with the evil. The old order had a great deal of good, one of the "goods" being a result of the evil; for slavery itself entailed a certain moral responsibility which the capitalist employer in free societies did not need to exercise if it was not his will to do so. This old order, in which the good could not be salvaged from the bad, was replaced by a new order which was in many ways worse than the old. The Negro, legally free, was not prepared for freedom; nobody was trying to prepare him. The carpet-baggers, "foreign" exploiters, and their collaborators, the native rascals called "scalawags," gave the Old South its final agonies. . . . The evil of slavery was twofold, for the "peculiar institution" not only used human beings for a purpose for

146

which God had not intended them; it made it possible for the white man to misuse and exploit nature herself for his own power and glory. The exploitation of nature is a theme that runs through all Faulkner's work; it adds a philosophical, even a mystical dimension to the conventional Southern myth.[52]

This Southern myth was certainly not Faulkner's invention, but bringing to bear upon it his own genius, viewing and shaping it with his troubled but fundamentally noble mind, he gave it its most powerful and far-reaching expression. And here the trouble begins. For the effect upon generations of readers has been to think of personally used myth as something very near fact. To see the South as a sort of second Eden, to trace doom through its families as indications of some tragic but inevitable Nemesis, these are but some possible ways of looking at a bewildering and disturbed history. For writers and critics to think of the matter otherwise is to let literature dominate life in an uncreative manner. The South is often recast according to the shape of Faulkner's thoughts, and he was a complicated and divided man. This is surely absurd. A society is a more complex and confused matter than any one man's vision of it can allow.

It is surely significant that of the writers I have considered not one has felt Faulkner as a creative force in their lives. The Fugitives and Faulkner enjoyed only cold relations; Walker Percy spoke of Faulkner as a curse for all practicing Southern writers. This is not to deny the force and indeed truth of his books; this is not to say that the writers may not admire and respond to them. But as an influence he has been, I suspect, unimportant on the major Southern novelists and disastrous on the minor ones. For what gives Faulkner's novels their unquestionable stature, their unique atmosphere is the strange marriage of Faulkner's psyche with a received but translated myth. It is the infusion of the personal that makes, say, *Absalom, Absalom* the agonizing affair it is, yet the myth serves to discipline the often inchoate tendencies of Faulkner's mind. One is saying, therefore, that Faulkner's books could only be written by Faulkner, and writers wanting to portray the South in the light of their own experience and sensibility had better forget about him.

Speaking to William Ray, Reynolds Price denied that Faulkner, to whom he paid tribute, had been any kind of model to him, or indeed to many Southern writers like him:

He just provides a *reminder* perhaps to certain young writers that the kind of language that they have grown up with and known all their lives in their kitchens and front porches is a language which is potentially the vehicle for works of serious fiction. And for me that particular understanding came not from Faulkner but from Eudora, whom I read and admired long before I ever got to Faulkner. I read Eudora Welty's early stories as a high-school student and knew immediately that I had grown up hearing stories exactly of this sort, knowing people who expressed themselves in exactly these same comic idioms, metaphors, similes, and my natural conclusion was—my own experience constitutes the potential building blocks for works of fiction, works of art! That would have been the chief thing that Eudora Welty's work did for me as a writer. As a human being, it's given me enormous pleasure and insight and understanding; but as a writer that was the great gift of encouragement her work gave me, I think, when I was fourteen or fifteen years old.[53]

Whereas not one of the writers I interviewed sang significant praises of William Faulkner, all without exception testified to their deep admiration for the work of Eudora Welty. I am not going to say that Eudora Welty is a greater writer than Faulkner—rating writers thus, one against the other, is a futile pastime—but she does seem to me the better creative example, as the tributes of her fellow Southern writers amply show.

From Oxford I made my way back to Nashville. A few days later I left for Atlanta, where I had been lent an apartment. Because I lived in Atlanta for two months and made many expeditions into the rest of Georgia from there, I have written the next chapter not so much as a travelogue as an attempt at a composite picture of Georgia as I experienced the life there.

6: THE TRAVELS

In Georgia

THE POLICE COURT in Atlanta seemed shabby and yet not altogether cheerless as I sat there at a rather early hour of the morning. Here the accused are brought to see if their cases warrant a trial. The room was quite full and already too warm, and it resounded with coughing and sneezing. Most of those awaiting the brief hearings were black. I had been taken to the police court, which was open to the general public, by a young lawyer I had met at a supper party the previous evening, and we sat in one of the front seats right under the eye of the fat, aging judge. The court was not as melancholy as I had expected because the informality with which many of the proceedings were conducted and the diversity of the people present imparted a certain partylike atmosphere. Nevertheless there is always something guilty about being a spectator at occasions which are of (possibly) grim significance for others. I thought of those lines by the English poet Walter de la Mare:

> *The Seraph scanned the murderer in the dock—*
> *The motionless Judge, beneath the courtroom clock,*
> *The listening jury, warders, counsel, clerk;*
> *Ay, one and all who shared that deepening dark;*
>   *And then, as I shunned to see*
> *He turned his burning eyes and looked at me.*[54]

Somehow the poem seemed the more relevant because no murderer was actually in the room. The shoddy misdeeds that had brought the men and women here were things one might well have done oneself. A large and sulky-looking girl was being taken to court by her father for charging expensive items to his account in an Atlanta store. A black youth had disturbed the peace by picking a fight with another when very drunk. Two old toothless blacks

149

in dirty, tattered clothes had shoplifted. Prostitutes of both colors were brought, completely unembarrassed, before the judge, and charged with misdemeanors.

Then came the major case of the morning: a white woman was bringing a charge of attempted rape against a black man. Her story was that she worked for the man as a secretary in a small firm housed in a multistory building in Atlanta. There was a brief power cut and, as her office had no external windows, she had been alarmed at the sudden descent of almost complete darkness. She had made her way to the corridor where there was a window, and here the defendant had also appeared. He had sat her down on a sofa and then had sat down himself beside her. He had put his arm around her, which she first thought was to comfort her, but then it had become clear from further gestures that comfort was not all he had in mind. When she then edged away from him he had asked, "Why not?" She had replied: "Because I don't want it!" Then the lights had come on and the defendant had returned to his office. A few minutes later he had called out to the plaintiff and she had risen from the sofa and gone in, thinking he wanted to dictate letters. But in fact he had thrown himself upon her, forcing her to the ground, and unzipped his trousers to reveal his penis. She had had great difficulty breaking free of him.

She told her tale in a controlled but cross tone of voice not angry or upset, as one might expect. Her story was punctuated with neatly phrased asides disparaging toward the man, as when she mentioned with a sneer how frequently he was late for work in the mornings. During her story the black defendant, a handsome man, wore a subdued and sheepish expression on his face. His pretty wife, some years younger than he, sat immobile listening intently in a seat close to mine.

Fifteen or twenty years ago the very notion of rape—successful or attempted—by a black man of a white woman would have aroused an hysterical reaction in white Southerners. Sometimes citizens took the law into their own hands and strung up a black they suspected, and this barbarous perversion of justice would be condoned by a Southern jury. Sometimes the black "rapist" received official punishment by being put to death in the electric chair. The hearing I watched that morning is surely a good illustration of the enormous changes that have occurred in recent years in the South. The judge, who had seemed somewhat dozy and abstracted when confronted by most of the wrongdoers, paid careful attention to this case. The defendant was treated with the utmost courtesy. There *was* a division in the room, however, which interested me very much; it was a division of the sexes. The white woman was aided by a black woman lawyer and the black man was defended by a white male lawyer. This may have been deliberate, making use of one common prejudice to combat another that often takes more rabid and violent forms. "That woman was a real bitch," I heard several white men saying after the hearing was over. Sad though sexism is, I cannot help thinking that the sex polarization in this instance was almost a tolerable price paid for avoiding the injustice of ascribing guilt to a person simply because of his or her race.

The remaining cases were not so engrossing as this, and as they went on I let my attention wander to the whole complex matter of black and white relations in the South as I had witnessed them. My first thought was of the separateness of the social lives of black and white. I received many invitations to Southern homes, particularly during my two month stay in Atlanta. None of these white Southerners appeared to have any black friends or even acquaintances. Bars and clubs tend to attract one race or the other, though restaurants, I noticed, were usually frequented by both black and white. If whites were in the ascendancy this reflected the ratio in the area. But this is, of course, itself very telling. Suburbs and residential districts are still exclusive by practice or design, and in the attractive part of Atlanta where I lived, near Emory University, I doubt if there were any black homes for several miles, at which point a noticeable architectural borderline was crossed.

How much does this matter? Would we worry if Irish or Italian immigrants lived, as indeed they tend to, in specific areas? But black/white tensions have involved profound irrational emotions which have repeatedly exploded into hideous violence. I sensed none of this during my time in the South, but I cannot help thinking that a little more daily jostling between the two groups would be healthier. In London, by no means irreproachable on the subject of racial harmony, I repeatedly see mixed couples, usually adolescent, flirting while waiting to enter a movie or while riding on the top of a doubledecker bus. In the South I never saw a single mixed couple. I was told that I would, but I never did. Many white Southerners use the term "nigger" freely, with a sort of cheerful contempt. Although enforced gentility of language can do no one any good, this cannot improve matters. During a long taxi ride from Covington, Louisiana, to New Orleans my white driver, who showed great solicitude toward me because of my laryngitis, continually shouted out "Dumb-assed nigger!" every time we passed a car driven by a black person. Many remarks about blacks, though not actually directed to them, would have caused unpleasant feelings if heard by their subject. In a North Carolina motel I discovered that I had lost my wallet and reported this to the white manager. Had there been any niggers near me when I made my way over to the motel, she asked, this being the obvious explanation for any loss of money. Niggers, I was often told, were rough in their lovemaking yet prudish about oral sex; niggers were frightened of the water because they still behaved as if they were back in Africa and had to avoid the crocodiles. "Do y'all have niggers in England?" I was asked, rather as if they were a species of insect pest. And I am sorry to say that during the very last moments of my time in America, when I was standing on the deck of the Queen Elizabeth II watching the wonderful waterfront of Manhattan, I was forced to listen to a man from Mississippi pressing me: "What did you think of them niggers down in Mississippi? Not the same as you and me, are they?"

This list could be amplified, but most instances seem to me to be essentially trivial. The very speakers of these deplorable remarks were also capable of other sentiments: "We Southerners haven't treated the blacks too good! I guess that's all over now." The fact that it is obviously *not* all over now only partially invalidates the new spirit of these remarks.

A sizable number of Southerners with whom I became friendly had been in school or college when enforced integration took place. They talked freely, almost lyrically, about this period—the hopes they had entertained when integration seemed imminent and both the difficulties and rewards of the first years. Often parents of both colors, perhaps still inhibited themselves in social cross-color relations, assisted their sons and daughters to establish contact with young people of the other race, urging them to offer friendliness despite the menacing provocation of opponents. And as it turned out there was not nearly as much violence as had been feared. In their hearts, I think, many Southerners welcomed the change, and a few of those who resisted integration in schools did so not so much for ideological motives as simply for fear of violence affecting their beloved children.

If I say that in their social life the races clearly divide I may be guilty of too narrow a definition of the word "social" (as well as of a generalization to which I am sure there are many triumphant exceptions). For all over the South now black and white mix at work or in other activities outside the home such as sports. Girls serving in stores and men employed by the same company establish warm relations from which a less compartmentalized society may well grow.

Outsiders are still only too happy to brand Southerners as a racially bigoted people with a penchant for cruelty. This is, first of all, to fail to take into account the multiple difficulties of the situation Southerners have inherited. It is also to fail to do justice to Southern behavior during the decade since integration. Southerners have in fact showed as much personal bravery and ability to reform themselves as any people in history. It is no easy matter to combat the legacy of decades of prejudice and hostility and to resist often intimidating peer groups. It took real courage for such men as the father of the lawyer friend who took me to the Atlanta court to insist on equal pay and rights for black and white in the firm he ran in a small Tennessee town. It took real courage for two brothers I met on the first day of school integration deliberately to walk across the schoolyard to where the black boys and girls stood. Such people were trailblazers, and they must be applauded.

But so too, perhaps, must another group of Southerners, those who were certainly once guilty of mean attitudes toward blacks but who now have not only accepted the new order but have accepted it gladly. Indeed, so distant has their previous stance become that today they often sincerely talk as if they had never felt otherwise. A cynic might say that such people only act differently because the social climate is different, and that this has only come about because of external imposition. This may be right, but I think it beside the point in addition to being destructive. Not many of us are heroes, capable of risking the censure or mockery of our fellows. The fact remains that at this moment in time, and indeed for the past few years, many Southern men and women are behaving with more virtue and tolerance than ever before.

Black readers may well argue that I have presented the situation almost entirely from the white Southerner's point of view and that not only are there still injustice and discrimination, but a true democracy of spirit between the races is still very far off. I remember the sad face of the girl on the bus leaving Memphis, and though I would not retract anything I have just said, I am afraid that my tone must smack of a superficial humanist's optimism. I say optimism because I make the assumption that attitudes are formed primarily in the conscious mind. The interested and sympathetic visitor to the South probably does consider the Southern racial situation principally on a conscious level (though it also arouses deep atavistic guilts and fears). Therefore such a person can easily proclaim that with goodwill white Southerners can put their past behind them. So they could if it were just a matter of rational knowledge, but it is no such thing. Resentment, fear, and a feeling of superiority or inferiority were imparted to Southerners, black and white, in their earliest childhoods. Even when reviewed in the light of adult experience and reason, these stories and points of view are still informed by a particular emotional quality. Patterns of events which add up to a spiritually constricting history have become a part of the Southern mind. Although intellectually the Southerner may come to perceive the limitations of these patterns, imaginatively they are always with him or her.

Southerners' difficulties are compounded by the fact that the black–white antithesis has played an important part in the development of their psyche. Even in societies where another race does not play a significant part, psychoanalysts have noticed that their patients frequently ascribe a different color to certain figures who are objects of fear or desire in their dreams and fantasies. A white man harboring an only dimly realized attraction, say, for an older white woman may dream of her as black. But for white Southerners, natural desires must have been awakened early in their lives by members of a group later realized to be taboo. This must cause serious ruptures and subsequent guilt at a deep level of the personality.

So when Southern writers from William Faulkner onward have told the rest of the world that race relations is not a matter that can be solved by a few legal reforms, they know what they were talking about. Their remarks did not spring from some strange chauvinism or the wish to preserve an ethically dubious status quo; they spoke from their knowledge of the complexities of the human psyche.

All the same I will venture to say that those writers were wrong

154

who declared that only cultural evolution and not imposed legislative reform was desirable for the South. For rational and humane ideas put forcefully into practice can and do work their way down into the deeper and murkier strata of the mind. If, for example, every black man suspected of attempted rape is treated in the same dispassionate but firm way that I witnessed in the Atlanta police court, this will establish itself as a norm. It may thus diminish and perhaps in time obliterate psychic white fears of the black man as violator requiring punishment.

To many sensitive black intellectuals the South is still no place to be. It is a matter of deep regret to me that I can include no black writer in this book; significant black novelists of Southern origin prefer to live elsewhere, which must be a telling point in itself. Ernest Gaines (born in 1933) is truly a major writer whose last book, *In My Father's House* (1978), is his best so far. It is a haunting study of a separated father and son in a rural Louisiana community. But though Louisiana is the setting of all his work and he thinks of himself as a Southerner, his home is in San Francisco. Yet I am confident that black writers who are resident Southerners will in the next decade make an important contribution to American literature.

After the dim light of the police court the full light of summer midday broke into my reverie. Downtown Atlanta is a pleasant place to be during lunch hour. People come out of the offices to eat snacks or sandwiches by the splashing fountains or in shady corners of the parks. "You wait till you get to Atlanta; you will never have seen so many beautiful women in your life," I was told, and indeed there do seem to be a remarkable number of them. The traditional grace and softness of Southern women combine, I suppose, with the elegance of a rich and sophisticated city.

Male Southerners are intensely proud of their women. It is a feature of Southern life that cannot be enough stressed. I had often read how women were the rallying image for fighting Southerners in the Civil War and had thought it a piece of romantic hindsight. But I do not think so any longer. I could not count the times I heard Southern men of all ages praising the abundant good qualities, manners and looks of Southern women. Many told me that they could never consider marrying or even having an extended relationship with a non-Southern girl. No other girl could possess the refinement, charm, warmth or sweetness. The mixture of gentle tenderness and virile pride that informs such talk is like nothing else

I have encountered elsewhere. It is also my impression that Southern men speak more freely and readily about love than most others. I suspect that were I more intimate with the countries of southern Europe I would make comparisons here. Perhaps the physical warmth and luxuriance of a country really do affect amatory attitudes.

Not that the Southern men who talked to me of their emotional lives spoke only of harmonious relationships. They acknowledged, indeed almost rejoiced in, love's tempests. Perhaps here again the climate plays a part, for nature in the South can certainly reveal a violent aspect. Certainly the incidence of crimes of passion in the South is statistically very high, and the figures may relate to Latin rather than Anglo-Saxon patterns.

If one needed confirmation of the importance to the Southern sensibility of passionate relationships with the opposite sex, then literature and music would provide it. Faulkner, Peter Taylor, Thomas Wolfe, Madison Jones, Robert Penn Warren, Allen Tate and Anne Tyler all assert the determining power of passion, an assertion not made by the majority of British novelists. As for music, from the black blues with its frankly erotic words and charged chords to vibrant rock 'n' roll numbers like "I Got a Woman," "One Night" and "Maybelline," Southerners have created a language of sexual response and passion for the rest of the world.

In Atlanta the hedonistic vein in Southern culture is augmented by the hedonism to be expected from a fast-growing boom city with a predominantly young population. My time in Atlanta compresses itself in my memory into a veritable collage of pleasures: restaurants; visits to clubs to hear progressive bluegrass bands and watch teenagers shrieking excitedly for "Raggerty Annie" or "Cotton Blossom Special"; parties given, it would appear, at the drop of a hat, indoors or outdoors; expeditions to the countryside beyond; visits to bars frequented by the smart and glamorous, and others by workers from rural Georgia; boating outings on glorious Lake Allatoona; raft trips on the Chattahootchie; outdoor concerts; long conversations over wine in friends' homes or in cafes; and lounging by suburban swimming pools to combat the devastating heat. Familiarity with the city made me feel a real affection for it, and even daily visions of that amazing skyline never failed to fill me with pleasurable awe.

All the same, when I heard Marion Montgomery and James Dickey exclaim against Atlanta, when I realized that their fears of its possible expansion into one of the largest cities in the world were not based totally on their hatred of the urbanization of the country-side, but on some quality in Atlanta itself, I could understand and even sympathize.

Presiding over downtown Atlanta are two enormous hotels, the Peachtree Center and the Omni, both proclamations of Atlanta's intention of being a major international conference city and capital of the New South. Each hotel complex contains areas open to the public, and in these a plethora of luxury shops, agencies, bars, clubs and restaurants can be found. The Peachtree is at once the more modernistic and, in its interior, the more baroque of the two. It has strangely shining waterfalls and pools and serpentine stairways like contrived obstacles in an expensive child's game. The Omni, as its name might suggest, is somehow more democratic in its appeal. At its center is a large, oval-shaped skating rink; above this stretch gallery balconies as in some outsize theater. These contain the fronts of a multiplicity of shops. But you can also look up from the rink and see a spectacular glass wall and the plant-festooned wall of the back of the hotel itself. Some people say the Omni is beautiful. Impressive it certainly is, and dazzling and enticing, too. But beautiful—no, not to me. I cannot divorce admiration for its architectural adventurousness from the distaste I feel for the credo it so proudly proclaims, that joy must come through spending and acquisition. When men such as James Dickey oppose Atlanta to the traditional South, they are making an earnest point; the Old South did not believe that joy resides in such things. It could never have created these triumphs of commerce, and I find it a little depressing that the contemporary visitor to Atlanta is automatically taken to these hotels as to the city's most prized sights. How can tier upon tier of luxury shops compare not only with the cathedrals and universities of the great European cities but with the subtle beauties of other Southern towns such as New Orleans, Charleston and Charlottesville?

Yet the first conference whose members I saw walking in force around these complexes was not made up of salesmen or show business people, but of Southern Baptist preachers; it had even brought Jimmy Carter to the town briefly. Turn on the television set in one of those swank hotel bedrooms and you may well see a popular program in which a faith healer works his wonders on a tense, fervent congregation. He urges evil spirits to come out of troubled faces, accompanying his imprecations with curious gestures. You may also see a certain Georgian politician beseeching his viewers to return to a racist society with contemptuous and calculatedly hysterical references to "niggers." The violent currents of Southern life still flow through sybaritic and postindustrial Atlanta.

> The change was not gradual; you could have stopped the car and got out at the exact point where suburbia ended and the red-neck South began. I would like to have done that, to see what the sense of it would be. There was a motel, then a weed field, and then on both sides Clabber Girl came out of hiding, leaping onto the sides of barns, 666 and Black Draught began to swirl, and Jesus began to save.[55]

This comes from James Dickey's ambivalently titled *Deliverance,* and its observation is a true one. The moment you have left the confines of Atlanta you enter a different culture.

One hot Sunday two friends took me to the area of their hometown, about an hour and a half's ride south of Atlanta. The farmland we drove through seemed to steam before our eyes. The song "Everything is Peaches Down in Georgia" and the official nickname of the Peach State are less relevant to the Georgia countryside now than they were a few years ago. Sudden and severe cold spells did such damage to the peach crop that the state's farmers have turned to other sources of revenue—corn, peanuts and hogs. We entered a belt of small mill towns, sober, hot, shut-looking places but surprisingly elegant in their layout. Then, shimmering in the distance, were the low wooded hills that I had seen from the other side when traveling from Newnan to Columbus. My friends drove to the entrance to a wood and we climbed down a path to where the welcome, cooling waters of a creek cascaded over rocks. Soon we had undressed and were riding the falls into swirling pools.

A group of young black men then entered the scene, intent on exactly the same pleasures we ourselves were enjoying. But this created no immediate bond of fellowship. A hostility emanated from them that soon became unmistakeable, and remarks offered in our direction were distinctly aggressive; asking if we felt we had a right to the creek. We preferred to leave the spot and walk down beside the creek to where it became narrower and the wood through it more entangled and luxuriant.

And then, half-wading down the stream, I was assailed by sudden pains. I cried out first with surprise, then with agony as jab after hot jab punctured my skin on my face, arms and hands. I had walked into a swarm of hornets. Though I was their principal target they also attacked one of my friends.

We made our way back to our original seat on the rocks above the little waterfalls. The black men had heard the commotion and asked what had happened. Of course when they learned, their manner changed immediately. They were sympathetic and proffered beer. Aggression was at an end.

Hornet stings, of which I had received about fifteen, can be dangerous if one has an allergy to them. Luckily I turned out not to have one, though I felt a little sick and faint. Somehow this served rather to heighten my appreciation of the countryside through which we drove back. Those small mill towns, those farmsteads—was this not the landscape of Flannery O'Connor's stories? Indeed, Flannery O'Connor (1925–1964) had lived for most of her tragically short life in Milledgeville, not many miles east of us.

Flannery O'Connor has become one of the saints of Southern literature. Many of the writers I visited spoke of her with something close to reverence. She is widely read, and not only in the South; English and French critics have approved her, and I think it would be fair to say that today she is, Faulkner excepted, the Southern writer most known and respected in the outside world, an honor previously enjoyed by the other Georgian woman novelist Carson McCullers. Perhaps the best recent work of serious criticism of her work is *The Question of Flannery O'Connor* by Martha Stephens, herself from Georgia and the author of a work of fiction, the tender and poignant *Cast a Wistful Eye* (1977).

Flannery O'Connor's very considerable reputation depends on two short novels, *Wise Blood* (1952) and *The Violent Bear It Away* (1960), and two volumes of stories, *A Good Man Is Hard to Find* (1955) and the posthumously published *Everything That Rises Must Converge* (1965). Sally and Robert Fitzgerald have collected together her extremely interesting essays *Mystery and Manners* which, along with a recently published volume of her letters edited by Sally Fitzgerald, are indispensable reading for anyone interested in the phenomenon of Southern writing.

In Flannery O'Connor we find a strange union of manner and matter. Her style is limpid and refined, her form spare and shapely; this may explain her predeliction for the short story, in which I think her greatest work was done. Every story is characterized by technical grace, each paragraph is pointed and purposeful, and the whole has the unity and compression we expect more from a poem than a work of fiction. This is especially remarkable considering the subjects and themes of the stories. They are populated by violent and obsessed people, closer to their own highly individualized Gods than to one another and capable of almost any emotional or physical enormity in defense of these private faiths. The enormities are horrifying indeed—the slaughter of a whole family, the burning out of someone's eyes with quicklime, the drowning of an affectionate idiot, and a child hanging itself. These are the subjects. The themes are metaphysical—the attainment of grace or the journey toward damnation in a fallen world, a world in which God is at once remote yet inexorably, fearfully, ultimately in charge and in which the devil has done a good deal of very thorough work.

Flannery O'Connor was a Catholic. The South is the setting of all her work and it is all-pervasive in it, and in its most idiosyncratic and primitive forms. It is also perhaps the staunchest and most fanatically Protestant community in the world. Flannery O'Connor herself wrote illuminatingly and convincingly on this paradoxical situation in several essays; the first is from "The Grotesque in Southern Fiction":

> Whenever I'm asked why Southern writers particularly have a penchant for writing about freaks, I say it is because we are still able to recognize one. To be able to recognize a freak, you have to have some conception of the whole man, and in the South the general conception of man is still, in the main, theological. That is a large statement, and it is dangerous to make it, for almost anything you say about Southern belief can be denied in the next breath with equal propriety. But approaching the subject from the standpoint of the writer, I think it is safe to say that while the South is hardly Christ-centered, it is most certainly Christ-haunted. The Southerner, who isn't convinced of it, is very much afraid that he may have been formed in the image and likeness of God. Ghosts can be very fierce and instructive . . .[56]

The following is from "The Catholic Novelist in the Protestant South":

> The image of the South, in all its complexity, is so powerful in us that it is a force which has to be encountered and engaged. The writer must wrestle with it, like Jacob with the angel, until he has extracted a blessing.
>
> It was about 1919 that Mencken called the South the Bible Belt.... Today Southern literature is known around the world, and the South is still the Bible Belt. Sam Jones' grandma read the Bible thirty-seven times on her knees. The rural and small-town South, and even a certain level of the city South, is made up of the descendants of old ladies like her. You don't shake off their influence in even several generations.... We have to have stories in our background. It takes a story to make a story. It takes a story of mythic dimensions, one which belongs to everybody, one in which everybody is able to recognize the hand of God and its descent. In the Protestant South, the Scriptures fill this role.
>
> The Hebrew genius for making the absolute concrete has conditioned the Southerner's way of looking at things. That is one of the reasons why the South's is a story-telling tradition. Our response to life is different if we have been taught only a definition of faith than if we have trembled with Abraham as he held the knife over Isaac.
>
> I think [the Catholic novelist in the South] will feel a good deal more kinship with backwoods prophets and shouting fundamentalists than he will with those politer elements for whom the supernatural is an embarrassment and for whom religion has become a department of sociology or culture or personality development. His interest and sympathy may very well go—and I know my own does—directly to those aspects of Southern life where the religious feeling is most intense and where its outward forms are farthest from the Catholic...[57]

There is, of course, a sting in the last paragraph above, aimed at the secular or freethinking reader; to criticize the content or ideology of the stories can be read as a criticism of religion itself. One who attacks them aims to dethrone the spiritual. This is an unfairness of which Flannery O'Connor is frequently guilty in both her essays and fiction. While I applaud her understanding of the fervent salvationist religion of the South and admire her artistry, I find myself far from satisfied with the vision of life her work upholds. But to express myself so smacks of the weak ineffectual humanism Flannery O'Connor continually derides in her work. Perhaps I should say instead that I dislike her vision exceedingly, though I do not see myself as an adversary of Christianity, either Catholic or Protestant.

Flannery O'Connor's stories show an extraordinarily adroit manipulation of events. Ingeniously contrived and often hideous fates will be traced for people usually maimed spiritually, physically or psychologically, and rendered with scant compassion, a virtue Flannery O'Connor anyway tends to disparage as a further token of humanist weakness. She also criticizes those readers who object to what they call her lack of verisimilitude. She feels she is attempting a deeper type of realism. As Flannery O'Connor insists on the metaphysical truth of her stories and claims she is giving us pictures of each person's relationship to the working of God's grace, I think it perfectly legitimate to suggest that the elaborate cruelties of both the novels and the short stories are features not of God's world but of Flannery O'Connor's private one. In her critical writing she dismisses those events and feelings that play so large a part in most lives—sexual love, work, social relations, family life, friendship and the pleasures of the senses—and which play only negligible parts in her own work. To believe in the possibility of human happiness or, worse still, in the alleviation of human suffering, is to invite Flannery O'Connor's unconcealed contempt. She inflicts ghastly sufferings on the well-meaning humanistic fathers in two related works, "The Lame Shall Enter First" and the novel *The Violent Bear It Away*.

She is morbidly fascinated by the maimed, the idiotic, the depraved, the insane and the feeble, and she pursues them with horrible experiences until at last she relents in a moment of gentleness which is translated into an epiphany of divine grace. It seems to me extremely dangerous to play at being God in this way. I applaud Flannery O'Connor for knowing exactly what she is doing in a literary sense, but I am not convinced, even after reading all of her intelligent critical writing, that psychologically she knew what she was doing. She does not concede (how could she?) that her imaginative gravitation to the bizarre and deformed is due to a strong vein of sadism. This is nonetheless revealed, I think, in the very deftness and coldly artistic contrivances of her short stories. Nor does she admit to her contempt for the healthy, the well-adjusted and the socially integrated. They are not only denied the author's mercy, but the light of God, it is tacitly stated, is forever withheld from them.

Flannery O'Connor's most extended work, *The Violent Bear It Away*, further reveals the limited nature of her reference. Kidnapped in early childhood by his great-uncle, a self-styled prophet and former inmate of a lunatic asylum, Tarwater has been brought up in the belief that one day the mantle of prophet will descend on him. After the old man's death Tarwater is simultaneously desirous, fearful and resentful at this prospect. In his orphaned condition he is befriended and almost adopted by his liberal uncle, an unhappy individual who has been deserted by his wife and left to look after their idiot child, whom he once attempted to drown.

The principal tension of the novel is provided by the struggle between Tarwater and his uncle over the baptism of the idiot boy, an act that the youth is seemingly intent on carrying out while his humanist uncle is equally intent on preventing it. The latter does not know that Tarwater is contemplating a blasphemous perversion of the holy rite as a way of freeing himself from the spell of his great-uncle. What he finally does is to mutter the words of the baptism service while holding the idiot down until he drowns under the surface of the lake's waters.

So much for the bare story. Its flesh is as eccentric and morbid as its bones and includes a terrible accident in which Tarwater's parents lost their lives; the uncle's treatment of the idiot child; Tarwater's obsessed vision of God's terrible swift mercy; a young mad girl possessed of a vision of salvation and evil; and a perverted criminal. Not once in the novel is there any idea of the ordinary stuff of life or of loving feelings returned. I am afraid that I can see the novel, for all the incisive intelligence behind it, only as a deeply sick document, a neurotic travesty of existence. I do acknowledge, however, Flannery O'Connor's artistic fidelity to her vision as something worthy of respect, and I am ultimately convinced of the fine character of the woman who left behind her such a glowing memory.

The undeniable fact remains that Flannery O'Connor means a very great deal to Southerners, both literary and otherwise. People told me that her stories were true to the ethos of rural Southern life, an opinion which for obvious reasons I am unqualified to challenge. I do not think the lives of the Southerners I encountered bore much resemblance to those of Flannery O'Connor's eccentric, obsessed people, but perhaps that is a foolish and philistine observation.

What Flannery O'Connor has surely done above all is to present, in remarkably shapely and sophisticated art, the apotheosis of an exceedingly important strand of Southern culture—its relentlessly individualistic Protestantism, perhaps the feature most derided by outsiders. Unfeeling and indeed hostile fun has been made of the South by radicals from Mencken onward for nurturing and harboring fundamentalists, Bible-beaters and self-appointed evangelists, castigating them as crazy peasants drunk on ignorant misconceptions of Scripture. Flannery O'Connor accords them instead a kind of dignity and pays them the compliment of taking them and their eccentric visions seriously; she sees them as real seekings after —and who knows, perhaps real findings—of God. This is a fine imaginative achievement, and one can see why Southerners are grateful to Flannery O'Connor for it.

All the same I cannot condone Flannery O'Connor's preference for these men and women, inebriated by their God, over more normal and integrated human beings, especially as I suspect her knowledge of them was cerebral rather than actual; nor does her art make me more sympathetic to what strikes me as a cruel and solipsistic brand of religion.

There is no greater admirer of Flannery O'Connor than the Georgian novelist Marion Montgomery (born in 1925). He knew her and was instrumental in her receiving a literary award—for *The Violent Bear It Away*—and he is currently at work on a vast critical work entitled *Homage to Flannery O'Connor*. His aim is to present her as the most significant literary challenge of recent times to both the Enlightenment and to the wooly philosophical and artistic thinking that has resulted from it. The book promises to be an interesting contribution to literary criticism.

The day was golden when I was driven by a friend to see Marion Montgomery at his home in the small country town of Crawford, a few miles from Athens, site of the University of Georgia. I liked Athens, from its old houses set in thick gardens along wooded avenues and its campus sprawling over hilltops to the views of the countryside below that every street seemed to provide. As we drove to Crawford the land seemed to reflect sunlight back at the sky.

164

It is hard for the outsider to appreciate Marion Montgomery's point that Crawford, so small, quiet and set in such rich and tranquil countryside, is almost a suburb of Atlanta. That city seemed so very far away to me. His house is a lovely one. Its front has a colonnaded porch behind which is a balcony that conjures up images of upper-class antebellum life. The garden was lively with Marion Montgomery's large family. He and I sat on the porch in the shade, welcome for it was midday and very hot. Later he drove me to nearby Lexington, the setting for his most ambitious novel, *The Fugitive*. The little hot town looked remarkably as he had described it. He pointed out the spot in the central square where a principal character first alights from the bus; he pointed out houses where other characters lived, the church they attended and a bulletin board which had provided inspiration for the plot. He also took me to the extraordinary Swinging Rock Park where a major event in the novel occurs. This is a huge boulder that one can touch and make sway backward and forward with only one's fingers. This stands in woodland; beyond it a creek showed tantalizingly, the hot air quivering above its waters.

Marion Montgomery is a man of gentle and warm manner, suggesting contentment in his life, home and work. He teaches English at the University of Georgia. His writing—self-aware, experimental (he is the only Southerner whose fiction can be so described), difficult of access and obsessive—presents a dark view of the human lot on earth and is set in a society which emphatically accepts this. *The Wandering of Desire*, in some ways his most immediate book, is a portrait of people dominated by a sin- and damnation-obsessed credo. But Marion Montgomery yet sees himself as a writer who can give conditional hope to his readers:

> We have to bear human foolishness, human absurdity, without resorting to making despair a virtue. Momentary despair—we can't escape that . . . I think I mean the existentialists' absurd —which has frightened too many of our writers out of wit and humor—is a prospect of the world we come to again and again. We can't escape coming to it. But it can't be enough just to come *to* it: one has to come *through* it. The ticket to it is the tragic eye, which I suspect is innate. The passport that allows us to come back from it we have to be given or earn—the humorous eye. Humor is a necessary complement to the tragic,

if one is to preserve what our age insists on calling "sanity." (I call it soul.) There are advantages of place and community and family to one's earning or being given that eye, I think. That is one of the gifts to the Southern writer that we haven't outgrown with our new arrogance.[58]

Georgia is the largest, richest and most populous of the Southern states and the most varied in landscape, from the Sea Islands and the swampy country around Savannah to the farm and mill town plains of the central counties; from the wilderness on the Florida border to the Appalachian territory of north Georgia; from the opulent suburbs of Atlanta and Marietta to old-fashioned communities near the Alabama and Tennessee borders. At the same time it seemed to me the state with the strongest sense of its own identity and the most glowing sense of pride in itself. This has been fortified of late by the presidency of Jimmy Carter and his importation of Georgia people to the White House. During the time of my stay in Georgia, Carter was suffering from a wave of wanton unpopularity all over the United States. He was a scapegoat for ills that could not logically be laid at his personal door. Georgians, for the most part, continued to speak of him with the same belief and pride that must have impelled them to vote for him for state office.

Though I respond to many kinds of scenery I must confess that hills and mountains, particularly high hills and low mountains, elicit the most intense reaction from me. The line in the Psalms, "I will lift up mine eyes unto the hills from whence cometh my help" has always seemed to me easy to accept. The wild wooded hills that rise beyond Rome, Georgia; the sharp wall of the Cohuttas, behind which are inviting, dramatic, forested rifts; the Blue Ridge country of rapids and steep faces, sudden lakes, dense trees, domed hills and valleys hazy with diffuse light—these excite me even in memory; at the time they filled me with joy in their beauty.

I went into North Georgia a great deal, staying with various friends and making expeditions with them. The country that stretches from Rome northward to the Tennessee border and Chattanooga and eastward through the Cohuttas to the North Carolina and South Carolina lines is full of associations for me; it has aroused an appetite and a longing in me that demand satisfaction through further visits.

I think now, back in England, of its flora and fauna and particularly of the kudzu that spreads over roadsides, fences, poles, walls and trees. James Dickey has captured the extraordinary impression of this ubiquitous plant, originally an import from Japan, and the awe that its persistence produces:

> *In Georgia, the legend says*
> *That you must close your windows*
>
> *At night to keep it out of the house.*
> *The glass is tinged with green, even so,*
>
> *As the tendrils crawl over the fields.*
> *The night the kudzu has*
> *Your pasture, you sleep like the dead.*
> *Silence has grown Oriental*
> *And you cannot step upon ground:*
> *Your leg plunges somewhere*
> *It should not, it never should be,*
> *Disappears and waits to be struck*
>
> *Anywhere between sole and kneecap:*
> *For when the kudzu comes,*
>
> *The snakes do, and weave themselves*
> *Among its lengthening vines,*
> *Their spade heads resting on leaves,*
> *Growing also, in earthly power*
> *And the huge circumstance of concealment.*[59]

I think, too, of the loud, throbbing chorus of bullfrogs croakingly addressing warm, starry nights (the victims of a barbarous country sport called "bullfrog-gigging"); of skunks gracefully inspecting trashcans on mountain roads; of deer seen valiantly swimming the considerable width of a lake; of a dog found at a camping site and adopted by my friends which drew admiring comments from various Southern boys; and of huge brilliant dragonflies skimming the water of small concealed, tranquil mountain lakes.

I think, too, of the glimpses of life in its towns and villages that I was afforded—in places like Cartersville, Calhoun, Dalton, Chatsworth, Dahlonega, Ellijay, Blairsville and Hiawassee. Saturday nights brought the Southern boys cruising around the central squares in their cars, showing off the cars (and their control of them) like male birds their plumage; visits to dark, bleak, smoke-filled poolrooms and bars; Sunday morning meant packing into small, severe wooden churches; other days we bought beer at gas stations and drank it while driving along hot, kudzu-lined roads. All these towns were dominated by their courthouse, often the first substantial building to be erected. (Dahlonega's is especially fine.) I also remember the peaceful dignity of the family life in the homes I visited.

The Appalachians are ancient mountains, and they have long been inhabited. Strange mounds in the vicinity of the Chattahoochee river indicate prehistoric peoples about whom little can be certain. Curious legends have accrued about pre-Columbian mountain-dwellers, the most curious of these being supposed visitors from Wales—"moon-eyed" men. What is certain is that Hernando De Soto in the mid-sixteenth century discovered thriving Creek and Cherokee Indian communities in the territory that is now Georgia. These tribes engaged in bloody battles against each other. Of the two the Cherokees have the more extraordinary story, for they were most "ready," so to speak, to receive the culture of their invaders. In Calhoun stand a statue and an arch which commemorate Sequoyah, part Dutchman and part Cherokee, who devised an alphabet for the Cherokee language. No people has ever become literate so speedily or so completely as the Cherokees. Three miles from Calhoun is New Echota, for thirteen years the capital of the federally recognized Cherokee Indian Nation. Alas, only sites and reconstructions, pleasing indications of contemporary interest, remain of this once flourishing center. It once contained government offices and even a printing house which produced a Cherokee language newspaper, the *Cherokee Phoenix*. In 1838 the nation was forcibly broken up after Andrew Jackson, president until 1837, realized the possibility that the Indians were living on land rich in minerals. He bulldozed through Congress a treaty expelling the Indians from Georgia, which eventually forced them to embark on the "Trail of Tears" to Oklahoma. It surprises me that more writers have not felt driven to the Cherokee story, especially as Georgians today seem to be atoning for this ugly episode in their history by an intense enthusiasm for Cherokee lore.

Not only did the Cherokee independent nation die in 1838 in Georgia, but the first American gold rush also took place with Dahlonega as its focal point. The gold lasted for about twenty-three years, and then the area returned to its ordinary country ways.

Life in the Georgia mountains has been hard, though not as hard as in Kentucky or West Virginia. Many of the smaller villages have to rely on summer tourism, when the townspeople sell folk toys, produce, and traditional delicacies. Hopefully not many of them will suffer the ghastly fate of Helen, which was once an ordinary mountain village but has been rebuilt in a crazy Alpine style. Its zany conglomeration of souvenir-stuffed chalets may attract visitors, but it is an insult to the beautifully tranquil hills and forest around it.

Between Ellijay, Hiawassee and Clayton the mountain landscape is of a numinous magnificence which no campsites or reservoirs can diminish. Tree, rock and rapid white water reign, the air is winelike with the scent of pines and flowers, and the eye can travel upward and see nothing but shining, fresh green. This is the land of James Dickey's *Deliverance* and of many of his poems. Indeed, the novel's canoe expedition has an antecedent in his poem "On the Coosawattee":

> *Into the slain tons of needles,*
> *On something like time and dark knowledge*
> *That cannot be told, we are riding*
> *Over white stones forward through fir trees.*
> *To follow whatever the river*
> *Through the clasping of roots follows deeply.*
>
> *As we go inward, more trunks*
> *Climb from the edge of the water*
> *An turn on the banks and stand growing.*
> *The nerves in the patches of tree-light*
> *On the ripples can feel no death,*
> *But shake like the wings of angels.*
>
> *With light hard-pressed to keep up*
> *Though it is in place on each feather . . .*
> *The stones beneath us grow rounder*
> *As I taste the fretted light fall*
> *Through living needles to be here*
> *Like a word I can feed on forever*
>
> *Or believe like a vision I have*
> *Or want to conceive out of greenness.*
> *While the world fades, it is becoming*
> *As the trees shut away all seeing,*

169

> *In my mouth I mix it with sunlight.*
> *Here, in the dark, it is* being.[60]

James Dickey is an appropriate poet to quote in the context of North Georgia, for he more than any other writer enjoys a psychic rapport with its wild country and has indeed become its most famous celebrant. As I looked at the rushing force of clear mountain water, beneath which stones gleamed whitely on the riverbed, I was pleased to reflect that I would shortly be seeing him. Though he has a small base in North Georgia, his home is in South Carolina and it was there that I visited him.

7: THE WRITERS

James Dickey

MY JOURNEY FROM ATLANTA to Charleston, South Carolina was
fraught and uncomfortable. I had found out that an overnight
Greyhound bus was scheduled to leave Atlanta not long after midnight and would get me into Charleston in time for breakfast.
When this bus, very late, at last arrived, it was only to disappoint
us—it had engine trouble. Into a replacement bus we passengers
filed to sit in irritated silence awaiting a driver. Without any explanation we were eventually told that the bus was not suitable for
us, and that passengers for Charleston should travel to Augusta,
Georgia, and change there. It was past three o'clock in the morning
when the Augusta bus pulled through the dark Atlanta streets
heading east. A baby began to cry and it wailed, piercingly, all
the way to Augusta. There we were all turned out, and an hour
passed in weary waiting for another bus; one came but was too full
and a second had to be found. I did in fact sleep on this one, and
when I woke up it was to see small houses with palmetto trees in
their yards. The palmetto is the emblem of South Carolina and a
symbol of its defiant spirit.

Perhaps it was because I was tired, but in the Charleston bus
station I read my map incorrectly. I soon found myself in a tangle
of scruffy though not unattractive streets containing a number of
seedy cafes and hotels. I went into one of the cafes to have some
much-needed black coffee. Inside a group of youths were drinking
can after can of beer and playing cards; their attention was at one
point directed by a black waitress to a large notice on the wall which
proclaimed that anyone using profane or obscene language would
be evicted from the cafe by the management. The coffee fortified
me less than I had hoped. After leaving the cafe I noticed graceful
wrought iron in front of the peeling walls of half-collapsed houses.

I looked into some pleasant if unkempt little yards, and I told myself what was partly true, that I liked the place. I was somewhat surprised, however, that it was so famous a city. But I wanted to see the harbor and Fort Sumter, and after asking two lolling young men the way there I realized how mistaken I had been in my directions.

Within an hour or so I decided that Charleston deserved all its fame and more. There can surely be no lovelier town; James Dickey says that it is one of the few American towns in which the main streets are not only pleasant to walk in but actually compel walking.

And he is right. One wants to walk slowly to admire the many felicitous examples of domestic architecture; to enjoy the glimpses of gardens, serene and lush with oleander, hibiscus and hydrangea; to savor the many delicate triumphs of wrought iron in balconies, garden gates and stairways. The tourist such as myself can take a trip around Charleston in a horse- or mule-drawn buggy. The young man who drove the buggy I took was unself-conscious and fast-talking. He said he was a Southerner by conversion, not by upbringing. He told us of Charleston's foundation over three hundred years ago; about its stature during the eighteenth and early nineteenth centuries as a center of commerce and the arts; about the Fort Sumter crisis; but one sensed that this was not where his real interests lay. Most of the tour was spent thus clopping leisurely down charming old residential streets, past "historic homes," and it was on certain aspects of these that he revealed his specialized fund of knowledge. He described the expenditure required to keep up almost any large house we passed, something which seemed to arouse in him an almost lyrical excitement. He knew how the owners had earned their money and hinted at future financial triumphs or setbacks. He spoke of grand costly parties held in the elegant rooms he pointed out; he touched on amorous goings-on both past and present. Indeed, at the end of the hour and a half one felt as if one had been inhabiting the pages of a Thackeray novel.

Charleston, I think, makes a special impression on the British visitor, for it provides a particularly agreeable demonstration of the deep and close kinship between British and American cultures. Bristol, Bath and such districts of London as Chelsea, Highgate and Highbury are the obvious comparisons. I am not saying that American civic and domestic architecture has not developed its own peculiar style, or that any street in Charleston could be mistaken for a British street—the very different climate sees to that. I am not even referring to the obvious fact that some of the older houses in Charleston date from the days of British colonialism. No, it is the conservatism (in the sense of cherishing the past), the cultivation of the charming and the soothing that links Charleston and other old Southern towns to Britain.

Overlooking the waterfront is a line of old houses known as "Rainbow Row" because of the different colors they are painted. Though Charleston Harbor is large, Fort Sumter is not difficult to recognize. Because the federal government did not recognize the right of secession and refused to give up its military bases in Confederate territory, the Civil War began with the order, "Fire on Fort Sumter." If it had not broken out over Fort Sumter it would have been somewhere else, but it seems somehow fitting that Charleston was the setting for the event. It is the largest and most prestigious city of South Carolina, and South Carolina was the very first state to secede. Secession seems to me (like the War of Independence) to demonstrate that vein of stubborn British determination not to submit which is also so important a constituent of the American character. Just as the colonists never showed themselves to be more British than when they rebelled against the British, so the Southerners never showed themselves more American (and thus British) than when they rebelled against the federal American government. It is appropriate that a city which suggests a fusion of the British and American spirits should be the site of this proud act of self-assertion, to say which is not to diminish or to cast a romantic haze over the bloody tragedy of the war itself.

Columbia, South Carolina, is where James Dickey (born 1923) lives and teaches. He also has a summer house near Georgetown, just over an hour's drive up the coast north of Charleston, and it was here that I visited him. This is swampy country and, away from the pleasures of Myrtle Beach and similar resorts, exceedingly mysterious. There are flat stretches of brackish marshland where a person can neither walk, swim nor boat. Only birds, brightly colored insects and reptiles, both dangerous and gentle, are at home there; the landscape seems to reflect the passing moods of the sky and betray even the slightest wind. Edgar Allan Poe knew this South Carolina countryside; it is said to be the inspiration and setting for "The Fall of the House of Usher," and certainly in this story and such poems as "Ulalume" references to it can easily be seen. Eudora

173

Welty, in an essay I have already mentioned called "Place in Fiction," speaks of the inextricability of the one from the other. Certainly one can understand that Poe's artistic imagination, even allowing for the traumas of his early life, might well have operated differently had he not encountered the changeable, soft, noisome and strangely enticing swamp country north of Charleston. Its flowers, trees and animals, James Dickey says, were a major reason for his choosing to work and live in South Carolina, in such a different environment from the North Georgia mountains he knew as a youth and praises in his poems and novel.

Perhaps the most striking feature of James Dickey's conversation is its imaginative and emotional adventurousness; he acknowledges no tedious social conventions that might prevent one from speaking of burning intimate concerns or asking others about their inner emotional life. I liked this about him immensely; I also respected him for it. He is a compelling man in his physical presence as well as in his speech. He said that after the success of *Deliverance* he appeared on a talk show where he was asked whether he saw himself as Ed, the narrator of the novel. Ed is surprised out of his rather gentle life into a realization of the darker but perhaps stronger forces within himself. Dickey said he didn't—if he resembled any character in the book it was Lewis, the man of obsessions who was determined to challenge nature with his own strength and who initiated the novel's fated expedition. James Dickey is indeed a man of contradictions, but he fully acknowledges them, and whatever agonies the conflicts cause him, they only add to his stature as a person and as a poet. With a record of intrepid war service he nevertheless speaks of a persistent admiration for Quakerism and the pacifist ideal. He admits to being able to understand the Fascist reverence for force and the superman, yet he has liberal convictions, a tenderness for all living things, and a love for the expression of this tenderness in art. He is a religious man, married to a Catholic wife, yet he confesses to times of despair when a wholeness of vision seems to be withheld from him. He has enjoyed public fame—he read the inaugural poem for his fellow Georgian, President Carter, a friend and admirer—yet no one clearly believes more in the private world of the passions and the mind. He was a crack athlete when young and even now is fascinated by sports, physical challenge and the life of action. He is triumphantly an artist and intellectual, with a wide, deep and idiosyncratic knowledge of literature and ideas.

After the war and college (which included a time at Vanderbilt) he taught at universities and worked for a number of years in advertising in both New York City and Atlanta. James Dickey recalls how one afternoon in his business office he sat down at his typewriter and wrote the following lines:

> *All dark is now no more.*
> *This forest is drawing a light.*
> *All Presences change into trees.*
> *One eye opens slowly without me.*
> *My sight is the same as the sun's.*[61]

These lines filled him with a strange excitement, for he felt they spoke with an urgent and personal voice that had so far eluded him. All that afternoon he worked at the poem that was to become "Sleeping Out at Easter," the account of a man who sleeps out in his backyard the night before Easter and awakes to thoughts of resurrection inspired by the trees around him. The poem is characteristic of James Dickey the mature poet, in its mystical feeling for nature, its sense of religious awe, and in its narrative of a man who has temporarily broken out of bourgeois living to confront the natural and in so doing discovers the supernatural as well.

James Dickey's major achievement is his poetry. Had the sensationally successful novel *Deliverance* never been written, his stature in contemporary American literature would be undiminished, which is not to disparage the novel in any way. I only wish that I could give his poems the attention they deserve, but alas, the scope of this book does not allow it. What I can do is to suggest some links between James Dickey the poet and James Dickey the novelist before discussing the novel itself.

There is a curious poem in the collection *Falling* called "The Sheep Child."

> *Farm-boys wild to couple*
> *With anything   with soft-wooded trees*
> *With mounds of earth   mounds*
> *Of pinestraw   will keep themselves off*
> *Animals by legends of their own:*
> *In the hay-tunnel dark*
> *And dung of barns, they will*
> *Say I have heard tell*

175

> *That in a museum in Atlanta*
> *Way back in a corner somewhere*
> *There's this thing that's only half*
> *Sheep   like a wooly baby*
> *Pickled in alcohol because*
> *Those things can't live   his eyes*
> *Are open but you can't stand to look*
> *I heard from somebody who . . .*

Into this half-human freak's dead, staring eyes James Dickey puts these beautiful lines:

> *I am here, in my father's house.*
> *I who am half of your world, came deeply*
> *To my mother in the long grass*
> *Of the west pasture, where she stood like moonlight*
> *Listening for foxes. It was something like love*
> *From another world that seized her*
> *From behind, and she gave, not lifting her head*
> *Out of dew, without ever looking, her best*
> *Self to that great need. . . . I woke, dying.*
> *In the summer sun of the hillside, with my eyes*
> *Far more than human, I saw for a blazing moment*
> *This great grassy world from both sides.*
> *Man and beast in the round of their need,*
> *And the hill wind stirred in my wool,*
> *My hoof and my hand clasped each other,*
> *I ate my one meal*
> *Of milk, and died*
> *Staring. From dark grass I came straight*
>
> *To my father's house, whose dust*
> *Whirls up in the halls for no reason.*[62]

I believe this poem expresses a deeply permeating vision of James Dickey's—that this sport of nature, doomed from gestation to non-survival, suggests a truth that lies below and beyond visible nature: that throughout creation there is a yearning for wholeness which is not capable of realization in this flawed world. Such acts as the coupling of a boy with a sheep point to a primeval bliss which we can partially recapture from time to time in other, less dramatic and doomed ways, and James Dickey is surely one of this century's supreme lyricists of these moments.

In that wild freak's blind eyes can be seen a power so intense that the bourgeois tourist, gaping at it, is frightened. James Dickey is obsessed by the way the bourgeoisie has concealed from itself the terror and joy of the natural world, shutting itself away with man-made comforts and man-made rules and shibboleths. Not that all apprehensions of the natural can be stifled, but too often the burial in civilization leads to an unreality of vision too strong to be fully cured. The Atlanta men in *Deliverance* have preserved enough atavistic feeling for nature to want to conduct their weekend experiment in the white water of North Georgia rivers. But even for the obsessive Lewis, with his dreams of self-sufficiency and his knowledge of and love for the wild, nature is not the reality, the battleground of forces and expression of universal truths that it should be; he has reduced too much of it to a self-centered game.

Violence in animals, violence in the elements and violence in men—James Dickey's vision makes little distinction between them. From his experience as a fighter pilot in World War II and Korea he has written some of the most moving war poetry of our time. Many describe his bombing missions, a subject about which he shows a passionate objectivity. But these poems do not differ significantly in tone from those describing hunting expeditions where the emotions of pursuer and pursued are caught in haunting stanzas in which a profound pity and a fierce joy in strength fuse together in strange, incantatory phrases.

What true difference is there between the hunterpilot or soldier and the hunterwolverine?

> *Let him eat*
> *The last red meal of the condemned*
> *To extinction, tearing the guts*
> *From an elk. Yet that is not enough*
> *For me. I would have him eat*
> *The heart, and from it, have an idea*
> *Stream into his gnawing head*
> *That he no longer has a thing*
> *To lose, and so can walk*
> *Out into the open . . .*[63]

James Dickey is addressing, in "For the Last Wolverine," a savage beast threatened with extinction. But are the appetites he apostro-

phizes here significantly different from those the narrator-hero of
Deliverance discovers inside himself when he determines to avenge
his companion?

The exciting story that *Deliverance* tells and its detailed, stimulating descriptions of canoeing, archery, hunting and guitar-playing
have perhaps obscured the novel's basic identity as the metaphor of
a tormented mind. It is a mind that cannot countenance the
blinkered, restricting nature of modern civilization yet cannot but
be appalled, bewildered and angered by the violent forces it encounters beyond. It is an uncomfortable work which does not
shrink from fear. Nevertheless James Dickey does suggest that
spiritual enrichment can come, perhaps not as spectacularly as one
might hope, from confrontation of the elemental and the evil in
life, and in a quiet way the narrator is the better for his ghastly experiences in the North Georgia mountains.

These experiences are, I think, too familiar through the excellent
film version to need more than a quick summary. Of the four men
in affluent middle age who go on a canoeing expedition, two are
held up by degraded mountain rednecks and one is forced at gunpoint to submit to buggery:

> There was no need to justify or rationalize anything; they were
> going to do what they wanted to. I struggled for life in the air,
> and Bobby's body was still and pink in an obscene posture that
> no one could help. The tall man restored the gun to Bobby's
> head, and the other one knelt behind him.
>
> A scream hit me, and I would have thought it was mine
> except for the lack of breath. It was a sound of pain and outrage
> and was followed by one of simple and wordless pain. . . . The
> white-haired man worked steadily on Bobby, every now and
> then getting a better grip on the ground with his knees. At last
> he raised his face as though to howl with all his strength into
> the leaves and the sky, and quivered silently while the man
> with the gun looked on with an odd mixture of approval and
> sympathy . . .[64]

The choice of buggery as the fate of Bobby, the most suburban
and limited in outlook of the four men, is an imaginative and important one. Humiliating and painful as well as the defiance of one
of the profoundest taboos of the American (and perhaps particularly
the Southern) male, it also constitutes a petty piece of wanton

malice, which makes a more fitting illustration of the promiscuous malignity that is such a frightening feature of our existence than any more serious assault would do. And it is precisely the gratuitous spite of the act, its nasty triviality, that goad the narrator witness into a state where he is ready to commit murder. As James Dickey explained to me, Bobby would, much as he disliked what happened to him, get over it easily enough. He is a lubricious kind of man to whom being buggered would not mean a great deal.

Drew, the sweetest in temperament of the four, and the most innocent in his attitude to life, is killed, and Ed, the narrator, kills a man he believes to be responsible. Lewis, the instigator of the expedition and a fervent believer in the ability of men to withstand the elements, is gravely wounded. All this happens in a setting which calls forth from all of them (with the possible exception of Bobby) delight, wonder and awe:

> I could hear the river running at my feet, and behind the woods were unimaginably dense and dark; there was nothing in them that knew me. There were creatures with one forepaw lifted, not wanting yet to put the other down on a dry leaf, for fear of the sound. There were the eyes made for seeing in this blackness; I opened my eyes and saw the dark in all its original color.[65]

And the outcome of these terrible events—what true resolution could there be? The narrator returns to his Atlanta life, for outwardly no change is possible. But inwardly he has been affected enough for a gentle revolution to take place in his psyche, though its outward expressions may not be noticeable to an observer. In accordance with symbolic truth and actual probability, the countryside through which the river ran—the scene of these lessons in the darkness of life—is submerged by the building of a dam:

> The river and everything I remembered about it became a possession to me, a personal, private possession, as nothing else in my life ever had. Now it ran nowhere but in my head, but there it ran as though immortally. I could feel it—I can feel it —on different places on my body. It pleases me in some curious way that the river does not exist, and that I have it. In me it still is, and will be until I die, green, rocky, deep, fast, slow, and beautiful beyond reality. I had a friend there who in a way had died for me, and my enemy was there.[66]

Deliverance, for all its universality of interest, seems to me a profoundly Southern book. This is not just because of its evocation of the contrasts between the city (Atlanta) and the country, of the Appalachians and their wild rivers, and of the mountain people, for these are superficial Southernisms and could in one sense have been written by someone not from the South (though they reveal deep intimacy of knowledge). No, it is Southern in its spirit. It is yet another version of the fall, that myth which peculiarly haunts the Southern mind and which we have found in Faulkner, Madison Jones, Allen Tate and Andrew Lytle. Here is the anti-Jeffersonian, anti-Enlightenment point of view with regard to nature that animated Madison Jones' earlier novels. We must not go out into the wilderness, which is a metaphor for the world, expecting that we can order our destinies, that its evils will be overcome by sense, pleasantness and preparedness. Yet, as in the works of all major Southern writers, nature is the object of a deeper passion than it ever is to the enlightened humanist. For these Southerners, a knowledge of its mysteries, which can never be more than partial, is cathartic for the human soul.

It was interesting and pleasant to me, too, to realize that when James Dickey wanted to illustrate the natural goodness of Drew, the "best" of the four men and the "friend who died," and to show the simple but real communication he had with his fellow humans, he made him a keen amateur bluegrass musician. James Dickey is himself a great bluegrass enthusiast and chose the music for the film, which may have done more to popularize the art form than any other single factor.

"Lonnie don't know nothin' but banjo-pickin'," the old man said. "He ain't never been to school; when he was little he used to sit out in the yard and beat on a lard can with a stick."

"What're we going to play, Lonnie?" Drew asked, his glasses opaque with pleasure.

Lonnie stood holding the banjo, looking off from us now with both eyes, the eyes splitting apart and all of us in the blind spot.

"Anything," the old man said. "Play anything."

Drew started in on "Wildwood Flower," picking it out at medium tempo and not putting in many runs. Lonnie dragged on the rubber bands and slipped the capo up. Drew started to come on with the volume; the Martin boomed out and over the dusty filling station. I had never heard him play so well, and I really began to listen deeply, moved as an unmusical person is moved when he sees that the music is meant. After a little while it sounded as though Drew were adding another kind of sound to every note he played, a higher tinny echo of the melody, and then it broke on me that this was the banjo, played so softly and rightly that it sounded like Drew's own fingering. I could not see Drew's face, but the back of his neck was sheer joy. . . . For the last couple of minutes of the song, Drew slid down and went over and stood beside Lonnie. They put the instruments together and leaned close to each other . . . and something rare and unrepeatable took hold of the way I saw them, the demented country kid and the big-faced decent man, the minor civic leader and hedge clipper.[67]

Northward my bus traveled up the coast road to North Carolina. At night all that could be seen were garishly illuminated "tropical" miniature golf courses, horrendous statues of giraffes and camels glowing in the dark, the lights of motel after motel, and just occasionally, for relief, a glimpse of dark shimmering water on which (so far) humans have been unable to impose their amusement baubles.

In North Carolina I was to see Reynolds Price, whose words on the South as a "Separate Country" had been a catalyst for me.

Reynolds Price

I MET REYNOLDS PRICE by appointment in the library at Duke University where he teaches. The library stands in the university's West Campus, a collection of flamboyantly Gothic Revival buildings set in extensive, lush parkland a mile or so from the center of Durham, North Carolina. The university is named after the tobacco magnate Washington Duke, a man whose great enterprise is shown in his having walked the 137 miles back to his home farm after the defeat of the Confederate army in which he served. It seems appropriate that Duke University owes its existence to tobacco, for tobacco is the principal crop of the surrounding countryside and provides the principal industries not only of Durham itself but of most other sizable towns in the area. And Reynolds Price's Mustian family, who feature lovingly in four of his works, are tobacco farmers. "Hell!" says young Milo Mustian, confronting the prospect of being a tobacco farmer all his life. "I don't even smoke."

For many years I had wanted to meet Reynolds Price, and had indeed corresponded with him. Born in 1933, he had his first novel published in 1962, *A Long and Happy Life*. I read it when I was a student at Oxford after my professor there, Lord David Cecil, recommended it to me as a first novel remarkable in both its artistry and its picture of life. So intense was my enjoyment of it that as soon as I finished it I immediately began reading it again. Since then I have read it, I suppose, a dozen times, and if any one work is responsible for my interest in the Southern novel, this is it.

A Long and Happy Life is a work of a quite extraordinary freshness. Its central character is a twenty-year-old girl, Rosacoke Mustian, who works as a telephone operator and lives with her family on a small-holding in the North Carolina countryside. Delight Baptist Church plays a considerable part in the life of her rural community, yet virginity is not a particularly treasured virtue. Rosacoke's brother Milo, among others, advises her that the only way she can keep her enigmatic and errant boyfriend, Wesley Beavers, is to give in to his sexual requests. Milo even sings her a bawdy song by way of counsel:

182

> *Pull up your petticoat, pull down your drawers,*
> *Give him one look at old Santy Claus.*[68]

Eventually, because she does in fact love him, Rosacoke accommodates Wesley, but as a result of this one act of lovemaking she becomes pregnant. This condition brings out in her self-indulgent lover a tenderness and an unsuspected fineness of spirit. Thus on one level the novel shows how a situation which has arisen through a pragmatic sexual ethic (healthy rural cynicism and modern liberation combined) can vindicate age-old wisdom about the sovereignty and redemptive nature of love. The novel ends at Christmas with the Delight Baptist Church's annual pageant in which the pregnant Rosacoke takes the part of Mary, holding in her arms a friend's baby:

> He seemed the safest thing still, seemed shut for the night, so while they sung the last verse around her . . . she looked on at him, and under her eyes his lips commenced to move, just the corners at first, slow as if they were pulled like tides by the moon, as if he might wake to end some dream, but his eyes didn't open, didn't flicker, and his lips pulled on till at last he had made what was almost a smile, for his own reasons and for no more than three seconds but as if, even in his sleep, he knew of love.[69]

It is a poetic close to the novel, but Reynolds Price commented in his interview with the French critic Georges Gary: "It has always seemed to me that the ending of *A Long and Happy Life* is a very bleak ending indeed. It happens to occur in a really lovely atmosphere, a Christmas pageant, a lovely ritualistic atmosphere; but the future of those two children was pretty bleak, and their child's was going to be just as bleak." The reader can indeed sense this at the same time as being stirred and inspirited by the tribute to love. *A Long and Happy Life* though it abounds in lyrical evocations of the countryside and of occasions of human happiness, cannot be accused of shirking the harsh side of existence. The novel opens with the funeral of Rosacoke's old friend, a black girl called Mildred Sutton who died giving birth to a child fathered by she didn't know whom. The central section of the novel is taken up with the death of Rosacoke's brother's baby and the effect of this on the other members of the family.

Perhaps what impresses one most about *A Long and Happy Life* is the triumphant individuality of the characters, who are presented by the author with mystery, affection and love. Rosacoke was based on the kind of girl he went to junior high school with, and her brother Milo, perhaps the richest of the portraits, is drawn from boys he knew in adolescence. Reynolds Price shows us his people by means of several devices he is to use extensively and very individually in his subsequent novels—the quotation of letters, particularly those between loved ones; badinage between friends and members of a family which sheds light on their mutual relationships and illumines all the personalities involved; and descriptions of moments when the characters confront their own sexuality and stand in acknowledged relationship to their own loins.

So real were the Mustian family and their neighbors to Reynolds Price that he has written three other works in which they appear, the moving long short story "A Chain of Love" (in *The Names and Faces of Heroes*), the novel *A Generous Man* (1966), and most recently a play, *Early Dark*, in which the events of *A Long and Happy Life* are presented again in dramatic form. "But," says Reynolds Price, "the play is not the novel dramatized. It is rather the same general set of actions, the same few people seen by a different man who stands elsewhere and sees otherwise. The story of the play differs therefore from the novel's as two alert but separate witnesses' versions of a complex event will inevitably and instructively differ."[70] This statement shows Reynolds Price's gift of seeing people and events as separate from himself, to be approached with wonder and with awe.

When I met Reynolds Price he had but lately returned from New York where *Early Dark* had received its first performance. He had been delighted with the performances of the young actors who had taken the parts of Wesley (a character he was fond of, though he observed that women readers have never cared much for him.) and Rosacoke; he praised them for the way they had tried to envisage these characters' lives away from the text, and he had hung photographs of them in his house. Reynolds Price has said in his conversations with William Ray (published by the Memphis State University Library): ". . . if I talk or think about my own work, I find myself thinking about it in the way that most critics think is awfully old-fashioned and corny and nineteenth century—simply as books about people, as books about other human beings. If I want to talk about my people, I essentially want to talk about . . . what Milo's life is or is not like as it seems to me: about what I think there is, in a very old-fashioned way, to learn about human life, human behavior, from the contemplation of a life presented truly and a little more neatly and visibly than would actually be possible."[71] But he does qualify this statement by saying: "I'm not *nuts* about the characters. I don't think they really have lives which continue after the book ends."

This, last remark indicates that the characters do not possess a fantasy significance for him. Nevertheless, they are very real to him. In conversation with me Reynolds Price gave me an account of how Milo would feel and talk about black people. This was not only interesting for the light it shed on a convincingly drawn fictional character, but in the way it illuminated the attitudes of Milo's kind of North Carolina country people.

Reynolds Price lives, by himself, about halfway between Duke University and the university town of Chapel Hill. He drove me to his house through pretty woodland. I remembered what he had written in an essay on the Southern novel in 1971:

> Today I can leave my house, midway between Duke University and Chapel Hill, walk five hundred yards and be in houses and among people, white and black, who could today conduct mutually intelligible, agreeing dialogues with their resurrected great-grandparents and who, for all that, do not see themselves as isolated islands of the past but as typical of the world around them. I can drive sixty miles to the house where I was born, in a town of two hundred; visit my aunts (whose mother—my grandmother whom I clearly remember—was kissed by General Lee in 1870), submerge with them gladly in days of memory—the scared hilarious appalling past we led through us again in the sacred forms (each word as rigid in its place and function as a phrase of the Mass, as productive of promise, release, joy). And not only I—my niece, age three, already listens closely to the same ceremonies; and though she is a visitor, how can I guess what strata are slowly, immovably depositing in her?[72]

Thus, apart from a three-year spell in England as a Rhodes Scholar at Oxford and a return visit there in 1961–1962, Reynolds Price has spent all his life in North Carolina. He attended Duke University as an undergraduate and returned there a teacher in 1958. ("I've really spent . . . my life within fifty miles, sixty-five miles of where you and I are sitting right now; and have no intention of spending the rest of it anywhere else, certainly no *hope* of spending the rest of it anywhere else.")

But he does see North Carolina as part of a greater whole:

> As I've said in several essays, the South is a country larger than France; and I can travel from Durham, North Carolina to Jackson, Mississippi, which is a distance of 800 miles, and find that people are still speaking almost exactly the same dialect that I have grown up with and known all my life, whereas I can go from Durham, North Carolina to Philadelphia, a distance of 400 miles, and find them speaking an utterly different dialect. . . . So it's not so much a matter of geographical distance as it is of a prevailing tradition over a large part of the country.[73]

In the grounds of Reynolds Price's house is a beautiful sequestered little lake; he asked me to be careful of copperheads as we walked to the front entrance of the house. Its interior reveals the same fastidious, individualistic artistry that distinguishes all his fiction. In the living room hang many pictures—a Picasso etching, works by Sutherland and Philip Sutton—and Japanese Noh masks and various Indian artefacts. Elsewhere in the house are fine Japanese prints. The fiction of Reynolds Price displays a careful composition and structural unity that are akin to a painter's (indeed, to be a painter was his first ambition), while they also possess certain ritualistic elements that make his interest in Japanese Noh and Kabuki eminently explicable. His last novel, *The Surface of Earth* (1975), in its multiple quests, the many generative and symbolic encounters between one character and another with their meaningful yet puzzling questions and answers, seems to partake of the nature of an antique and mysterious ritual.

Reynolds Price is a handsome man with large liquid dark eyes and the most mobile face of anyone I have ever met. He has a beautiful deep voice, mobile, too, in its inflections. His conversation is imaginative, intimate, personal and yet entirely unegotistic, and makes completely organic yet always stimulating changes from the serious to the humorous, from the public to the private, from the almost metaphysical to the gossippy and back again, all the time retaining a certain unity of tone.

I had written to him three years before my visit on the subject of his latest novel, *The Surface of Earth*, immense in size, ambition and achievement and by far his greatest work so far. Between *A Long and Happy Life* and this latest work came two novels, *A Generous Man* (1966) and *Love and Work* (1968), two volumes of short stories, *The Names and Faces of Heroes* (1963) and *Permanent Errors* (1970), and a rich and memorable volume of essays, *Things Themselves* (1972).

A Generous Man is a strange book. I can think of nothing else quite like it, and I think it requires more than one reading. At its center is fifteen-year-old Milo Mustian whom we met, nine years later on in his life, in *A Long and Happy Life*. The Milo of the second novel differs importantly from the Milo of the first. At twenty-four Milo had a coarseness, a bluntness of response to emotional predicaments, though we can sense a lurking but dormant sensitivity at times. The Milo in *A Generous Man* is however—for the few days that the novel covers—a radiant being, casting life-enhancing light on all with whom he comes in contact. When the novel opens it is morning; the night before, Milo lost his virginity and now he has found a new self. He rejoices in the sexual identity that has, it seems, descended like a gift upon him, and this innocent delight he communicates to those around him, men and women, old and young. Reynolds Price spoke of this rejoicing as something he thought very American, and in particular very Southern, but he asked me whether I had during my own adolescence encountered certain youths who, a little in advance of their fellows, were in some way transfigured by their own awareness of a newly burgeoned sexuality. And of course I had. Milo further reminds certain people he comes across of a dead man, Tommy Ryden, with whom he seems to have some special kinship. Indeed, Tommy's ghost makes an appearance during the course of the story.

This last fact alone should indicate that *A Generous Man* is not the realistic novel that its predecessor was, that it has an almost *Magic Flute*-like nature with its initiations into manhood and its searches and eruptions of the preternatural. The narrative tension of the work is provided by a quest of a curious kind. Lost in the woods are Milo's simple brother Rato, Rato's beloved old dog suspected of being mad with rabies, and a python called Death which has escaped from a traveling show and whose thoughts we are later given! A search party is organized to find the missing, and Milo is a key member of it, though he finds other things as well pertaining to his recent assumption of manhood. The symbolic nature of the search party is emphasized in the prayer that Milo somewhat reluctantly speaks to the other members:

Milo's lips were suddenly separate from his face, red and long and as clearly, firmly lined on his skin as if worked with a blade and intended for silence. But they moved, opened and this was provided—"Today we are hunting three valuable things that have given some pleasure to several people. My brother Rato is valuable to us. His mad dog Phillip is valuable to him. And death is valuable to the Provo ladies. Help us to always remember that, all day today. Help us be worthy of what we are hunting. Help us to live with whatever we find."[74]

These last words have an ironical significance. The generosity referred to in the title is that of which any youth could be capable after discovering the richness of sex. As the local sheriff says to Milo: "It is eleven twenty-five, a clear broad morning that will be noon soon. You are fifteen, a man, and the Lord has hung gifts on you like a *hatrack*. . . . Don't wait, don't wait. Don't think it's morning when it's late afternoon."

And yet Milo's transfiguration is to be short-lived, however he may later deploy his sexual powers. After Milo and the missing Rato have met in a deeply touching scene, what can Milo do but return home and prepare for the life of tobacco farmer that he has always known awaits him? Reynolds Price comments:

But then what on earth would Milo have done had he left home? All right suppose Rato is actually dead; suppose Lois really agrees to follow him; what the hell is he going to do? At *best* he can go to Raleigh or Richmond or Norfolk or some nearby city—Henderson, North Carolina—get a job, you know, working in a carwash or feed-and-seed store. The boy is quite unequipped to pursue the sort of knight-errantry that he seems to have in mind, that he seems to feel is required by the situation of the world. . . . He's doomed. He goes on to become this rather raucous, burnt-out jokester that we see . . . [in] *A Long and Happy Life*.[75]

I used to feel that *A Generous Man* was too teasing a blend of the realistic and the non-realistic. I no longer think this; it now seems to me a shapely and haunting whole. All the same, I do think that its fantasy elements prevent its having the wider emotional reference of Reynolds Price's first and last novels.

The Mustian family are country people of scant education (though they are complex psychologically). The hero of the third novel, *Love and Work*, is a university teacher like his creator; his is a highly educated sensibility, steeped particularly in the major poets of English literature. Yet for me *Love and Work* is Reynolds Price's least satisfactory novel—Thomas Eborn, the main character, is only partially alive. He never lives for me either as a member of a university faculty or as a married man; on the other hand, his reaction to his mother's death is finely done, and even better is his attempted re-creation of his parents' courtship through their own words. These pages make us realize the creative elements missing elsewhere in the novel. Yet in its exploration of parent-child relations it marks a step forward.

Perhaps of all Reynolds Price's writings between *A Long and Happy Life* and *The Surface of Earth* some of the short stories and essays are the most successful. The title story of *The Names and Faces of Heroes* is a beautiful account of the relationship between a father and his young son (whom he affectionately nicknames "Preacher"); it is partially autobiographical and anticipates the final section of Reynolds Price's latest masterwork. "Uncle Grant" is a heartfelt portrait of an old black associate of his family. And the essays of *Things Themselves* cover in personal, idiosyncratic but thorough ways many subjects including Milton, Rembrandt, the Southern novel, and the much admired Eudora Welty:

> *The Optimist's Daughter* is Eudora Welty's strongest, richest work. For me, that is tantamount to saying that no one in America has yet shown stronger, richer, more useful fiction. All through my three readings, I've thought of Turgenev, Tolstoy, Chekhov . . . and not as masters or originals but as peers for breadth and depth.[76]

Reynolds Price made preparations for *The Surface of Earth* for twelve years before he began writing it. Its topography and chronology are very precisely worked out. North Carolina and Virginia constitute the novel's setting in place; in time it moves from May 1903 to June 1944. The events of 1903 and 1904 dictate the happenings and relationships of the greater part of the novel, and so may need summarizing here.

Forrest Mayfield, a high-minded schoolmaster, intellectual, and, despite his years (he is thirty-two), still a virgin, falls desperately in love with one of his pupils. Eva Kendal is sixteen years old and comes from a long-established land-holding family. Apart from a much older sister, Forrest himself has virtually no family; his mother is dead and his father disappeared when he was only a boy, and perhaps because of this lack he cannot conceive the damage Eva will do to her kin and to herself if she runs away with him. Nevertheless she does so, her family renounce her, and Nemesis would seem to follow. While giving birth to a son Eva experiences the most appalling agony, and meanwhile her mother, overcome by her daughter's recalcitrance, kills herself. This terrible act—itself a reenactment of an earlier tragedy—is crucial to the destinies of Forrest, Eva and their child. For Eva leaves her husband to return to the home she has betrayed and violated, there to expiate her crime by her devotion to the other members of the family. She takes with her her baby son Robinson. Forrest, brokenhearted and desolate, then embarks on a search for his own lost father.

This sequence of events engenders tensions which are felt—and have to be worked through—not only by the protagonists themselves but by their relations and descendants. Eva tells Forrest after their separation that she is still grateful to him for his love. "But I also know I was wrong, wrong to think you were all that watched or joyed in me. There were others, from the start. I didn't know or just didn't see—I've been good at blindness and have suffered for that. I've made them suffer. Some of them still do, need me and suffer both."[77]

Pain is thus seen to be inextricably bound up with even the happiest of our actions, even those done for love (something symbolically emphasized in the agonies, mortal or near-mortal, which are experienced in childbirth by almost all the women in the book). Reynolds Price is surely reminding us in this opening section of the biblical account of man's fall from grace, a parallel borne out by Eva's very name and by Forrest's remark to her: "I know you had your reasons; I never understood them. I doubt you do, whatever you say. I doubt any human since Adam understands any true full reason." The novel suggests that full understanding of any event is not possible for us. Eva's mother, in the letter she writes her daughter before her suicide, says: "I do not want to live in a world that will harbor and succor a heart like yours . . . you have torn the lives of others by seeking the sole satisfaction of body." But Eva and Forrest's lovemaking, despite its tragic repercussions, is shown as something pure, lovely and good, qualities found in other love passages later in the novel.

As I have already said, the story of Eva and Forrest determines but does not constitute the main body of *The Surface of Earth*. For its central figure is the son of their brief, doomed union, Rob Mayfield. He has a certain kinship to the Milo Mustian of *A Generous Man*, both in temperament and in the situation in which we first fully encounter him, and Reynolds Price agreed with this when I put the similarity to him.

At the opening of the second book of the novel Rob is seventeen, handsome and ardent in his confrontation of life. He is soon to prove his sexual capabilities and the light of the proud, newly fledged male still attends him. He lives with his mother's family in a state of ignorance of anything concerning his father. The quests of Rob Mayfield form the central action of the novel. His first quests are for his parents—a quest of the spirit in the case of his mother, who seems to him almost unbearably remote. He is unaware of why she has withdrawn from life. Rob's search for Forrest parallels, of course, Forrest's own earlier quest for *his* father. Then come Rob's quests for himself; these involve sexual experience, love and a tragically brief marriage. The fulfillments, or attempts at fulfillment, of these quests lead inevitably to repetitions and reenactments of the earlier quests. In the last part of the novel, set at the time of World War II, Rob searches and is searched for by his own son, Hutch.

Throughout the novel there is a sense of movement, of the driving desire to attain rest and to find one's proper spiritual home through the ceaseless journeys the realization of this desire must entail. This "yearning for rest" is summed up in the book's epigraph from St. Augustine: "But You the Good which need no good, rest always, being Yourself Your rest. What man can teach another man that? What angel an angel? What angel a man?"

It should be clear that the sum total of Rob's relationships, of these searches of father for son, son for father, father for surrogate son and son for surrogate father can stand as a metaphor for the author's vision of life. As in myth, the meaning of the novel is to be sought in the sequence of events itself and in the interrelationship of the characters, for these embody major constituents of the human psyche. *The Surface of Earth* is thus a presentation in fictional form of the deepest urges and wishes of the human personality, of the cyclic discoveries each person has to make throughout life of his or her own identity.

The ambitiousness of this fictional enterprise is increased by the fact that Reynolds Price attempts a resolution of the themes of quest and quarry. His belief in fiction as an enhancing force in life— testified to in his essays on his own work and on other people's and in his conversation with me—means that he ends this vast novel with his hero finding the peace of mind and spirit that has been denied him for much of his restless career. He finds this through a full confrontation of the diverse elements in him, by acknowledgment of the many currents of love flowing within him, and by the realization too of his own unique individuality. Rob's young son Hutch also has his part to play in the resolution of the novel's many-stranded problems. For Hutch can be seen as the culmination, as it were, of these generations of emotionally estranged yet also emotionally interlinked individuals. It is surely of great significance that this sensitive, gentle, loving boy wants to become an artist. In his life, by his future work, Hutch will harmonize the varying and warring strains of his family, will vindicate its sufferings and give its emotional history shape and meaning. And his achievement as a painter will, one supposes, be analogous to Reynolds Price's as a writer.

For Reynolds Price's art in this novel is fully equal to the magnitude of the tasks he has set himself. For all the book's length, its intensity and pace of narrative are unflagging. And it has tremendous formal beauty. As in a symphony, themes appear only to be transformed and then restated; incidents, objects and conversations stand in contrapuntal relationship, one to another and acquire symbolic stature. Intricately done, too, is the generous use of dreams—dreams in which the characters undergo strange and significant mutations which in turn influence their waking behavior and reactions, dreams in which the dreamers apprehend their own and others' metaphysical predicaments. Both types of dream contribute to the overall emotional and imaginative effect of the novel.

Yet the novel's complex mythic structure never dwarfs its people. As in the author's other books they move seemingly independently of their creator, who often appears to stand in the relation of a caring confidant—hence his copious use of their letters, richer and subtler even than in the previous works. *The Surface of Earth* contains a veritable gallery of fully and sympathetically drawn people —Forrest and Eva, Eva's spinster sister Rena, Forrest's black kinsman and helper Grainger, and above all Rob Mayfield himself. Rob, so intimately and lovingly apprehended, is at once the novel's center and its finest achievement. There is, one feels, no aspect of him that Reynolds Price has not thought out, yet ultimately he remains, as every human being should, a mystery.

The novel in my view is a great one; indeed, I think it stands unsurpassed among fiction written in the English language since World War II. Its effect is a cumulative one for all its many incidental beauties, and it is hard to give satisfactory examples of its art. All the same I want to try. Here is Rob writing a letter to his cold, distant mother while on vacation; he is writing in the belief that his mother has suddenly revealed an inner warmth for him:

> God-knows-where, near Fayetteville
> May 22, 1921

Dear Mother,

I hope you are well and all happy at home. This will show I am well despite the mosquitos (the one on my forehead right now feels shod). Happy I will not claim to be. Was it you that made me go on this party or was I really fool enough to come, free-will? Anyhow I'm here and will stay, if I live, for the whole promised week; but you may not know me on my return—swollen past recognition with bites or wasted to nothing with chills and fever. Get the chill tonic out! . . .

I am getting plenty of time to think about my future that Aunt Rena is always preaching about. What I think is this, I will come on back at the end of this party and take the depot job with Uncle Kennerly. Who knows, I may own the railroad eventually—all ladders have bottoms—but in the event I can live there at home and help you out any way needed. You may recall that I have thought a long time about going off for a little at least and testing myself elsewhere, anywhere, *away*. You know too I guess that the point of that plan was hoping to force you to ask me to stay. For a while it looked bad! But what you gave me the morning after commencement turned the tide.

Now Mother, you can rest assured that whatever the next months and years hold for any of us in the way of trouble and loss, Rob will be on hand to offer his hand for what it's worth.[78]

What pathos there is in Rob's very young male appeal to his mother, how touching and noble, too, are his assurances of future devotion!

Here is a letter written by Rena, so strong, so lonely, to Rob on the eve of his wedding. Rob has been the true center of Rena's emotional life, though with the unintentional cruelty of youth he never, while living at home, appreciated his aunt's feelings. Now he receives this letter from her, accompanied by an old photograph:

Rob,

This is you and me nineteen years ago. I was clearing out the stable, much against Eva's will. She had tried to argue me out of it all morning, saying if I couldn't stand a little manure underfoot, Father had good strapping men for the job. I told her "None better than me," and went. So she had the grace to leave me alone for two hours, when I'd almost finished. Then she woke you up from your nap and dressed you—Eva made the sailor suit—and taught you a sentence to say to me. Then you both came to get me. Eva brought her Kodak. You were meant to stay with her, well back from the stable, and call out to me "Your beau is here." Then Eva would snap my picture as I came to the door all embarrassed (I never knew at *what*; there was surely no beau, in the yard or on the moon). She had just got her camera as a gift from Father; took her five years to stop catching people off balance. Anyhow you said your piece and I heard you; but I thought you said "Your boy is here," and I still think you did (what did you know of beaux?) so I trudged to the door with my rake to see you—me dirty as the rake—and you ran toward me while Eva was sighting ...

Well, I thought you were mine from then on out. I had prized you before, since the day she brought you home after Mother's death. But I took this as proof, and you never let me doubt it all the years since."[79]

Are not three lives illuminated by this letter—Rob's, Eva's and Rena's?

Much of Rob's career is a sorry affair, marked by confusion and indulgence. Toward the end of the book Rob makes love to a black woman he had known in his youth:

> He was speechless with thanks—for old help renewed with no prior claim of sacrifice or debt. He was not so much young and starting again as *himself* again. He felt what he'd always been in his depths (however long buried, drowned, assaulted, ignored) —a strong, gentle boy named Robinson Mayfield, who meant only good to the world and himself and would live to achieve it as trees do leaves, in silent perfection, the absence of doubt, a natural skill.[80]

It seems to me one of the novel's major triumphs that we feel this also.

Later that evening Reynolds Price took me out for a Mexican dinner in the enchanting neighboring town of Chapel Hill, home of the University of North Carolina. He was kind enough, too, to ask me to stay the night in his house. We talked into the small hours and then again over breakfast, eaten outside on the terrace.

At the time of my visit he had recently published *A Palpable God*, best described in the words of its subtitle: "Thirty Stories from the Bible with an Essay on the Origins and Life of Narrative." His interest in biblical narrative is revealed in the chronicles of *The Surface of Earth*. He said that he had been a Christian since his childhood and had never seriously departed from the faith, though he very rarely attended a church service of any kind. He said he had an eighteenth-century attitude to religion in many ways; he found inner piety and convictions very hard to talk about.

I praised the delineation of the black character Grainger in *The Surface of Earth*, and this led him to speak of the blacks in the South. He thought that many Southern children, particularly boys, had had their first experience of feminine warmth and care, unalloyed by genteel restrictions on demonstrativeness or notions of duty, in their relationships with their black nurse or servant. Where he had grown up in the countryside of east North Carolina there had been more blacks than whites. His father had often said that many of his greatest friends were black; boys in their early years were often able to forget color differences in their games, and later on sporting activities could unite them. All the same, people of his father's generation would not have been able to sit down to dinner

195

in their homes with black guests, and they rarely questioned the prevailing social code that there was a natural and unbridgeable gap between black and white. He said that had I traveled through the South in the days before desegregation I would have found the same friendliness between black and white that I had often observed on my present trip. Nevertheless, this did not mean that a cruel barrier did not exist. He thought, however, that the sexual advantage allegedly taken of black girls and women by white males had been much exaggerated, since emancipation anyway. Out of a wide range of acquaintance he could think of only a very few white men who had done so.

He thought Southern writers had benefited by the separation geography had imposed on them, preventing them from leading the literary coterie life that he thought too many English or New York writers led to the detriment of their art. Though he thought of himself as the "original indoors person," he found it of incalculable importance to himself and to his writing that he lived in the country. And I was reminded of what he had written in that fine essay on Southern literature, "Dodo, Phoenix or Tough Old Cock":

> So rocks and trees condemn our folly and our virtue, chasten our fret as buildings never can—scratch a farmer and find the tragic sense of life—yet they still can console us because they will submit to the pathetic fallacy, will absorb all our emotions, not simply our destructive emotions. Or—if consolation is impossible or irrelevant—illumination, clarification; because they offer us the only objects of meditation in the presence of which the literally human qualities of man can be distanced, comprehended, calmed, controlled. That is not merely the experience of Wordsworth and all the novelists of the world till 1922 but of Aeschylus, Jesus, Oedipus at Colonus, King Lear . . . many more than half of the people of the South still live in close proximity with a nature that beautifully, grandly asserts its permanence.[81]

As I traveled away from Durham in the bus I thought about Reynolds Price's remarks on the speech unity of the South. Of course, to a linguist there would be obvious differences from one region of the South to another, but to the visitor—and, it would seem to the insider, too—there is a common Southern way of talking which binds together the members of the various states. It is like no other accent in the world. It has a charm, a melancholy and a certain slowness that suggest a belief in taking time in dealings with other human beings. And, of course, it is by his accent that the Southerner is identified by others, and invites and receives conditioned responses. And Southerners say "yall" ("you all") every bit as much as they are meant to. This could be interpreted as another proof of the Southerner's seeing him or herself and others not in isolation but as part of an organic group. At any rate, I am inclined to think of it like that.

North Carolina was where Anne Tyler grew up, the youngest novelist of those discussed in this book and the subject of my last chapter. She attended Duke University and was taught by Reynolds Price. She now lives in Baltimore.

Anne Tyler

Row houses slipped past him in endless chains, with clusters of women slumped on all the stoops, fans turning lazily behind lace curtains, parlor windows full of madonnas and globe lamps and plastic flowers alternating with windows boarded up and CONDEMNED signs on the doors. Children were drinking grape Nehis. Men scuttled out from package stores with brown paper bags clutched to their chests. "Are you still sure you want to stop in Baltimore?" Peter asked.[82]

This passage from *The Clock Winder* (1972) is an excellent impressionistic rendering of Baltimore as it presents itself to someone approaching the city from the south. Indeed, some of its more dilapidated streets drew forth sad comments from other passengers on the bus as we drove in. Despite the old houses in Roland Park, the pleasant residential streets near Johns Hopkins University (Anne Tyler's own part of Baltimore), and its rather impressive situation, Baltimore is an ugly city. Anne Tyler, who confesses to a certain affection for it, thinks of Baltimore as a Southern city, and I agree with her.

It has certainly partaken of Southern history. The largest city of a slave-holding state uncertain of its future direction in the troubled prelude to the Civil War, its people were chastised for their Secessionist sympathies. Union troops were jeered at and pelted with missiles by the citizens as they marched through Baltimore. Provoked, the soldiers fired on the crowd and a number of people, mostly civilians, were killed. As a result Lincoln ordered the occupation of Baltimore by the army and the imprisonment of leading local pro-Confederates. Now a large black and Catholic population, a certain raunchiness in the downtown section particularly, the crumbling grandeur of some of its older houses, and the picturesque scruffiness of its artisan streets give it as strong a cousinship to New Orleans, Louisville and even Nashville as to Philadelphia or Boston. Anyway, its Southernness is probably to be found more in the attitudes and lifestyles of its families than in anything available to the visitor. Anne Tyler, a North Carolinian by upbringing and education, is in a position to assess this aspect.

Anne Tyler, married to an Iranian psychiatrist, with two daughters, is a beautiful woman with a quiet, intense and thoughtful manner. She is articulate about her work and expressed pleasure at the excellent reception her last novel, *Earthly Possessions*, received in both the United States and Britain. But I got the strong impression that her writing is a very private affair. It is the delineation of individuals and the spheres in which they find themselves that obsesses her, not her own fortune in the commercial or literary worlds. In this as in other ways she seemed to me very much a sister to her fellow Southern writers Walker Percy, Eudora Welty and Reynolds Price, and the fact that hers is a more urban life than theirs and that she is geographically closer to Washington, D.C., and New York is of little importance.

Anne Tyler told me of the great excitement she had felt in her teens on first reading Eudora Welty; here seemed to be a way of looking at and understanding the world that she herself knew. In particular some lines from the story "The Wide Net" made an impression on her:

> "She's smart too, for a girl," he said.
> "She's a lot smarter than her cousins in Beula," said Virgil. "And especially Edna Earle, that never did get to be what you'd call a heavy thinker. Edna Earle could sit and ponder all day on how the little tail or the "C" got through the "L" in a Coca-Cola sign."[83]

It is easy to understand, in the light of the work she was to do, why Anne Tyler responded to these lines: their humorous, affectionate delight in another person's idiosyncrasy is something abundantly present in all her own novels. It is something that can be detected in the very first sentences of her first book, *If Morning Ever Comes* (1964). "When Ben Joe Hawkes left home he gave his sister Susannah one used guitar, six shelves of National Geographic, a battered microscope, and a foot-high hourglass. All of these things he began to miss as soon as he hit New York."

Highly characteristic of her is a paragraph describing Ben Joe only a few pages later:

> Ben Joe started reading the society section (of the newspaper), holding it upside-down in front of him. He had started learning to read when he was three, but his parents wanted him to wait until school age; they made him stand facing them when they

read him bedroom stories, so that the book was turned the wrong way around. It wasn't until too late that they realized he was reading upside down. Usually he read the right way now unless he was bored, and then upside-down words came to his mind more clearly. He held the newspaper at arm's length and frowned, studying an upside-down description of a golden anniversary where the couple had had another wedding performed all over again.[84]

The list of objects left by Ben Joe tells us that he is a fairly ordinary person, whose manners and tastes would not normally arouse comment. The account of his reading habits, however, lets us know that he has—as each of us surely has—certain quirks and tastes peculiar to himself which, when seen in combination with his other characteristics, render him a unique being. Anne Tyler has the ability to see people in terms of both the qualities they share with others and those that make them endearingly or bewilderingly different.

Ben Joe's double way of reading the newspaper can be seen as analogous to his creator's way of reading people. We get the feeling that her characters are taken from communities or households which the author might have known herself; her novels work on us largely through their seeming verisimilitude, through the exactness of Anne Tyler's ear and eye. But her people are often compelled into highly idiosyncratic lifestyles or relationships by imaginative drives and visions that might surprise someone casually meeting them. Saturated in a sense of reality though they are, Anne Tyler's novels contain many instances of curious, wilful or wayward behavior, but never any acts that we could not imagine coming up in the course of ordinary gossip.

Gossip or the local newspaper do not seem incongruous in connection with Anne Tyler's work, highly sophisticated though her art is, any more than in the work of Peter Taylor or Eudora Welty. Indeed, the central action of *A Slipping-Down Life* (1970) sprang from something that Anne Tyler read about a wild Elvis Presley fan. It would come as no surprise were we to learn that the kidnapping of Charlotte in *Earthly Possessions* originated from a similar source, or that Anne Tyler wrote about the eccentric Emerson family in *The Clock Winder* or the individualistic Pecks in *Searching for Caleb* (1977) because she had overheard local gossip about real people. Anne Tyler stressed the importance to her of the person-centeredness of Southern talk. In other places, she said, a story was told because an event was remarkable. In the South stories were told about and around individual people. That story would lead on to others, each illustrating some facet of the man or woman under discussion. She had learned much from talking to both white and black workers in the North Carolina tobacco fields as a schoolgirl. Their burning interest in people, in all their varieties, habits and unpredictabilities, had an immense influence on her.

Anne Tyler described herself to me as "the original commune child." She grew up in a series of utopian communities in North Carolina, most of Quaker connection. Her father was an ardent Quaker and pacifist. She says that as a girl she spoke two languages, that of her family and their circle, and that of some of her friends; she knew well people from the "white trash" class. So Anne Tyler stood at enough distance from the world of her youthful aquaintances to be able to see them with an interested curiosity, while her own background gave her insight into the way people attempt to live out their idealism. This last insight bears its finest fruit in *Searching for Caleb*. Moreover, a ready contrast was presented to Anne Tyler in her early years which has surely enriched her fiction, the contrast between the ideology and enlightenment that characterized her own family and the traditional conservative mores of the rural South.

Anne Tyler was very young indeed—twenty-three and twenty-four respectively—when her first two novels were published. These she now virtually disowns, though they can now be enjoyed in paperback editions and have by no means been forgotten by the public. The second, *The Tin Can Tree* (1965), contains many good things—the feeling of James, the central male character, for his invalid brother Ansell; Joan's relationship with the Pike family, who adopt her after their bereavement; James' photography—but it is too static in some parts and too jerky in its forward movements in others to rank with the rest of Anne Tyler's productions. But its predecessor, *If Morning Ever Comes* (1964), is a delightful novel distinguished by a rare and wholly unsentimental sweetness.

It recounts the unexpected homecoming from New York City to a little North Carolina town of a gentle, thoughtful young man who is the only son of a large family. The novel presents us with

Ben Joe's relationships to his grandmother, mother, his dead father's mistress, his tempestuous elder sister Joanna, who also returns home after a long absence, and to a former girl friend. The novel anticipates Anne Tyler's maturer work in its absence of irony in the delineation of human quirks and foibles; like Reynolds Price, she makes much use of badinage between members of a family or between people who know one another well in order to illuminate personality. It is also characteristic of its author in its delighted rendering of the humdrum and in the importance it attaches to kindly, warm sexual relationships.

I know of no woman writer who writes more sympathetically about men than Anne Tyler; she can describe them with affection as well as with stronger emotions and sees them not as objects of desire or embodiments of impersonal forces but simply as individual beings. She said she had always had happy experiences of men; she enjoyed good relations with her father and three brothers and is now happily married. But I also think that Anne Tyler's novels bring to fruition a peculiarly Southern quality of tenderness where sexual relations are concerned. This quality is present in *If Morning Ever Comes* as it is in its successors. The following is Ben Joe traveling back to New York on the train with his former girlfriend, now his fiancée, asleep by his side:

Behind his own eyelids the future rolled out like a long deep rug, as real as the past or the present ever was. He knew for a certainty . . . the exact look of anxiety that would be in Shelley's eyes when they reached New York. And the flustered wedding that would embarrass him to pieces, and the careful little apartment where Shelley would always be waiting for him, like his own little piece of Sandhill transplanted, and asking what was wrong if he acted different from the husbands in the home-making magazines, but loving him anyway, in spite of that. And then years on top of years, with Shelley growing older and smaller, looking the way her mother had, knowing by then all his habits and all his smallest secrets and at night, when his nightmares came, waking him and crooning to him until he drifted back to sleep, away from the thin warm arms. And they might even have a baby, a boy with round blue eyes and small struggling feet that she would cover in the night, crooning to him too. Ben Joe would watch, as he watched tonight, keeping guard and making up for all the hurried things that he had ever done. He shifted in his seat then, frowning; what future was ever a certainty? Who knew how many other people, myriads of people that he had met and loved before, might lie beneath the surface of the single-faced person he loved now?[85]

In one respect, however, *If Morning Ever Comes* is not very typical of its creator; it is somewhat episodic and lacks firm structure, as Anne Tyler herself points out. Normally she sees the action of her novel as a single entity, with the end (though usually undramatic and admitting of many possibilities) implicit in the beginning.

Such is the case in *A Slipping-Down Life,* the first novel of which Anne Tyler feels proud. Indeed, she speaks of it with great tenderness. Fat, not very clever, teenaged Evie, daughter of a somewhat aloof school teacher, develops an obsession for an eccentric, handsome young rock singer called Drumstrings Casey. The nature of his musical routine is unusual:

> [Evie] heard a clanging of guitar strings, a patter of drums which sometimes subdued the guitar into a mere jingle at the end of a beat, and a strong reedy voice that softened consonants and spun out vowels. "Nnhnn!" he said occasionally, close to the microphone. Then the singing stopped, but the music went on. Drumstrings turned his narrow, unseeing face toward the audience.
> "*Why do you walk on my nerves this way?*" he asked suddenly. Evie turned and looked around her.
> "*Have I got to tell you again? Have I got to say it?*
> *We met him on the mountain. He was picking blueberries.*
> *She was emptying trashcans.*
> *Don't leave now!*"
> The guitar grew louder, and the drums along with it. The song started up no different than before, with the same blurred words. Not many people clapped when it was over.[86]

Disconnected sentences and remarks overheard or read are an inextricable part of Drum's act, which Evie responds to with such frenzied enthusiasm (though she is not musical) that she later cuts his name in her forehead with her nail scissors, but backward so that the letters can only be read in the mirror. Drum is not a little embarrassed by this, and he is not attracted to Evie, anyway. But his manager persuades him of the publicity advantages, so she is courted, with the outcome that Evie and Drum marry. Though their marriage has its tenderness, it has no solid foundation and founders.

A Slipping-Down Life deserves, in my view, minor classic status. For with humor, compassion and artistic economy it presents the history of a relationship that has a metaphorical significance for our current age, one in which pop music is a principal medium by which a male asserts his attractions and powers over the female (a medium which moreover originated in the South). The novel also illuminates the hunger for excitement that devours even the least likely people, such as fat Evie, and small though its canvas is, it provides valuable insights into that amorphous, often emotionally undirected section of society, the lower middle class.

Anne Tyler's subsequent four novels—*The Clock Winder*, *Celestial Navigation* (1974), *Searching for Caleb* and *Earthly Possessions* can be seen as a group, for they possess certain important features in common. Each book is densely populated; starting with a family or household, Anne Tyler introduces a diversity of people who regularly impinge on these few interrelated lives—lodgers, clients, neighbors, parishioners, obscure family connections, boyfriends or girlfriends or relatives and so forth. The Southern regard for the family and the community—so strongly present in the work of Faulkner, Eudora Welty, Peter Taylor and Reynolds Price—accounts in part for this; so too, I feel, do Anne Tyler's feelings for the Russian novelists she studied at Duke University. Chekhov and Turgenev also present, in shapely works of fiction, a large gallery of related persons who define themselves in part through these diverse relationships. From the Southern tradition and the Russian masters, too, may come another conspicuous feature of Anne Tyler's mature work: without sacrificing unity, each book contains and makes an appeal to a wide range of emotions which follow one another in a succession that always seems utterly convincing. The author from the start has suggested a mystery and ultimate unpredictability in her characters. Thus Timothy Emerson in *The Clock Winder* seems to us, as he does to the heroine, Elizabeth, a bumbling, sensitive, kindly buffoon, though like her we have uneasy glimpses of the world of pain inside him. His suicide comes as a sudden shock to us

204

as it does to Elizabeth and to his family, especially when we remember how amused we were at his earlier behavior. But then we think, as we surely would in life, that we ought to have known, we ought to have realized.

Yet Elizabeth recovers from the effect of the appalling action she witnesses. She does not forget Timothy, of course, but his memory becomes overlaid with other experiences. The last chapter of the novel shows her happily married to Timothy's brother, who had long loved her. How then can we define the emotion with which we close the book? All of Anne Tyler's novels escape emotional pigeonholing in this way, both overall and in their parts. Her concern is with both the complexity of human beings and the complexity of life which thrusts tragic and ludicrous situations alike on them.

Because of her interest in a variety of people and the experiences they have, Anne Tyler's novels cover considerable periods of time. But because each of her novels springs from a single vision, a unified picture of a life or several intertwined lives, she is not content to write a sprawling, middle-brow chronicle. Each novel attempts an experiment with form in its presentation of the characters in time. *The Clock Winder* gives us a series of dramatic pictures of Elizabeth and the Emersons from 1960 to 1970. The last of these, she felt, required a sudden change of vision and perspective in order for us to see more completely the people whose fortunes we have been following. Consequently the last pages are presented through the eyes of both the Emerson son with whom we have been least concerned and his delightful foolish young wife. This device seems to be a complete success, and it may have suggested the more elaborate narrative experimentation of *Celestial Navigation*. Like *The Clock Winder*, this novel uses dramatic pictures to present the differences in the characters and their mutual relationships over a long period (in this case thirteen years). But here each succeeding picture is presented through the vision of a different person. The novel in part demanded this, for its central character, Jeremy Pauling, with whom Anne Tyler says she feels a special empathy, is a very eccentric person—reclusive, affectionate, life-shy, and psychologically unable to go beyond the block in which his house stands—as well as a talented and imaginative sculptor. In order for us to accept him, it is necessary that we see him from a variety of viewpoints, including his own.

Anne Tyler's next book, *Searching for Caleb*, is perhaps her richest and most ambitious. She described writing it as like being a guest at a large and marvelous party. Here is an even more individualistic family than the Emersons of *The Clock Winder*, and there are more generations, too (four to be exact). This and the eccentric, peripatetic lifestyle of the married couple at the book's center, Justine and Duncan, must have posed considerable problems for the author. How would she handle such complex and diversified matter? In fact she relies on two devices—an extended flashback and a quest by two of the characters for a lost relative. Both are interesting in themselves, but I think that they necessarily involve certain sacrifice of artistic unity. Our attention is directed away from what is surely the dominating theme of the book, the way tender love triumphs over the difficulties imposed on Duncan and Justine's marriage through Duncan's wilful, erratic temperament. But when our attention *is* focused on Duncan and Justine we are often deeply moved, and Anne Tyler's handling of their relationship proves her, I think, to be a novelist of the first rank.

Here Justine remembers her early fascination for Duncan, her wild cousin:

But Duncan Peck was an evil, evil boy, and all his cousins worshiped him. Duncan was prankish and reckless and wild. He had a habit of disappearing. (Long after she was grown, Justine could still close her eyes and hear his mother calling him—a soft-voiced lady from southern Virginia but my, couldn't she sing out when she had to! "Dun-KUNN? Dun-KUNN?" floated across the twilit lawn, with no more response than a mysterious rustle far away or a gleam of yellow behind the trees, rapidly departing.) While the rest of the cousins seemed content to have only one another for friends, Duncan was always dragging in strangers and the wrong kind of strangers at that, ten-year-old boys with tobacco breaths and BB guns and very poor grammar. His cousins took piano lessons and hammered out "Country Gardens" faithfully for one half hour a day, but all Duncan would play was a dented Hohner harmonica—"Chattanooga Choo Choo" complete with whistles and a chucka-chucka and a country-sounding twang that delighted the children and made the grown-ups flinch. His great-grandma complained that he was impudent and dishonest. It was perfectly obvious that he was lying to any adult who asked him a question, and his lies were extreme, an insult to the intelligence. Also he was accident-prone. To his cousins that was the best part of all. How did he find so many accidents to get into? And such gory ones! He never just broke a bone, no, he had to have the bone sticking *out*, and all his cousins crowding around making sick noises and asking if they could touch it. He was always having a finger dangle by one thread, a concussion that allowed him to talk strangely and draw absolutely perfect freehand circles for one entire day, a purple eye or an artery opened or a tooth knocked horizontal and turning black. And on top of all that, he was never at a loss for something to do. You would never see *him* lolling about the house asking his mother for ideas; he had his own ideas, none of which she approved of. His mind was a flash of light. He knew how to make the electric fan drive Richard's little tin car, he could build traps for animals of all kinds including humans, he had invented a dive-proof kite and a written code that looked like nothing but slants and uprights. Tangled designs for every kind of machine littered his bedroom floor, and he had all those cousins just doting on him and anxious to do the manual labor required. If he had been a cruel boy, or a bully, they never would have felt that way, but he wasn't.[87]

It is easy to imagine the delights of such a person and easy too to imagine how difficult these very qualities would make him later on in his life, for the adult world beyond the family may not provide the cushioning necessary for the comfortable gratification of his whims and vagaries. But I think it is a triumph of Anne Tyler's art that, through all the reverses and humiliations of Duncan's career, (all of which mean hardship for his wife) neither the reader nor Justine ever loses sight of the engaging youth he had been.

Nevertheless I consider Anne Tyler's most recent novel her finest. *Earthly Possessions* has a formal beauty, a freedom from the self-indulgence one feels at times in *Searching for Caleb*, and a heartening extension of sympathy. The novel opens with the kidnapping at gunpoint of Charlotte Emory at the very moment that she is withdrawing money from her bank in order to leave her preacher husband. Alternate chapters present Charlotte's journey southward to Florida with her captor and her autobiography, from her lonely early years to the tense recent months of her marriage. This alternation is beautifully carried out, most noticeably in the last quarter of the novel when past and present begin to converge. What is outstanding in this novel is what I have praised in its Southern peers *The Golden Apples, The Fathers,* and *The Surface of Earth*—the lovingly apprehended, complete individuality of each character in an organic and ordered work of art. From the imaginative, eccentric Charlotte herself, whose eccentricity only becomes apparent as the novel goes on (so convincing is Anne Tyler's assumption of her voice), to her pathetic, obese mother (whose death is movingly described with a strange fusion of horror and nobility of vision) and her haunted preacher–husband Saul and his three doomed brothers, all have a triumphant life of their own. But of all the portraits, perhaps the best and most original is that of Charlotte's kidnapper Jake, a likeable young man whose attempt at a bank robbery is his only real crime. His motives are convincingly presented as being informed by a kind of foolish chivalry: he wants the money in order to help his featherbrained, pregnant girlfriend Mindy, herself a delightful and touching creation.

In some ways Jake is related to Drumstrings Casey in *A Slipping-Down Life.* Though I think his delineation shows her kinship with Eudora Welty and Reynolds Price, I can think of no other novelist who could have portrayed him and Mindy quite as Anne Tyler has. Here Jake talks about his friend Oliver, whom he hopes to see in Florida where he has driven himself, Mindy and Charlotte:

> "When the two of us got out of training school," Jake said, "why I would drop over to see him sometimes. He didn't live all that much of a distance. He lived with his mom, who was a real estate lady. I would find him home reading, all he done was reading. We'd ride around, go out for a hamburger, you know how it is. I really had a good time with that Oliver. But only if his mom wasn't there. His mom was so brisk and dry of voice. Never smiled unless she was saying something mean. Like she'd say, 'Back so soon, Jack?' She always called me Jack, which is definitely not my name. That can grate on a person. 'Funny,' she'd say, 'I thought you were here just yesterday. No doubt I was mistaken.' With that small sweet smile curling up her mouth while she was talking. I hate a woman to do that."

"That's how *my* mother did you," said Mindy. "You just have this knack, I believe." She told me, "My mother used to be so rude to him! Now she pretends he's not alive and never will mention his name. I ask in my letters if she's seen him and all she'll answer back is how many inches of rain they've had. He could fall down dead and *she* wouldn't tell me. To her he's dead already."[88]

Anne Tyler excels, too, at rendering the places her characters inhabit—Charlotte's photography studio, Saul's church and the motel where Jake's admired friend Oliver lives. Though she doubtless has a long fiction-writing career ahead of her, I do not think she could possibly write a better novel than *Earthly Possessions*.

In addition to being the youngest of the writers I have dealt with in this book, she is a fitting last choice for another reason. Emphatically a Southerner, she admits into her fiction the very stuff, the transient and perhaps permanent, of contemporary American life. For that reason it is appropriate that she lives in Baltimore, frontier city of South and North.

Anne Tyler drove me down to the bus station in downtown Baltimore. Snow lay in random piles in yards and on the sides of streets. The sky was pinky-gray with the promise of more snow to come, and the late afternoon was very cold. For I have cheated here; Anne Tyler was in fact the first and not the last of the authors I interviewed. I went to Baltimore to see her in March, a few weeks before the southward train journey with which this book opened. But I want it to end with her, with the youngest carrier of a Southern tradition which contains Eudora Welty, Reynolds Price and (at a tangent, so to speak) Peter Taylor, a tradition which stands in contrast to, though in happy juxtaposition with, the other great Southern tradition, which derives from the Vanderbilt Fugitives and Allen Tate, and includes Walker Percy, Madison Jones, Marion Montgomery and James Dickey.

But perhaps I also have a psychological motive in ending this way. As I think of myself on that wintry day in Baltimore, bleak high-rise buildings rising against a snow-laden sky, I think of all that was still before me then—crossing the Blue Ridge, my first sight of the Mississippi, Atlanta dazzling in the morning sunshine, wooded hills rising abruptly above the golden Georgian countryside —and I feel I am beginning my travels all over again.

EPILOGUE

AN OFTEN-QUOTED PARAGRAPH from Truman Capote's *Other Voices, Other Rooms* (1948), a precociously sophisticated first novel set in the swampy countryside of Louisiana and Mississippi, reads:

> The gentle jog of John Brown's trot set ajar the brittle woods; the sycamores released their spice-brown leaves in a rain of October: like veins dappled towers of jack-in-pulpit cranberry beetles sang of their approach, and tree-toads, no bigger than dewdrops, skipped and shrilled, relaying the news through the light that was dusk all day. They followed the remnants of a road down which once had spun the wheels of lacquered carriages carrying verbena-scented ladies who twittered like linnets in the shade of parasols, and leathery cotton-rich gentlemen gruffing at each other through a violet haze of Havana smoke, and their children, prim little girls with mint crushed in their handkerchiefs, and boys with mean blackberry eyes, little boys who sent their sisters screaming with tales of roaring tigers. Gusts of autumn, exhaling through the inheriting weeds, grieved for the cruel velvet children and their virile bearded fathers; Was, said the weeds, Gone, said the sky, Dead, said the woods, but the full laments of history were left to the whippoorwill.[89]

How sensuously evocative of a sad, decadent culture and its strange, lush, forlorn home these incantatory sentences are! Evocative perhaps, but not for me. I cannot relate this passage and others like it to the South I have experienced. While the past is indeed evident everywhere you travel in the South, while certain houses and indeed certain communities do seem to speak the past more than the present, I visited no places which inspired in me or even suggested the mood of Capote's story. Nor did the ways of life, attitudes and conversation of the people I met suggest it.

210

On the contrary, as I hope these pages have conveyed, the South struck me as a remarkably vigorous and virile society, passionate, and not without its primitive aspects—a readiness to resort to force; a readiness to voice and indeed act upon instinctive fears, likings or aversions; and an inclination to express exuberant joy in both religion and secular life. These characteristics are in some measure counteracted by the precepts both of a stern Greco-Roman code with its premium on honor, duty and dignity, and of a puritanical religion. But neither Stoicism nor Southern Baptism, any more than the passions they ameliorate, is tainted with decadence.

The vigor of the South, of course, has been abundantly paid tribute by many better writers than myself, but the idea of its decadence has also had strong currency, especially north of the Mason-Dixon line. Certain passages of Faulkner's, the whole of Tennessee Williams' and Truman Capote's work and pages of Carson McCullers' do indeed partake of this quality and have helped popularize this notion of the South. There must be a reason for this. In considering it, we can ponder too the famous Southern literary preoccupation with freaks, eccentrics and outcasts, with sudden explosions of blazing schizoid emotion. How has so vigorous a society produced a literature which features these phenomena so prominently?

My tentative explanation of both the decadence and the prevalence of freaks in Southern writing lies precisely in the virility of the culture. Leaving aside certain special coteries and institutions, and such exceptional places as Charlottesville and Charleston, the South seems a society which both in its active and its leisured life inclines but little to the intellectual and aesthetic. It places great emphasis even now on physical handsomeness, athletic prowess and strength in men and on loveliness, charm and poise in women. Young men and women who have strong artistic interests but do not fulfill these social requirements may tend from an early age to view themselves as misfits or freaks and so to identify with those who fall more literally into this category. In the same way, if they are to feel a connection with their place of origin and upbringing at all, it may be to its aspects of loss that they will turn. In the shattering of antebellum refinement and style they may see a distorted reflection of their own situation, of a sensibility shattered by the crudities of a philistine world.

This, I must insist, can only be a partial explanation. Of course,

211

rural communities that are turned in upon themselves and inbred are always apt to produce human oddities, idiots and deformed people; such villages too may contain eccentrics humored by their society, which has helped to create the oddities in the first place. But I still cannot help feeling that the principal reason that Carson McCullers and Flannery O'Connor wrote about so many freaks is not because Georgia was fuller of them than elsewhere, but because it was not! When Flannery O'Connor tells us that the Southerner sees the freak as a metaphor for the incomplete human being who lives without Christ, I think she is grossly intellectualizing the situation.

The strong traditionalism of Southern society does mean, I think, that the unconventional person, which the artist is often likely to be, has a hard time in adolescence. In recent times most liberal views were apt to be given an hysterical reception in the rural South; it might have been as much as one's life was worth to espouse a code opposed to the white Southerner's hard line. In the more recent past the South tended to take a strongly pro-Vietnam War attitude and to refuse to tolerate youthful dissent more single-mindedly than elsewhere in the United States. It is not surprising, then, to learn that some writers had miserable childhoods or that a number of "misfit" young men turned to homosexuality, a practice which the average Southerner appears to hold in rabid abhorrence. The agonies and unhappy histrionics of Truman Capote and Tennessee Williams, often expressed with strange and beautiful poetry, reflect not the miseries of Southern society but the interior anguish of their own homosexual predicaments, to which that society has perhaps driven them. In the course of my travels I met several homosexual Southerners, and while I believe that homosexuality can often be emotionally fulfilling and indeed enriching, I could not but think that, had these individuals lived in a different society with less narrow role definitions, some of them might have had more "normal" sexual and domestic relationships.

But for those artists who can weather the problems of their own departure from the norm, the culture of the South is a marvelous cornucopia of riches. Again contrary to certain views, which fix on antebellum plantations and their rich, well-bred families, I am of the opinion that it is a powerfully vernacular culture. Unlike the cultures of England or New England, to which I have heard the larger South compared, it has very little of the bourgeois about it,

212

either in that class's virtues or limitations. This makes the Southern novelist what I firmly believe him or her to be, no matter his or her family of origin—a natural democrat. All Southern writers can and do write about all classes with charity, understanding and knowledge. This may spring from the more traditional class structure of the Southern countryside, but not wholly, for this general democracy of approach cannot be found among a comparable group of English or French writers. No, it is surely because the Southern artist or intellectual knows the stirring, passionate, vital, musical, religious, narrative and rhetorical culture which the Southern population, both white and black, has uniquely evolved. Faced with this the artist cannot but respond with love and gratitude.

The upper-class college boy and the farmhand can meet as equals over the delights of guitar-picking; the religious emotions of the doctor's wife correspond visibly with the transports of the black salesgirl. No wonder Southern writing is distinguished by the respect its writers show toward the people they write about.

Religion must also account for this. The South is still a very devout society, and its writers perhaps the only remaining literary body in the world of which the majority are convinced Christians. Peter Taylor and Anne Tyler profess no religion, though they appear to be influenced in their art by certain of its consequences on their society; for the rest, Madison Jones, Walker Percy, Allen Tate, Andrew Lytle, Eudora Welty, Marion Montgomery, the late Flannery O'Connor, James Dickey and Reynolds Price are all Christians of varying degrees of orthodoxy. And it is worth noting that four of these people are Catholics, though I venture to say profoundly influenced by the Protestantism around them. The religious view of a human being—as the creation of God, the dwelling-place of both good and evil, and the possessor of an immortal soul— makes certain prevalent existentialist twentieth-century visions of humanity unacceptable. Even Walker Percy, the writer most profoundly influenced by existentialism and perhaps the one most inclined to look on life in its light, has intellectually wrestled against it and turned instead to the traditional Christian values. Their veneration for the individuality and freedom of people, their love for humans against all odds, seems to me Southern writers' single greatest quality.

Religion, too, must account for the spirituality that informs the great Southern novels. *The Sound and the Fury, Look Homeward,*

Angel, The Golden Apples, Clock without Hands, The Fathers and *The Surface of Earth* all show a certain intense spiritual atmosphere emanating from the inner lives and preoccupations of the characters; this spirituality is the more intense, I think, for the solidity of the settings. It is this feature above all others which calls for comparison with nineteenth-century Russian masters of fiction. Here, too, people for whom the social and the mundane constitute only a limited part of life move in a world vividly apprehended and described.

Another result of the domination of religion in the South on its writers is their inclination toward mythic presentations of life. Scrupulously faithful to their observations of life though many of them are, they arrange events and confrontations between their characters in patterns which add up to mythic statements. *The Fathers, The Violent Bear It Away, The Golden Apples, The Surface of Earth*, almost all the major novels of Faulkner and Madison Jones, and Lytle's *Velvet Horn* all can be thought of as individual attempts at myth, which is something dependent on an appeal to the fears and wishes that we all share in our secret buried selves.

The Southern saturation in the Bible, as Flannery O'Connor and Reynolds Price have observed, must be held partly responsible for this feature of Southern literature. So, too, must the myths in which the Southern past is so often encapsulated, though this almost certainly itself derives from the Bible-reading habits of its people. All the writers, with the possible exception of Anne Tyler, are profoundly concerned with the South's past, though this may not be directly expressed in their fiction. The terms myth and history come to seem nigh interchangeable at times when reviewing Southern culture. From Southern talk and books we receive emotionally charged presentations of the past which are of such intensity and frequency that in one sense it scarcely seems to matter where one begins and the other ends. Both play a part in determining the Southern imagination and character.

All the same one has to stand back and try to work out for oneself the Southern story that has haunted not only Southerners themselves but readers, music-lovers, cinema-goers and historians all over the Western world. And so, with diffidence and aware of its inevitable limitations, I offer my own.

The White Southerners descend largely from the Scottish and the Scottish–Irish, as many of their names suggest. In their new

214

country they retained many of the features of the societies they had left: a salvation-oriented Protestantism, with its tendency to put personal closeness to God above ethical obligations; a sense of the supernatural and the providential; an ability to express themselves emotionally in music, singing and dancing; a lively oral tradition; an intense feeling for the extended family; and a reverence for the martial. The South, however, unlike Scotland and Northern Ireland, is hot and luxuriant. This factor made inevitably for some changes in the Scottish/Scottish–Irish culture together with certain others—notably the addition of an English element, more easy-going and with certain defiantly upper-class mores lacking in the Scots, and the "peculiar institution" of slavery with its far-reaching effects on both whites and blacks. The South became and still is today a far more hedonistic society than its originals, far more concerned with and frank about sexual passions, and less concerned with productivity as an end. Its agrarianism and the retention of certain pioneer values meant that, to a lesser extent than the rest of America east of the Mississippi, the South never really developed a bourgeoisie.

But the society Southerns found themselves in gave full play to two more dubious inheritances from British culture. These were the plantation mentality, already expressed in the Ulster plantations of the seventeenth century, whose legacy is the bitter tragedy of contemporary Northern Ireland; and the Calvinistic disposition to the idea of election, even outside the strict sphere of theology, so that theological promise was converted into a social separatism. The seventeenth-century Covenanters fighting the British forces in the Scottish Lowlands thought of themselves as divinely appointed and favored, and so did many of the Southerners who fought the Unionists in the American Civil War.

The inevitable defeat of the smaller, poorer, traditionalist, agricultural South by the larger, richer, more forward-looking, commercial North meant emotional difficulties of enormous proportions for the men and women who lost. The defeat intensified their sense of apartness, of separateness. They had been better and braver than all others; they had sinned more grievously than any previous society—indeed, they were repeating Man's Fall and expulsion from Eden.

Southerners retained the Scottish and Irish ability to hold the past very close. Even now as one travels around the South one finds it difficult to believe that the Civil War happened over a century ago. But of course, vivid memory is a common characteristic of the defeated everywhere, as Allen Tate reminded me. The defeated cherish the sufferings they have endured as proof of the cruelty of the victors.

Perhaps it is inevitable that the literature of a brave and vigorous people who suffered defeat makes a profound psychic appeal to the rest of the world. We are all the victims of defeat sooner or later, in some form or other, and defeat after struggle is the easiest with which to identify. Moreover, the guilt of the Southern past—the unjustifiable nature of plantation slavery; the cruelties, vendettas and bloodshed that hideously and liberally punctuate its pages— enforces this appeal. We know ourselves to be guilty of sins, some committed, some mere whispers in our hearts, but all malevolent to our fellow humans. None of us can stand before the world with shining virtue, undeserving of the blows of fate; all the same, we would like to feel that we could. We also know that we have much of which to be proud. In a sense, therefore, we are all Southerners, hence the directness with which their literature speaks to us.

The South is a complex society, as any of fifty million, no matter how homogeneous or united by its past, must inevitably be. There are many features of Southern life with which I am not happy. There must be an easier communion between black and white, and a less pervasive and narrow sense of machismo. I think in both cases Southern life would be considerably enriched. On the other hand, it is my firm conviction—the greater after writing this book —that the South possesses as considerable a body of living creative writers as any society in the world today, and one with distinct superiorities and strengths all its own. One simply needs to consider the works that were published in the seventies—*The Optimist's Daughter, Deliverance, The Surface of Earth, In the Miro District, Lancelot, A Cry of Absence* and *Earthly Possessions*, to see a testimonial of the South as a significant and valuable center of literature unsurpassed by any other.

Honoring this fact and the interesting men and women responsible for it, I review my time in the South. I think of the beauty of its landscape; the justly famous hospitality of its people; the company of the friends I made there; the charm of its small towns and old houses; the luxuriance of its trees and flowers; the courage of its recent social accomplishments; the power of its music; the per-

216

vasiveness of its history; and the indefinable spiritual quality that informs and determines it. Then I remember that popular tune of my adolescence and say to myself, "In the South is where I want to be!"

SELECT BIBLIOGRAPHY

Wendell BERRY (born 1934)
Nathan Coulter (novel) 1960
The Broken Ground (poems)
1964
A Place on Earth (novel) 1968
Findings (poems) 1969
Openings (poems) 1969
The Long-Legged House (essays)
1969
Farming (essays) 1971
The Memory of Old Jack (novel)
1974

James DICKEY (born 1923)
Into the Stone and Other Poems
(poems) 1960
Drowning with Others (poems)
1962
Helmets (poems) 1964
Buckdancer's Choice (poems)
1965
Poems 1957–1967 (poems) 1968
The Eye-beaters, Blood, Victory,
Madness, Buckhead and Mercy
(poems) 1970
Deliverance (novel) 1970
Butch to Byzantium (essays) 1973
Jericho: The South Beheld
(nonfiction) 1974

Madison JONES (born 1925)
The Innocent (novel) 1957
Forest of the Night (novel) 1960
A Buried Land (novel) 1963
An Exile (novel) 1967
A Cry of Absence (novel) 1971
Passage through Gehenna (novel)
1978

Andrew LYTLE (born 1902)
Bedford Forrest and His Critter
Company (biography) 1931
The Long Night (novel) 1936
At the Moon's Inn (novel) 1941
A Name for Evil (novel) 1947
The Velvet Horn (novel) 1956
The Hero with the Private Parts
(essays) 1966
A Wake for the Living (family
memoir) 1975

David MADDEN (born 1933)
Cassandra Singing (novel) 1969
The Shadow Knows (short
stories) 1970
Bijou (novel) 1974

Marion MONTGOMERY (born
1925)
Dry Lightning (poems) 1960
The Wandering of Desire (novel)
1962
Darrell (novel) 1964
The Gull and Other Georgia
Scenes (poems) 1970
The Fugitive (novel) 1971

Walker PERCY (born 1916)
The Moviegoer (novel) 1961
The Last Gentleman (novel) 1966
Love in the Ruins (novel) 1971
The Message in the Bottle
(essays) 1975
Lancelot (novel) 1977

Reynolds PRICE (born 1933)
A Long and Happy Life (novel)
1962

The Names and Faces of Heroes
(short stories) 1963
A Generous Man (novel) 1966
Love and Work (novel) 1968
Permanent Errors (short stories)
1970
Things Themselves (essays) 1972
The Surface of Earth (novel) 1975
Early Dark (play) 1977
A Palpable God (translations)
1978

Allen TATE (born 1899)
Mr. Pope and Other Poems
(poems) 1928
Stonewall Jackson (biography)
1928
Jefferson Davis: His Rise and Fall
(biography) 1929
"The Immortal Woman" (short
story) 1933
"The Migration" (short story)
1934
The Mediterranean and Other
Poems (poems) 1936
Reactionary Essays on Poetry and
Ideas (essays) 1936
The Fathers (novel) 1938
Poems 1922–1947 (poems) 1948
Essays of Four Decades (essays)
1959
Poems (poems) 1960
The Swimmers and Other Poems
(poems) 1971
Memoirs and Opinions (essays)
1976
Collected Poems 1919–1976
(poems) 1977
The Fathers (revised edition)
(novel) 1978

Peter TAYLOR (born 1917)
A Long Fourth and Other Stories
(stories) 1948
A Woman of Means (novel) 1950

The Widows of Thornton (short
stories) 1954
Happy Families Are Alike (short
stories) 1959
Tennessee Day in Saint Louis
(play) 1957
Miss Leonora When Last Seen
(short stories) 1963
Collected Stories of Peter Taylor
(short stories) 1969
Presences: Seven Dramatic Pieces
(plays) 1973
In the Miro District and Other
Stories (short stories) 1977

Anne TYLER (born 1941)
If Morning Ever Comes (novel)
1964
The Tin Can Tree (novel) 1965
A Slipping-Down Life (novel)
1970
The Clock Winder (novel) 1972
Celestial Navigation (novel) 1974
Searching for Caleb (novel) 1976
Earthly Possessions (novel) 1977

Eudora WELTY (born 1909)
A Curtain of Green (short stories)
1941
The Robber Bridegroom (novel)
1942
The Wide Net (short stories) 1943
Delta Wedding (novel) 1946
The Golden Apples (linked short
stories) 1949
The Ponder Heart (novel) 1954
The Bride of the Innisfallen (short
stories) 1955
Losing Battles (novel) 1970
One Time, One Place
(photographs) 1971
The Optimist's Daughter (novel)
1973
The Eye of the Story (essays)
1978

FOOTNOTES

1 Eudora Welty, *Eye of the Story*, Random House, 1978. Excerpts from the works of Eudora Welty are reprinted by permission of Russell & Volkening, Inc.

2 Anne Tyler, *Earthly Possessions*, Alfred A. Knopf, Inc., 1977.

3 Alan Lomax, *Folk Song USA*, New American Library, 1947, 1975.

4 Carson McCullers, *Clock without Hands*, Houghton Mifflin, 1961.

5 Carson McCullers, "The Mortgaged Heart" in *The Mortgaged Heart*, edited by Margarita G. Smith, Houghton Mifflin, 1971.

6 Reynolds Price, *Things Themselves*, Atheneum, 1972.

7 Charles P. Roland, *The Confederacy* (History of American Civilization Series), University of Chicago Press, 1960.

8 Allen Tate, *Collected Poems 1919–1976*, Farrar, Straus & Giroux, Inc., 1977.

9 Tennessee Williams, *A Streetcar Named Desire*, New Directions, 1947

10 Eudora Welty, *The Bride of the Innisfallen*, Harcourt Brace Jovanovich, 1955.

11 Madison Jones, *A Cry of Absence*, Crown, 1972.

12 Madison Jones, essay in *The Sewanee Review*.

13 Madison Jones, *A Buried Land*, Viking, 1963.

14 Madison Jones, *A Cry of Absence*, Crown, 1972.

15 *Ibid.*

16 Madison Jones, *Passing through Gehenna*, Louisiana State University Press, 1978.

17 Walker Percy, *The Moviegoer*, Farrar, Straus & Giroux, Inc., 1961.

18 *Ibid.*

19 Walker Percy, *Lancelot*, Farrar, Straus & Giroux, 1977.

20 Allen Tate, "The Migration", *Yale Review*, September 1934, reprinted in *The Fathers and Other Fiction*, Louisiana State University Press, 1977.

21 *Ibid.*

22 Donald Davidson, *Poems 1922–1961*, © Copyright 1924, 1927, 1934, 1935, 1938, 1952, 1961, 1966 by Donald Davidson, University of Minnesota Press, Minneapolis.

23 Allen Tate, *Memories and Essays, Old and New*, 1976.

24 Twelve Southerners, *I'll Take My Stand*, edited by Donald Davidson, © 1930 Harper and Row, Copyright renewed 1958 by Donald Davidson, introduction copyright, 1962, 1977, Louis D. Rubin, Jr.

25 John Crowe Ransom, "Antique Harvesters", *Selected Poems*, 3rd edition, Alfred A. Knopf, Inc., 1963.

26 Donald Davidson, *Poems 1922–1961*, see no. 22.

27 Robert Penn Warren, "Bearded Oaks," *The Selected Poems of Robert Penn Warren*, 1923–1976, Random House, 1976.

28 Thomas Wolfe, *The Web and the Rock*, Harper and Row, 1939.

29 Twelve Southerners, *I'll Take My Stand*, see no. 24, essay copyright, 1962, 1977, Virginia Rock.

30 Andrew Lytle, "The Working Novelist and the Mythmaking Process", *Daedalus*, Journal of the American Academy of Arts and Sciences, Vol. 88, No. 2, 1959.

31 Peter Taylor, *In the Miro District and Other Stories*, Farrar, Straus & Giroux Inc., 1977.

32 *Ibid.*

33 *Ibid.*

34 *Ibid.*

35 Allen Tate, *The Fathers*, Putnam, 1938, revised edition Louisiana State

University Press, 1977.

36 *Ibid.*

37 *Ibid.*

38 *Ibid.*

39 *Ibid.*

40 Allen Tate, *Collected Poems 1919–1976*, Farrar, Straus & Giroux, Inc., 1977.

41 Eudora Welty, *One Time, One Place*, Random House, 1971.

42 Eudora Welty, *A Curtain of Green*, Harcourt Brace and World, 1941.

43 *Ibid.*

44 *Ibid.*

45 Eudora Welty, *The Eye of the Story*, Random House, 1978.

46 Eudora Welty, *The Wide Net*, Harcourt Brace and World, 1943.

47 *Ibid.*

48 *Ibid.*

49 Eudora Welty, *The Robber Bridegroom*, Harcourt Brace and World, 1942.

50 Eudora Welty, *The Golden Apples*, Harcourt Brace and World, 1949.

51 *Ibid.*

52 Allen Tate, *Memories and Opinions 1926–1974*, Swallow Press, 1975.

53 Reynolds Price, *Conversations with William Ray*, Memphis State University, 1976.

54 Walter de la Mare, "One in the Public Gallery," *The Collected Poems of Walter de la Mare*, Faber & Faber, 1969.

55 James Dickey, *Deliverance*, Houghton Mifflin, 1970.

56 Flannery O'Connor, *Mystery and Manners*, Occasional Prose, selected and edited by Sally and Robert Fitzgerald, Copyright © 1957, 1961, 1963, 1964, 1966, 1967, 1969 by the Estate of Mary Flannery O'Connor. Copyright © 1962 by Flannery O'Connor. Copyright © 1961 by Farrar, Straus & Cudahy, Inc. (now Farrar, Straus & Giroux, Inc.). Reprinted with the permissions of Farrar, Straus & Giroux, Inc.

57 *Ibid.*

58 Marion Montgomery, in *Kite-Flying and Other Irrational Acts*, edited by John Carr, Louisiana State University Press, 1972.

59 James Dickey, *Poems 1957–1967*, Wesleyan University Press, 1967.

60 *Ibid.*

61 *Ibid.*

62 *Ibid.*

63 *Ibid.*

64 James Dickey, *Deliverance*, Houghton Mifflin, 1970.

65 *Ibid.*

66 *Ibid.*

67 *Ibid.*

68 Reynolds Price, *A Long and Happy Life*, Atheneum, 1962.

69 *Ibid.*

70 Reynolds Price, *Early Dark*, Atheneum, 1977.

71 Reynolds Price, *Conversations with William Ray*, Memphis State University, 1976.

72 Reynolds Price, *Things Themselves*, Atheneum, 1972.

73 Reynolds Price, *Conversations with William Ray*, see no. 71.

74 Reynolds Price, *A Generous Man*, Atheneum, 1966.

75 Reynolds Price, *Conversations with William Ray*, see no. 71.

76 Reynolds Price, *Things Themselves*, see no. 72.

77 Reynolds Price, *The Surface of Earth*, Atheneum, 1975.

78 *Ibid.*

79 *Ibid.*

80 *Ibid.*

81 Reynolds Price, *Things Themselves*, see no. 72.

82 Anne Tyler, *The Clock Winder*, Alfred A. Knopf, Inc., 1972.

83 Eudora Welty, *The Wide Net*, Harcourt Brace and World, 1943.

84 Anne Tyler, *If Morning Ever Comes*, Alfred A. Knopf, Inc., 1964.

85 *Ibid.*

86 Anne Tyler, *A Slipping-Down Life*, Alfred A. Knopf, Inc., 1970.

87 Anne Tyler, *Searching for Caleb*, Alfred A. Knopf, Inc., 1976.

88 Anne Tyler, *Earthly Possessions*, Alfred A. Knopf, Inc., 1977.

89 Truman Capote, *Other Voices, Other Rooms*, Random House, 1948.

INDEX

222